Language and Meaning

Studies in Functional and Structural Linguistics (SFSL)

Taking the broadest and most general definitions of the terms functional and structural, this series aims to present linguistic and interdisciplinary research that relates language structure — at any level of analysis from phonology to discourse — to broader functional considerations, whether cognitive, communicative, pragmatic or sociocultural. Preference will be given to studies that focus on data from actual discourse, whether speech, writing or other nonvocal medium.

The series was formerly known as *Linguistic & Literary Studies in Eastern Europe (LLSEE)*.

Volume 55

Language and Meaning. The structural creation of reality
by Christopher Beedham

Language and Meaning

The structural creation of reality

Christopher Beedham

John Benjamins Publishing Company

Amsterdam / Philadelphia

™ The paper used in this publication meets the minimum requirements of
American National Standard for Information Sciences – Permanence of
Paper for Printed Library Materials, ANSI z39.48-1984.

Library of Congress Cataloging-in-Publication Data

Christoper Beedham
    Language and Meaning : The structural creation of reality / Christopher Beedham.
       p. cm. (Studies in Functional and Structural Linguistics, ISSN 0165-7712 ; v. 55)
    Includes bibliographical references and index.
         1. Structural linguistics. 2. Generative grammar. 3. Russian language--
Grammar, Comparative--German. 4. German language--Grammar, Comparative--
Russian. I. Title. II. Series.
    P146.B38   2005
    410'.1'8--dc22   2005048394
    ISBN 978 90 272 1564 2 (Hb; alk. paper);
    ISBN 978 90 272 1569 7 (Pb; alk. paper)

John Benjamins Publishing Co. · P.O. Box 36224 · 1020 ME Amsterdam · The Netherlands
John Benjamins North America · P.O. Box 27519 · Philadelphia PA 19118-0519 · USA

to Anna and Stephanie

Table of contents

List of figures

List of tables

Preface

This book brings together my research in the linguistics of modern English, German, and Russian over the last 30 years, updates it with the inclusion of only recently acquired data and recently developed ideas, some of it not yet published in the journals, and makes it all accessible to a wider audience by focussing on English, with German and Russian backing up the presentation in separate sub-sections. I have written the book with three audiences in mind: the professional linguist and researcher; students of linguistics; and the general public. The book is based on a short course entitled 'Issues in Structural Linguistics' which I gave as guest lecturer in the Department of Foreign Literatures and Linguistics, Ben-Gurion University of the Negev, Israel, in January 2002, at the invitation of Prof. Yishai Tobin. That course has since become part of my general linguistics teaching at the University of St Andrews, in a course originally called 'Structural Linguistics' but now called 'Saussurean Structuralism', which has also fed into the book. I have used mainly English examples, but have included separate sub-sections on German and Russian at the end of certain key chapters. Although I have tried to write the German and Russian sub-sections so as to be accessible to the non-specialist in those languages, they may be omitted without major detriment to an understanding of the book as a whole.

I owe a huge debt of gratitude to Yishai Tobin, for supporting my work both to the extent of inviting me to teach the course in his Department on which this book is based, and for inviting me to submit the book to the Benjamins series, Studies in Functional and Structural Linguistics, of which he is co-editor. I am also grateful to the following people for their help and advice: Chris Gledhill, Wendy Anderson, Kormi Anipa, Clive Sneddon, Leslie Stevenson, Matthias Müller, Norbert Schaffranek; and to an anonymous reader for Benjamins, whose meticulously detailed and constructively critical comments led me to make numerous improvements to the original version. I am grateful also to the students who took the courses on which the book is based between 2000 and 2005. You helped me by telling me things I did not know, by producing analyses which I had not thought of, and by saying 'I don't understand, say that again', and when I did say it again I realised either that the analysis was wrong and needed revising or that I was explaining it badly and when I finally explained it properly I actually understood it properly for the first time myself. Every class you helped me to a deeper understanding of the issues, time and again I went home after a class and changed something in the book in the light of our discussions.

The drawing of the jellyfish conversation on p.17 is by Andreas Prüstel. Some of the research presented was supported by the British Academy.

Introduction

Language is the most human of all human attributes. More than just a means of communication it is our vehicle of thought. We cannot imagine human beings without language, and if we came across another creature with language in our sense we would say it was human or human-like, or intelligent in the way that humans are. Language impinges upon every sphere of human activity, including all the sciences, from physics through sociology to literary criticism. It is no exaggeration to say, therefore, that linguistics – the scientific study of language – is the most important scientific discipline of them all. Within linguistics the most important question of all concerns meaning: how does language mean, how do words and morphemes[1] mean what they mean? When we ask that question we do not do so historically and etymologically. Of course, in a historical sense the answer to the question is straightforward and familiar: a word means what it means because it has inherited its meaning from an earlier stage of the language. But we do not pose the question in that way, historically or diachronically, we pose it synchronically, to use the Saussurean terms. How does language mean synchronically? Another way of phrasing the question is: What is the relationship between language and thought/perception? How does language influence thought/perception? Does language come first, and then thought and perception, or do thought and perception come first, and then language? To answer these questions we will turn to the structuralism of Ferdinand de Saussure, the topic of our first chapter.

CHAPTER 1

Saussurean structuralism

Saussurean structuralism, like any great intellectual movement, is elusive, open to interpretation, and fraught with controversy. To start at the beginning, Ferdinand de Saussure is acknowledged as the founding father of modern linguistics and yet Yishai Tobin claims that "the 'Saussurean Sign Revolution' did not really take place in linguistics", and almost called his book *Semiotics and Linguistics* 'Structuralism: The Revolution that Never Happened' (Tobin 1990: 13; Beedham 1999b: 1,13). Moving to the end, the famous final sentence of Saussure's *Cours de linguistique générale*, "... l'idée fondamentale de ce cours: *la linguistique a pour unique et véritable objet la langue envisagée en elle-même et pour elle-même*",[2] which asserts that *langue* not *parole* is the proper object of investigation in linguistics, is apparently not from the mouth of Saussure himself but from the pen of the editors of the *Cours*, Bally and Sèchehaye, thus allowing linguists of that persuasion to say that maybe we could investigate *parole* after all (Saussure 1972: 476–477; Hartmann 1999). And backing up to the middle, the indivisible linguistic sign, consisting of *signifiant* (form) and *signifié* (meaning), does not of itself tell us whether we should start with the *signifiants* – with form – and move from there to the *signifiés* – to meaning – or do it the other way round and start with meanings and move from there to forms. In this chapter we will address these questions in a general way, picking them up again in later chapters more concretely, where we will focus on the passive construction and irregular verbs.

The basic tenet of Saussurean structuralism is that a language is a system whose units are determined by their place in the system, not by some outside point of reference such as reality.[3] Although the units which Saussure had in mind initially were phonemes, which are not meaning-bearing but meaning-distinguishing, he soon moved on to the meaning-bearing units words, morphemes, and syntagms. Saussurean structuralism is a theory of meaning, which opposes the referential account of meaning. According to the referential theory reality pre-exists language – language comes along later and labels the already existing bits of reality. For example, tables and chairs, dogs and cats, exist independently of language. A language like English then calls tables *table*, chairs *chair*, etc. According to Saussure, on the other hand, if one tried to envisage reality without language there would be no reality as we know it, instead there would be an amorphous mass of nebulous, indistinguishable stuff, no pieces of furniture, no types of animals, just a great big uninterpretable blob (Saussure 1983:110). It is only once language is there that bits of reality become recognisable and distinguishable. Language creates the reality that we perceive: *In principio erat verbum* 'in the beginning was the Word'.[4] In fact, there are two processes happening at once. One is that reality takes shape under the influence of language, the other is that language takes shape under the influence of reality. This is the origin of the idea that the linguistic sign is indivisible, i.e. *signifiant* and *signifié*, form and meaning, cannot be separated.[5]

The referential theory of meaning is the older one, and the one held by the laywoman, but can be easily knocked down. It sounds plausible enough when one has concrete objects such as tables and chairs in mind, but what about abstract concepts such as love, hate, socialism, episcopalianism? A parent can point to a chair and say [tʃeə], and the child can imitate him, but you can hardly point to episcopalianism, whilst the child imitates you saying [ɪpɪskəˈpeɪliənɪzəm]. What is the piece of reality that pre-exists function words such as *of, and, the*? What about grammatical endings and their meanings? How many mothers have you seen pointing to past time and saying 'That's *-ed*'? Or rather, 'That's [t], [d], or [ɪd], depending on the phonetic environment'? Take derivational morphemes such as the noun-forming suffixes in English *-tion*, *-ment, -ness*, the adjective-forming suffixes *-al, -ic, -ous*, with their meanings. Or take case endings such as German *der den des dem* Nom., Acc, Gen., Dat., with their meanings. With none of these can one point to a piece of reality and say 'that is *of*', 'that is *-tion*', 'that is the nominative case'. It is ridiculous to suggest that these very precise and very specific meanings pre-existed language. They clearly did not, they clearly were created by the specific structure of the language concerned. A considerable part of the world we inhabit and speak about consists of abstract notions such as these, not concrete objects. Berger and Luckmann 1966 emphasised that every society and every age constructs its own religion, science, and politics, despite the fact that the people in each society think that their particular version represents the one and only objective truth. I would go a step further and say that even concrete objects are constructs of language, the five senses, and other biological properties of humans, as maintained, for example, by Berkeley and Kant (see below in this chapter). The referential theory of meaning, with its idea that there is such a thing as objective reality which pre-exists language, is plain wrong and in dire need of replacement. The structuralist revolution is indeed a revolution that

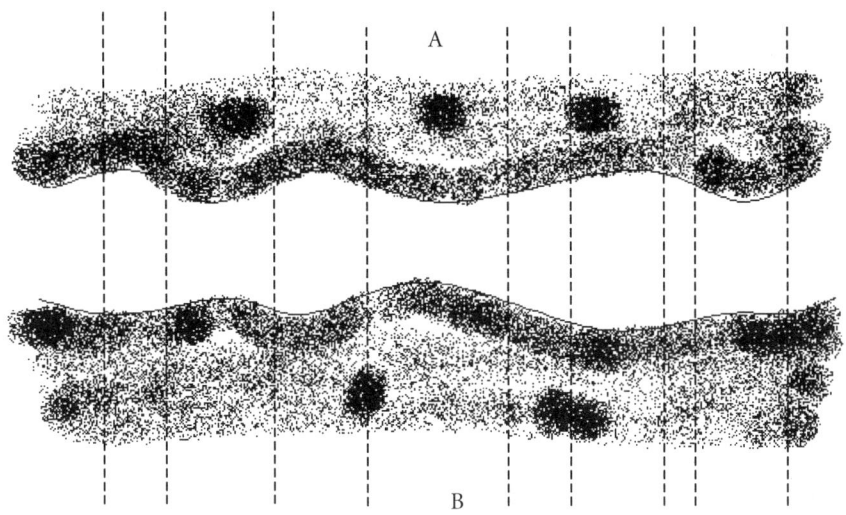

Figure 1. The genesis of language and reality simultaneously, in the sign (based on Saussure 1983:111)

never happened, and in this first chapter it is with some urgency that we revisit some familiar concepts of Saussurean structuralism.

The *Cours* contains a useful diagram of the way in which reality and language take shape simultaneously, which is reproduced here in Figure 1. Portion A of the diagram represents the undifferentiated grunts and groans of pre-language, whilst portion B represents vague, amorphous precognition. The dotted lines represent language. The dotted lines cut through portions A and B simultaneously, and could do no other than cut through them simultaneously. The divisions of language – phonemes, morphemes, words, syntagms, etc. – take shape at the same time as the divisions of reality, and the two processes, concept formation and language formation, could do no other than happen at the same time.

Language is not a nomenclature, a list of names for things. Rather, meaning happens by a process of signification, not naming. Words are signs, with a value in a system. The sign consists of two parts, *signifiant* and *signifié*, signifier and signified, form and meaning, as shown in Figure 2, which is based on another diagram given in the *Cours*. The *signifiant* is the counterpart to the *signifié*, i.e. the sign is indivisible, indicated by the arrows: "A linguistic sign is not a link between a thing and a name, but between a concept and a sound pattern" (Saussure 1983:66).

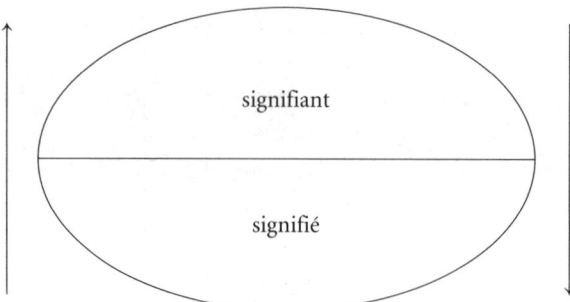

Figure 2. The binary, indivisible sign, with meaning (*signifié*) buried beneath form (*signifiant*) (based on Saussure 1972:158)

Figure 2 is based on the diagram in the *Cours*, but it is not an exact reproduction of it. I have changed it slightly. The original diagram appears with *signifié* on top and *signifiant* underneath, but I have put *signifiant* on top and *signifié* underneath (I did the same for Figure 1). The reason is that I want to align myself with one side of the debate about whether to go from form to meaning or from meaning to form,[6] and it is from form to meaning that I go in my own work. Although many linguists who consider themselves to be structuralists work in the other direction, it seems to me that it follows naturally from the basic tenets of structuralism that one should start with form and move from there to meaning, indeed the study of language is a search for meanings, as Tobin (1990:64) puts it. For example, the subject of the sentence is formally defined as the noun phrase in initial position in the stylistically neutral sentence (or as the noun in the Nominative case in languages with a case system), and semantically defined as usually the agent of the sentence (though it may also express patient, perceiver, instrument, and many other meanings). Some linguists start with the semantic notion of 'agent' and ask the question: How is 'agent' realized in this or that language? That is the semantic approach. Other linguists start with the formal notion of subject, and ask: What are the meanings of subject in this or that language? That is the formal approach.

Both approaches are possible precisely because the sign consists of both *signifiant* and *signifié*. And many linguists work in both directions in a perfectly reasonable and sensible way.[7] But it is my contention that the form-to-meaning approach is fundamentally structuralist and likely to lead to new discoveries, whereas the meaning-to-form approach goes against the grain of structuralism and tends towards making no advances in linguistics. The reasons are twofold. Firstly, as linguists it is our job to examine language, not reality. The linguist who starts with meanings, i.e. reality (in Saussurean terms 'concepts'), is in effect an amateur psychologist, dilettante anthropologist, amateur physicist, etc. But we do not want to be amateur anything, we want to be professional linguists. Given that reality and language take shape together, as Saussure says, it is language which is the overt manifestation of reality and which precisely as linguists we are privileged to examine. Secondly, as we saw above and which again is a fundamental part of structuralism, there is no such thing as objective, non-linguistic, pre-linguistic reality anyway (because reality only takes shape under the influence of language). Meanings and the reality we perceive arise in and through language and linguistic forms. There is, in fact, no such thing as looking at meanings separate from and devoid of form. Linguists who examine meanings do so, without realising it, on the basis of a formal analysis which they bring with them ready-formulated to the task at hand (see 'Methodological implications' at the end of Chapter 3 'The Passive').

By way of illustration let us take the passive construction, anticipating somewhat Chapter 3. Semantically oriented linguists are inclined to take it for granted that actives and passives are cognitively synonymous – for example, *Jack built the house* is cognitively synonymous with *The house was built by Jack* – and that the subject in passives is patient, and to cast around for other constructions in which the subject is patient, e.g. *The cakes are selling well*, and to call these 'notional passives'. But formally speaking the passive consists in English of *be* + V-*ed*, and the first question we have to ask is: What does *be* + V-*ed* mean? Traditionally passives and their underlying active are indeed said to be synonymous, but it will be suggested in Chapter 3 that actives and passives are not cognitively synonymous, rather, the passive with *be* + V-*ed* has the meaning 'action + state', i.e. the expression of a new state arising on the subject as the result of a preceding action (hence the subject is patient). Contrary to common assumption and superficial appearances the meanings of forms are not obvious and self-evident. Linguistics is a search for meanings – form determines meaning.[8] *Be* + V-*ed* may mean 'action + resultant state' and it may not, the arguments for one meaning or another have to be presented, the case has to be made, which we will do in Chapter 3. In this debate about meanings one sees the indivisibility of the sign in the fact that if you believe that actives and passives are cognitively synonymous then for you formally speaking the passive will be a voice of the verb, whereas if you believe the passive means 'action + state' then for you the passive will be formally an aspect of the verb. But more about that in Chapter 3.

Another great Saussurean dichotomy is the distinction between synchrony and diachrony. Diachronic means historical. A synchronic approach to language is one which makes a cut in the passage of time and analyses a language as if it were in a steady state, ignoring the numerous historical factors and influences which led to that state. One can analyse a modern language synchronically, but equally one can analyse an earlier stage of a language synchronically; e.g. Latin, an early stage of the Romance family of languages, is studied at school synchronically, not historically. Indeed, in order to pursue historical linguistics one *must* first analyse a language synchronically, two stages thereof, an earlier one and a later one, and then follow the changes which led from the earlier stage to the later stage (Saussure 1983:79–100). For example, in studying the history of German one would perform first a synchronic study of (say) Old High German, then a synchronic study of Middle High German, and then *and only then* is one in a position to embark on a study of the changes which led from Old High German to Middle High German. That is to say, diachronic linguistics presupposes that a synchronic study – to be precise, two synchronic studies – have gone on first. In other words, diachronic linguistics is fundamentally synchronic in nature.

My own work is concerned with the synchronic study of modern German, Russian, and English, i.e. I do not work historically. An important element in that synchronic work is the hypothetical nature of grammatical descriptions. That is to say, a grammatical description – for example, the kind found in traditional grammar – is not a statement of obvious facts, but a theory (in the pre-Chomskyan sense) or hypothesis. Of course, a theory or hypothesis is open to refutation, if the right data and arguments can be adduced to refute it, and the search for new data and new arguments to refine and improve existing grammatical descriptions is a stock in trade of my work, as for all linguists carrying out research into the modern language. However, regrettably I have to say that my experience of the reaction of some historical linguists to my work – I emphasise some, not all – leads me to think that they in their research do not normally contemplate revising existing synchronic descriptions. For example, I have proposed that the passive construction, usually described as a voice of the verb (derived from an underlying active), is an aspect of the verb, as alluded to above, and that the irregularity of the English strong verbs is probably an artefact of an incorrect analysis, and a new, phonotactic approach to them will hopefully lead to rules by which we can predict those preterit and 2nd participle forms which at the moment are bizarre lexical idiosyncrasies (see Chapter 5). But over the years I have sometimes encountered incomprehension and hostility from historical linguists – particularly those who also write pedagogical grammars of the modern language – a hostility which seems to boil down to their inability or reluctance to countenance the notion that the traditional synchronic analyses – the passive is a voice of the verb, the strong verbs are a historical vestige with no synchronic regularity in them – might be wrong and replaceable. When it comes to the modern language they seem not to have a Saussurean synchronic approach at all, and I can only assume that in their own historical work they do not have it there, either.[9] Thus it is that – ironically, since Saussure was himself a historical linguist – the linguistics of the modern language is Saussurean in outlook, whilst much of historical linguistics would appear to be atomistic in a non-Saussurean way.

Why should this be? One possibility is as follows. A stock in trade of all sentence-grammarians concerned with the modern language is to work with invented sentences and to test them for their grammaticality with native speakers. Depending on the results you get you propose a new (synchronic) analysis, or not. Historical linguists cannot do this, for obvious reasons – there are not many speakers of, for example, Old High German around to test invented sentences on.[10] On the other hand, Saussure, who conceived the synchronic method as a historical linguist, did not have that opportunity either, so that can't be right. Or maybe the kind of synchronic linguistics practised by linguists of the modern language, influenced as it is by using invented test sentences on native speaker informants, is different to the one proposed by Saussure and practised by historical linguists today? Another possibility is that historical linguists are simply distracted from the synchronic by the diachronic work which they have to do. If you are concerned only with the modern language there is no diachronic part to your work to be distracted by – you have no choice but to work synchronically. Another possibility is that historical linguists simply take umbrage at the temerity of someone analysing a language non-historically, and resent the popularity of the linguistics of the modern language, which they see as happening at their expense. I don't know what the answer is, but I would put it to historical linguists: In your research do you carry out synchronic analyses of earlier stages of the languages you are studying? If so, do you simply keep on the traditional synchronic analysis of a given stage, or do you consider revising it?

In the 19th century linguistics meant historical linguistics, and Saussure was part of that tradition. In the 20th century and thus far in the 21st century linguistics means the linguistics of the modern language, and it is supposed to be Saussurean (notwithstanding Tobin's lament that the Saussurean revolution never happened, because linguists neglect the indivisibility of the sign and the maxim 'one form:one meaning' (see p. 3)). What seems to have happened is that linguists adopted the synchronic part of Saussure's work (or tried to, anyway), but applied it to the modern language only, dropping the diachronic part. At the same time many (though not all) of those linguists who carried on doing historical linguistics dropped the synchronic part of Saussure's method. Strange, but true.

Returning to structuralism generally, Saussure's *langue-parole* dichotomy is also in peril. *Langue* is the abstract system or structure of language, whilst *parole* is the concrete realization of the system in actual speech or in texts (a 'text' can be spoken or written). The accepted wisdom is that the whole point of Saussure making the *langue-parole* distinction was to emphasise that *langue* is the proper object of investigation in linguistics. But then three things went wrong. Firstly, in America in the 1950's structuralism somehow ended up looking at the distribution of linguistic units in texts. This was a conflation of and misunderstanding of *langue* and *parole*, leading to a methodology which was very different to Saussurean/European structuralism, so different that it received a different name, viz. American structuralism or distributionalism (Robins 1967: 210, 1980: 293, 1999: 69; Helbig 1983: 80–84). Whereas European structuralism was and still is concerned with the occurrence or combinability or distribution of items in sentences, that is to say in the grammarian's abstract, idealised sentence, i.e. in *langue*, American structuralism was concerned with the distribution of items in utterances or texts, i.e. in *parole*.

The second thing to go wrong was that Chomsky came along with his competence-performance distinction, to muddy the waters. Competence, later known as I-language (internalised language), is the native speaker's knowledge of his language and its rules, the grammar in the speaker-hearer's mind. Performance, later known as E-language (externalised language), refers to actual utterances by individual speakers in specific (spoken or written) texts, including all the slips of the tongue, hesitations, etc., that happen in real speech. Clearly competence or I-language is similar to *langue*, and performance or E-language is similar to *parole*. Chomsky's point was that the true object of investigation in linguistics is competence or I-language. This might have been good news, except that the grammar that Chomsky envisaged was a generative grammar. Under the generative method the linguist postulates or assumes certain 'devices' or 'principles' or 'parameters', e.g. transformations, underlying structures (previously called deep structures or D-structures), lexical features, components of grammar and their make-up, etc. etc., and expresses his assumptions in a 'formal' notation which he devises as and when needed as he goes along, making up his assumptions. The notation consists of a mixture of symbols borrowed from computer programming languages, logic, and mathematics, and symbols which are abbreviations and mnemonics which the linguist introduces himself. The result is a generative 'theory' or 'grammar' or 'model' (Gross 1979). The assumptions are never properly tested empirically, and no matter how outrageous and unlikely the assumptions are, they are justified by saying that they are part of competence or the I-language or Universal Grammar (UG), and it is the linguist's task to elucidate the I-language or UG. In effect, competence or I-language is a licence to assume. More of this in Chapter 4, but for the moment it is clear that Chomsky's overturning of Z. S. Harris's corpus and *parole* orientation was not a return to *langue* but heralded instead the advent of the misguided enterprise known as generative grammar.[11]

The third thing to go awry with Saussure's *langue-parole* dichotomy happened when linguists found themselves in a position where, if they wanted to do grammar, i.e. in *langue*, it had to be generative grammar, descriptive grammar was no longer acceptable. The response of many linguists, in the Anglo-American and English-speaking world at least, was to leave (sentence-)grammar altogether and move into areas such as sociolinguistics, pragmatics, speech act theory, and text grammar, which are all part of *parole*. Apart from a small yet significant number of people who continue to practise theoretical descriptive linguistics, most linguists today, if they work within *langue*/competence are generative grammarians, and if they work descriptively/experimentally they are working on *parole*. Either way Saussure's *langue*, as advocated in the final sentence of the *Cours*, is lost.

For the sake of clarity I have spoken of *langue* and *parole* as quite distinct entities. But they are, of course, both part of language and are interconnected with each other (Saussure 1983: 18–20). Every language change which eventually makes it into *langue* starts off in *parole*; deixis intrudes into sentence-grammar from *parole* (see Bühler 1990); ideally, when native speaker informants make judgements about the grammaticality of an invented sentence (the stock in trade of the *langue*-oriented (sentence-)grammarian), they do so entirely on the basis of intuition, but they sometimes end up doing it by imagining a context in which the sentence might occur, and when they do that they are in the realms of *parole* (granted that real contexts in real texts underlie all grammaticality judgements and intuitions); and we will see in Chapter 6 that *parole* findings feed into work on *langue*. Nevertheless, it is valid to distinguish between the grammarian's abstract sentence and actual utterances in texts, and in my view it is the former, it is *langue* and sentence-grammar, which constitutes the core of linguistics.

Saussure claims that language is a system whose units are determined by their place in the system, *un système où tout se tient* 'a system where everything hangs together', as Meillet put it.[12] In other words, language is systematic, and everyone knows that grammar consists of rules. But where does that leave exceptions to rules, which, again, everybody knows about, especially anyone who has learnt a foreign language and had to memorise them? Familiar exceptions such as strong or irregular verbs, and less familiar ones such as non-passivizable transitive verbs? Anticipating somewhat Chapter 7, the standard answer is that there are always exceptions in grammar, and we have to live with them; there is nothing we can do about them. But that seems to me to be wrong. The existence of a large number of unexplained exceptions to a rule contradicts the basic idea of a language being a Saussurean system. It is inherent in the definition of Saussurean system that everything has to be in there, there can be nothing left outside the system, not hanging together with the rest of the system. So why do (unexplained) exceptions arise? It seems to me that they arise to the extent that the grammarians have got it wrong. If a rule is correct and valid it will have no exceptions. If a rule has exceptions it is not wholly right.

There flows from this train of thought a crucial methodological point. Unexplained lexical exceptions offer us the perfect opportunity to home in on the flaws and weaknesses of a grammatical analysis, and to do so in an empirical manner by asking why those lexical items do not conform to the rule, what is special about them, and investigating them in detail. One works at the interface of grammar and lexis. One takes a grammatical rule and analyses the (unexplained) lexical exceptions to it. In Chapter 5 we look at irregular or strong verbs like *drink drank drunk*, and before that, in Chapter 3, we will examine verbs which are – or used to be – unexplained exceptions to the rule that all and only transitive verbs form a passive, viz. transitive verbs which do not form a passive, e.g. *to resemble*. We will see in Chapter 3 that if one recognises that the passive construction with *be* + V-*ed* is an aspect of the verb, not a voice of the verb, as alluded to above, then it becomes clear that it is lexical aspect which prevents some verbs from forming a passive. Furthermore, if one recognises that the passive with *be* + V-*ed* means 'action followed by resultant state', it also becomes clear that verbs which are atelic (also known as aterminative), i.e. which cannot express an end-state, will not be compatible with the passive. More of that later, but for now let us note that the special role of exceptions in grammatical research follows naturally from the structuralist tenet that a language is a system whose units, e.g. grammatical word-forms and morphemes, are determined by the place which they occupy – or are considered in a given analysis to occupy – in that system.

We started out this chapter by saying that language creates the reality which we perceive: *C'est le point de vue qui crée l'objet* 'it is the point of view which creates the object' (Saussure 1983:8), to give another famous quotation from the *Cours*. This idea is immediately apparent to anyone who knows a foreign language and interacts with its native speakers. Each language divides reality up differently, i.e. each language has its own grammar and lexicon, and all the native speakers of a given language believe that the divisions and the reality that their particular language provides and which they grew up with is the obvious, natural, objective, and true one.[13] They believe this even though the very existence of numerous languages, each with its own way of dividing up reality, contradicts the idea of there being one true way of dividing up reality. But it is not only language, it is other attributes of the human species which contribute to our perception of reality. First and foremost are the five senses: vision, hearing, smell, taste and touch. If we did not have the five senses the reality that we perceive would be very different. The five senses arise from certain biological properties that humans happen to possess. But surely all the human attributes – biological, physical, chemical, and psychological – contribute to our perception of reality? Other creatures, e.g. cats, spiders, jellyfish, must surely perceive reality differently to us. And then the question arises, is it merely a matter of perception, or something more? Does objective reality exist, and cats and spiders see it differently to us? Or, in line with Saussure, is there no such thing as objective reality at all, rather, is it that reality is a product of every species' perceptual apparatus? In philosophy the view that without an observer the world does not exist is known as 'subjective idealism' and was famously held by Berkeley, who wrote:

> It is indeed an opinion strangely prevailing amongst men, that houses, mountains, rivers, and in a word all sensible objects have an existence natural or real, distinct from their being perceived by the understanding. But with how great an assurance and acquiescence soever this principle may be entertained in the world; yet whoever shall find in his heart to call it in question, may, if I mistake not, perceive it to involve a manifest contradiction. For what are the aforementioned objects but the things we perceive by sense, and what do we perceive besides our own ideas or sensations; and is it not plainly repugnant that any one of these or any combination of them should exist unperceived?
>
> (Berkeley 1998: §4)

Kant also held this view in part, calling it 'transcendental idealism':

> Thus the order and regularity in the appearances which we entitle *nature*, we ourselves introduce. We could never find them in appearances, had not we ourselves, or the nature of our mind, originally set them there . . . .
>
> However exaggerated and absurd it may sound, to say that the understanding is itself the source of the laws of nature, and so of its formal unity, such an

assertion is none the less correct. (Kant 1933: A125, A127; quoted in Stevenson 1982: 335; see also Stevenson 1981)

Although we are fooled into believing that the reality which we perceive is the true and objective one, and really there, the fact of the matter is that it is not, it is a construction and artefact of our biological properties. One learns so much about the realities of other societies by talking to foreigners in their language, if one could talk to another species of animal, e.g. a jellyfish, I think the conversation might go something like this:

CB: Hello, jellyfish, how are you? You do realise the universe is hard, don't you. For example, this piece of driftwood is hard.

JELLYFISH: No it isn't, it's squidgy.

CB: Yes it is, it's hard, touch it.

(*CB touches and knocks the driftwood – knock knock*)

JELLYFISH: (*touches the driftwood – squidge*) See, it's squidgy.

CB: Ah yes, but it only *appears* squidgy to you because you have no tactile skin and hard bones.

JELLYFISH: True, and it only *appears* hard to you *because* you have skin and bones. If you didn't have skin and bones it wouldn't appear hard to you. The hardness is not there objectively to be felt by every creature, irrespective of their biological makeup. Your biological properties determine what you perceive.

CB: Alright, I'll show you how hard the universe is. If I pick you up and drop you from a great height onto the sand, then you'll see how hard the universe is!

JELLYFISH: [*Thinks*: "Typical aggressive human!"] I wouldn't advise that. It would prove nothing. The only reason that your action would hurt me is that I happen to be the size I am. Imagine if I were smaller than the smallest sub-atomic particle in the sand. I would pass right through the sand, without even knowing it was there. So once again we see that the universe, not just as perceived but as it is, depends on physical and biological attributes of the perceiver. Beauty is in the eye of the beholder, and reality is in the senses of the perceiver.

CB: Hmmm, clever, maybe you're right. Anyway, it's been nice talking to you, I'm off, now. Bye.

JELLYFISH: Bye.

The notion that without an observer the world does not exist is counter-intuitive, and appears to contradict our immediate apprehension of the world. But many things in life – scientific facts, as they say – are counter-intuitive.

We used to think the earth was flat: it took physics, intrepid travellers, and photographs from outer space to show us that the earth is round. And yet it still seems bizarre and contrary to our immediate experience that we are stuck to a ball of rock spinning through space, and don't fall off. It sounds equally perverse to claim that the world is a product of the perceptual apparatus of the observer, and that the world does not exist but for the observer, yet it is true.[14]

The question arises, to what extent is the fact that the human perceptual apparatus, especially language, creates the reality which we perceive a merely philosophical observation, of interest only to intellectuals and linguists, and to what extent is it something psychologically real, which touches us all in our consciousness with important and specific consequences.[15] Two familiar areas of debate amongst linguists, anthropologists, and psychologists here are colour terms, and words for snow in the language of the Eskimos. Does the fact that different languages divide up the colour spectrum differently affect the way in which the speakers of those languages see colours (Berlin & Kay 1999; Hardin & Maffi (Eds.) 1997)? Do native speakers of the Eskimo-Aleut languages, who are reportedly but controversially said to have several words for 'snow', perceive snow differently to native speakers of English, which has only one word for 'snow', viz. *snow*?[16] The answer to the general question is a varied one, I think, depending on which aspects of language and life you are talking about. Let us take grammatical distinctions first. German has a rule which says the verb in a main clause always appears in second position: *Ich war gestern im Theater* 'I went to the theatre yesterday' and *Gestern war ich im Theater* 'yesterday I went to the theatre'. English has a different rule, viz. the order is always subject-verb, i.e. we say *I went to the theatre yesterday* and *Yesterday I went to the theatre*, not **Yesterday went I to the theatre*. Are these two different rules psychologically real in the minds of German and English speakers respectively? Yes and no. Yes, they are psychologically real because language resides in the human mind and therefore everything linguistic is psychological. But no, in the sense that these two rules are purely grammatical rules which do not affect the consciousness, mentality or *Weltanschauung* of German and English speakers in any significant or noticeable way. The same argument applies to aspectual distinctions which Russian speakers make and English speakers do not make, and to definite/indefinite article distinctions which English speakers make but Russian speakers do not make.

Let us turn now to lexis. What is the impact of the linguistic creation of reality on lexis? For some parts of the vocabulary of a language the impact is fairly trivial. For example, the fact that German has one word, *Kissen* 'cushion; pillow', where English has two, viz. *cushion* and *pillow*, is not a major impediment to mutual understanding between nations. The same applies to *realia*, amusing and much talked about though they may be, such as in German *Wurst* 'sausage meat wrapped in a skin and served hot as sausages or sliced and served cold as cold meat', *Lederhosen* 'leather shorts, lederhosen', and *Bildungsroman* 'bildungsroman (novel concerned with the intellectual or spiritual development of the main character)', or *pub, kilt,* and *pantomime* in English. There is an element here of the manipulation of conceptual categories by language but not an insuperable one. But the linguistic creation of reality starts to become noticeable and serious in the area of language and politics. To give just one example, in 2003 Britain assisted America in its invasion of Iraq. Some Britons supported the invasion, whilst others opposed it. But the supporters of the invasion had the language in which the debate was held in Britain on their side. The minister responsible for the British armed forces at the time, Geoff Hoon, was called the Defence Minister. The term Defence Minister not only implies but even asserts[17] that Mr Hoon was the minister responsible for the defence of Britain, indeed for the self-defence of Britain. But opponents of the war felt that the invasion was an act of aggression, not (self-)defence. And yet they were not able to re-name Mr Hoon and his job title the War Minister, or the Aggression Minister, or the Minister for Naked Imperialism. The language of the debate and the conceptual categories which it created worked against the opponents of the invasion and made it difficult for them to get their message across. The Ministry of Defence, by virtue of its very name, cannot be said to have instigated an act of aggression, and indeed a statement like 'the Ministry of Defence initiated an act of aggression' sounds like a self-contradiction. If language determines thought, for speakers of English it is literally unthinkable, as in George Orwell's *Nineteen Eighty-Four*, that the Ministry of Defence might initiate an act of aggression. Or at least, it requires a huge intellectual or cognitive effort to resist the pressure from the language and to think that thought. In this instance the linguistic creation of reality and the fact that form determines meaning had a crucial and serious impact on the psychology of speakers.[18]

One of the most important grammatical constructions in the history of the debate about the relationship between form and meaning is the passive, for the simple reason that under the traditional voice analysis, i.e. the practice of deriving passives from an underlying active, there is a conflict between the apparent synonymy of actives and passives on the one hand and the huge difference in form between the two constructions on the other. We will examine the passive in Chapter 3, but in order to prepare for that we will now look at the grammatical category aspect.

CHAPTER 2

Aspect

Aspect is one of the two principal means in language of expressing time, the other one being tense. The main tenses which linguists usually recognise are past, present, and future. Typical aspects, on the other hand, are the progressive, perfect,[19] stative, telic, atelic, perfective, imperfective, durative, etc. Whereas tense locates an event relative to the moment of speech as past, present, or future, aspect is an expression of the way in which an action/event passes through time, e.g. as a continuous/extended activity, as an event with a final result, as the beginning of an action, with emphasis on the intensity of an action, etc. In this chapter we will define and explain each term as it comes up for discussion, but for your convenience a Glossary of Aspect Terms is provided on pp. 207–212.

In order to avoid confusion with tense let us first of all clarify what the tenses are. In doing so we will distinguish clearly between the form and the meaning of the tenses. Let us start with the form of the tenses. Most linguists now believe that it is best to restrict the notion of tense formally to inflection on the verb only (Quirk et al. 1985:176). That means that the past tense in English, e.g. *worked*, is a tense, because it is formed with -*ed*, and the present tense, e.g. *She works*, is a tense, because it is formed with -*s* (and Ø). But the future tense, e.g. *She will work*, is not really a tense, it is a modal construction, because it is formed with *will* + infinitive, in which *will* is a modal verb.

The supposed meanings of the tenses are reflected in their names. The past tense means past time, the present tense means present time, and the future tense, for those who still think of it as a tense, means future time. The practice of calling grammatical categories after their meanings is an invidious one and goes against the grain of structuralism, not to mention common sense.[20] The reason is that, as we said in Chapter 1, linguistics is a search for meanings, and if we commit ourselves to a meaning for a given form by naming the form after its supposed meaning, it makes it difficult to change our mind about its meaning in the light of further research, unless we change its name every time (Quirk et al. 1985:175). Moreover, it is irksome and impractical

when different scholars give their own names to a form reflecting their particular view of its meaning, thus multiplying terminology. There is a narrow and
parochial benefit to the bellicose, axe-grinding linguist in having semantically
motivated terms, since they are easier to use and every time you use them the
semantic point you are trying to make is reinforced. But if one takes the longer
and wider view they are harmful and ultimately self-defeating. The solution
adopted by the American structuralists of the 1950s was to number grammatical categories instead of naming them, so that nouns were 'Words of Class 1',
verbs were 'Words of Class 2', etc. (see e.g. Fries 1952). It did not catch on.[21]
There are other ways, though, of referring to a grammatical category without
referring to its supposed meaning. If it is a morphological category we can talk
about 'the -ed form in English', for example, instead of saying 'the past tense'.[22]
Another solution is to use the opaque name with a classical root (opaque from
the perspective of modern English (of course, not opaque to those who happen
to know ancient Greek and Latin)), where one exists, which hints at a meaning
without necessarily committing us to it. For example, the term 'preterit' comes
from the Latin *praeteritum*, meaning 'past'. The term preterit etymologically
speaking invites us to believe that -ed in English means 'past'. But we can decline the invitation. It is well-known that words move away from their original
meanings and motivations, and end up only loosely connected to their ety-
mons, so that we can ask the question 'What does the preterit mean? Is it past
time? Maybe it does, but maybe also it means something else?' without self-
contradiction. If we use the term 'past tense', on the other hand, the question
'Does the past tense mean past time?' or 'Does the past mean past?' would be a
self-contradiction. For that reason it is better to use the term 'preterit' and not
'past' to refer to the form -ed in English.

Of course, I am speaking here of theoretical linguistics, not pedagogical
grammars. In pedagogical grammars, especially for foreign learners, it is a
completely different matter. Obviously, the foreign learner has to be told the
meaning of forms, moreover, it would certainly not do to say 'this is the form,
and we think it means this, but we are not sure'. But for the theoretical linguist it is different. The theoretical linguist must give himself the opportunity
to change his mind about the meaning of a form by not committing himself to
a meaning in the name of the form.

Unfortunately there are no alternative names available and commonly
known for the present tense and the future tense, so we will have to continue to
use them, since I have enough on my plate in this book without fighting battles
to introduce new terminology here, there and everywhere. Thus so far we have
two terms which refer exclusively to formal categories, viz. tense and preterit;

two terms which may be used to refer exclusively to meanings, viz. time, and past; and two terms which are used to refer both to the formal category and its meaning, viz. present, and future.

We are now ready to deal with aspect, and we will again distinguish clearly between formal realization and meaning. Aspect is formally realized in three different ways in the world's languages: (i) Auxiliary + Participle; (ii) lexical aspect (also known as *Aktionsart*); (iii) compositional aspect. If we take each of these in turn, English has two recognised Auxiliary + Participle aspects, the progressive and the perfect. The progressive is formed with the auxiliary *be* and the 1st participle ending in *-ing*, as in the sentence *She is reading a book*. Turning to meaning, the progressive portrays an action as on-going or continuous (Quirk et al. 1985: 197–198). The perfect is formed with the auxiliary *have* and the 2nd participle in *-ed*, as in the sentence *She has read the book*. Although there are several sub-meanings of the perfect, its most general meaning is 'past action with current relevance' (Quirk et al. 1985: 190; McCawley 1971; R. Lakoff 1970: 844–845; McCoard 1978).[23]

Turning to our second formal type of aspect, lexical aspect, although English does not have morphological lexical aspect like Russian, i.e. lexical aspect realized by specific morphemes which attach to words (see below in this chapter),[24] it does have syntactic[24] lexical aspect, viz. one can see the lexical aspect a verb has by the way it reacts to being combined with the progressive and the perfect.[25] For example, it is well known that some verbs, e.g. *to know*, cannot combine with the progressive, or at least, they resist it, thus the sentence **She is knowing the truth* is under normal conditions ungrammatical. It is common practice amongst grammarians to infer from this fact that verbs like *to know* have a special lexical aspect, usually called stative. Stative verbs, as their name implies, express a state.[26] Although an action can readily be expressed as on-going or continuous a state cannot – hence stative verbs are incompatible with the progressive (Quirk et al. 1985: 200–202; Leech 1971: 14–29; Palmer 1974: 70–77; R. L. Allen 1966; Lyons 1977: 706–707). Thus stative verbs in English are an example of lexical aspect, formally recognisable by virtue of the fact that they are incompatible with the progressive. It is important to emphasise that, although because we have formal proof of their existence (viz. their incompatibility with the progressive) it makes sense to give them a meaning and say they are stative, it would not do to attempt to identify a class of stative verb solely on the basis of meaning. If such a class of verb had no formal consequences in the language it would be pointless. But there is a formal consequence, incompatibility with the progressive, and on the basis of that formal evidence we can proceed to posit a class of verb, stative.

A similar trick can be performed with the perfect, but with regard to sub-meanings of the perfect, not grammaticality. Grammarians recognise at least two distinct sub-meanings of the perfect, the continuous perfect and the resultative perfect. Consider sentences (1)–(4):

(1)   He has lived in Scotland for 20 years.

(2)   I have known her since 1990.

(3)   The taxi has arrived.

(4)   She has broken her doll.

Sentences (1)–(2) have a continuous meaning, i.e. the situation described continues to the present time. In (1) the implication is that he still lives in Scotland, and in (2) the implication is that I still know her. Sentences (3)–(4), on the other hand, have a resultative meaning, i.e. the action described leads to a result. The result in (3) is that the taxi is here, and in (4) the result is that the doll is now broken. The resultative perfect means, then, 'action + result'. The point of interest for us here is that it depends on the lexical aspect of the verb which sub-meaning of the perfect you end up with. If the verb has the lexical aspect telic – a telic verb is one which expresses inherently an end-point – it leads to a resultative perfect, whilst if the verb has the lexical aspect atelic – without an end-point inherent in its lexical meaning – it leads to a continuous perfect. The end-point is necessary to become the result in the meaning 'action + result' of the resultative perfect. The verbs *to live* and *to know* are atelic, i.e. do not express an end-point in their lexical meaning, and so (1)–(2) are continuous perfects, whilst the verbs *to arrive* and *to break* are telic, i.e. they have an end-point inherent in their lexical meaning, and so (3)–(4) are resultative perfects (Leech 1971; Dillon 1973; McCoard 1978: 142–144).[27] Once again, although these lexical aspects are not morphologically marked on the verb they do reveal themselves in the way in which the verbs behave in combination with an Auxiliary + Participle aspect, this time the perfect. This criterion with the English perfect is not as good as the other criteria given in this chapter, because it is semantic, and relies on our ability to interpret sentences semantically. The others we give are formal and rely on the grammaticality of sentences, that is, they rely on our ability to say whether a sentence or expression is grammatical.[28] But English grammarians seem confident about their ability to recognise a continuous perfect and a resultative perfect, so I have included them here anyway, even though it goes against my desire always to have formal evidence for the existence of a lexical aspect.

The possibility or impossibility of the perfect participle appearing in attributive position, i.e. before the noun, also indicates lexical aspect of the verb, and we are back now, thankfully, on the safe ground of formal evidence. For example, in English you can say *the departed guests, an escaped prisoner, the vanished treasure*, but you cannot say *the arrived immigrant, *the died man, *the left man*. The determining factor is the lexical aspect of the verb. Zandvoort (1962: 48–49) called intransitive verbs which allow attributive use of their 2nd participle 'mutative' verbs, by which he meant verbs which express a change of location or state. On the basis of this formal evidence we can say that in English *to depart, to escape, to vanish* are mutative, whilst *to arrive, to die, to leave* are non-mutative. True, we have come a cropper once again semantically, since semantically the latter three verbs, *to arrive, to die*, and *to leave* would appear to be no less mutative in meaning than the former three verbs, *to depart, to escape*, and *to vanish*. So Zandvoort's semantic characterization needs some refinement, to say the least. But as long as we approach it from the formal test of with or without a possible attributive 2nd participle we will be on firm ground, and we can identify a viable sub-set of verbs.

Turning now to our third way in which aspect is realized formally we come to compositional aspect. Aspect is not determined by the verb alone, but by certain other elements of the sentence which appear with the verb, viz. the subject, object, and adverbials, i.e. aspect is compositional (Verkuyl 1972, 1993; Kabakčiev 2000; Friedrich 1974; Brinton 1988: 36–51; Freed 1979: 10–14; Zifonun et al. 1997: 1867, 2048–2050). Consider the sentences in (5):

(5) a. A guest arrived.
     b. The guests arrived.

One of the tests for telic versus atelic aspect – remember, telic means with a built-in end-point, atelic means without an end-point[29] – is the possibility of co-occurrence with a durational time phrase like *for hours*. If an expression can combine with *for hours* it is atelic, if it can't it is telic. This is because the conclusive and terminative nature of a telic expression, i.e. its built-in end-point, clashes with the durational or temporally extended meaning of the phrase *for hours*. If we apply the *for hours* test to (5a) and (5b) we see that (5a) is telic – because (5c) is ungrammatical – but (5b) is atelic, because (5d) is grammatical:

(5) c. *A guest arrived for hours.
     d. The guests arrived for hours.

Both (5a) and (5b) contain the same verb, *to arrive*, so clearly it is not the verb which causes the difference in aspect between them. But they differ in their subjects, and it is indeed the subject which causes the difference. (5a) contains the singular subject noun phrase *a guest*, bringing about telic aspect, whilst (5b) contains the plural subject noun phrase *the guests*, bringing about atelic aspect. Aspect, then, is not just dependent on the verb, it is a function of the subject as well.

The object also determines the aspect of a sentence. Consider the sentences in (6):

(6) a. John is singing.
     b. John is singing a song.
     c. John is singing songs.
     d. John is singing five songs.

Another test for telic versus atelic aspect is as follows. Looking at (6a), suppose that John is interrupted in his singing. Will it be true to say that John has sung? Yes. Looking now at (6b), if John is interrupted will it be true to say that John has sung a song? No, because (6b) has an end-point in it and John is prevented from reaching that end-point by being interrupted. (6a) on the other hand has no end-point in it, which can be seen from the fact that, if interrupted, it is still true that John has sung. So (6a) is atelic, whilst (6b) is telic.

But it is not merely the presence or absence of an object which determines aspect, the type of object matters as well. Look at (6c). Remember that (6b), with an object, was telic. If in (6c) John is interrupted is it true to say that John has sung songs? Yes. So (6c) is atelic, i.e. by changing the singular object noun phrase *a song* to the plural object noun phrase *songs* we have changed the aspect from telic to atelic. Looking now at (5d), if John is interrupted is it true to say that he has sung five songs? No. So by changing the indefinite object noun phrase *songs* to the definite object noun phrase *five songs* we have changed the aspect back again to telic (Comrie 1976: 44–45). Obviously not just the presence of an object but the type of object present affects the overall compositional aspect of a sentence.

Adverbs also affect the compositional aspect of a sentence. Durational adverbs like *for hours*, *all day*, induce a durative interpretation, whereas punctual adverbs like *at five O'clock*, *yesterday*, induce a perfective interpretation. If a durational adverb is put together with a punctual verb the result is an ungrammatical sentence, as in (7b) below:

(7) a. They drank whisky for hours.
     b. *They broke the bottle for hours.   (Verkuyl 1972)

The role of adverbs in compositional aspect can also be seen in the following examples: *the newly arrived immigrant, a well-read woman, a soft-spoken person.* Here we see that the verbs *to arrive, to read, to speak,* which do not normally allow their 2nd participle to be used attributively, do allow attributive use if an adverb is present (Quirk et al. 1985: 1327). This could only be because the adverb changes the lexical aspect of the verb, from non-mutative to mutative, to use Zandvoort's terms.

We have seen that the aspect of a sentence is affected not just by the verb but by the subject, object, and adverbials as well, i.e. aspect is compositional. We may note three things from this. Firstly, there is a similarity between the structuralist tenet that a language is a system whose units are determined by their place in the system, and compositional aspect. Both the structuralist point and the aspect point manifest themselves in the sentence, the structuralist point in terms of which sentences are grammatical, the aspect point in terms of which particular aspect the sentence will turn out to have. John Lyons hit the nail on the head when he wrote (1977: 714): "Few parts of a language system illustrate better than its aspect-system does the validity of the structuralist slogan: *Tout se tient*".[30]

Secondly, we see how it was that lexical aspect acquired such a bad name for itself, as some linguists said 'English has lexical aspect, here are some examples', and other linguists reacted by quite easily producing counter-examples, in which a verb did not have the aspect it was supposed to have. The counter-examples are made possible by the fact that aspect is compositional, not just a matter of verb meanings.

We may note thirdly how absolutely crucial it is to have a formal, not semantic, approach to aspect, particularly when comparing languages. Every language is a structure *sui generis*, i.e. a unique structure, and never more so than in its aspect system. It is therefore wrong to transfer aspects from one language to another, for example to claim that English might have an imperfective/perfective distinction as in Russian. It is true that there are semantic similarities between e.g. Russian imperfective, French *imparfait*, and English progressive (Comrie 1976: 46), but for most purposes of linguistic analysis the differences are more important than the similarities.[31] It is also misguided to take a word in one language with its aspect, translate the word into English, and say the English translation must have that aspect as well. Finally, it is wrong to take a concept, e.g. words for 'to sleep', and say that that concept or meaning must be one aspect or another (and in the case of 'to sleep' it would be durative), in any language that one cares to take. The lexical aspect that a word has arises from the lexico-grammatical system of which it is part, and only from that system. The lexical aspect of a word arises from the system to which it belongs and we can only see its lexical aspect in that system, i.e. we can only see its lexical aspect on the basis of formal criteria such as morphology and syntax.[32]

The insistence that particularly in aspect we must work formally ties in with the point made earlier, in Chapter 1, that language creates reality. Let us take the English progressive as an example. As we said, the English progressive presents an action/event as on-going or continuous. But does that meaning exist independently of the English progressive? Ask an Englishman – or any native speaker of English – and they will say yes, of course, I can see it in my mind's eye, even now. But ask a 'foreigner', i.e. somewhat whose native language is not English, and they will say certainly not, it does not exist in my native language and it is an area where I make mistakes in English, even as an advanced learner of English. To the non-native speaker of English it is obvious – painfully obvious – that the meaning of the English progressive does not pre-exist the form, it is a meaning which arises from the presence of the form *be + V-ing* in English, and only from that form. This point is as obvious to the non-native speaker of English as is the notion to the non-native speaker of Russian that the meanings of the Russian perfective/imperfective distinction are idiosyncratic to the grammar of Russian. To the Englishman struggling to learn Russian it is obvious – painfully obvious – that the Russian perfective/imperfective semantic distinction does not pre-exist language, in this case the Russian language, it is not hovering out there somewhere, waiting for Russian to come along and label it. It is created by the grammar of Russian, and exists only in the context of the lexico-grammatical system of Russian. Our native language fools us into believing otherwise, but the truth of the matter is that reality does not exist except that it is created by language and languages. Linguists must therefore work from form to meaning, not from meaning to form, and aspect of all categories must be approached formally, not semantically.

Aspect in Russian

The language which is most associated with aspect is Russian, and a few minutes spent examining the Russian aspect system will be time well spent. Most verbs in Russian have two forms, an imperfective and a perfective form. Typically the imperfective form is simplex, and one adds a prefix to obtain the perfective form:

Imperfective	Perfective	Prefix
pisat' 'to write'	napisat'	na-
delat' 'to do'	sdelat'	s-
čitat' 'to read'	pročitat'	pro-

It can be seen from these examples that lexical aspect in Russian is a completely different kettle of fish to lexical aspect in English. In Russian the fact that we are confronted with a different aspect of a verb is obvious and indisputable because it is indicated by a prefix. In English, on the other hand, we have to resort to the syntactic properties of verbs, in particular the way in which they combine with the progressive and the perfect, in order to obtain formal evidence of a lexical aspect. It is in this sense that lexical aspect is overt, i.e. morphologically marked, in Russian, but covert in English, i.e. only discernible syntactically (syntax in the sense of combinatorial possibilities).

The meanings of imperfective and perfective aspect in Russian are as follows. The imperfective aspect expresses an action from within, as on-going. The perfective aspect, on the other hand, expresses an action from outside it, surveying an action as a whole, from its beginning to its end.[33] The imperfective is the unmarked member of the pair, perfective the marked member, i.e. if a verb is being used neutrally, without any special reference to the aspectual characteristics of the action described, the imperfective is chosen (Русская грамматика 1980: 583; Бондарко 1971; Isačenko 1962: 347–350; Forsyth 1970; Wade 1992: 258–259; Pulkina & Zakhava-Nekrasova 1960: 208). The following examples may illustrate the difference:

Imperfective	Perfective
Včera ja pisal pis'mo	Včera ja napisal pis'mo
'Yesterday I wrote a letter'	'Yesterday I wrote a letter (from beginning to end)'
Učenik sidel i delal uroki	Učenik sdelal uroki i pošel guljat'
'the pupil was sitting and doing his lessons'	'the pupil did (all) his lessons and went for a walk'
Zavtra ja budu čitat' rasskaz Gor'kogo	Zavtra ja objazatel'no pročitaju rasskaz Gor'kogo
'tomorrow I shall be reading a story by Gorky'	'tomorrow I shall certainly read the (whole) story by Gorky'
	(Pulkina & Zakhava-Nekrasova 1960: 298)

The English glosses are given here in a manner which emphasises the semantic difference between imperfective and perfective. However, under most circumstances the second imperfective example would be translated into English as 'the pupil sat and did his lessons', the third imperfective example as 'I shall read', i.e. exactly the same as the perfective. This is partly because the English verb forms *sat, did, read* can be understood in both a Russian-style imperfective and a Russian-style perfective way, depending on the context, and partly because in Russian the imperfective is used under neutral conditions, when no particular attention is being paid to aspectual considerations.

Often the addition of a prefix to a verb changes not just its aspect but its lexical meaning as well, either in terms of a nuance or more drastically, so that a different verb, i.e. semantically speaking a different verb, is produced. For example, we said above that the perfective of *pisat'* 'to write' is *napisat'*, with the prefix *na-*. But there is also *zapisat'* with the prefix *za-*, which means 'to note, make a note of', and with the prefix *pod-* you get *podpisat'* 'to sign'. Isačenko (1962:385) says, quite rightly, that the imperfective-perfective distinction in Russian is an oversimplification, and that one must take account of what he and others call *Aktionsarten*, that is to say, most verbs in Russian enter a series of derivations involving several prefixes and suffixes, they do not exist in just pairs. To give another example, we said above that the perfective of *delat'* 'to do' is *sdelat'*, with the prefix *s-*. But there are many other prefixes which can be added to *delat'*. Wolkonsky and Poltoratzky (1961:84–85) give the following 14 verbs derived from or related to *delat'*, and more could be added:

verb	prefix
delat' 'to do'	
vdelat' 'to insert'	v-
vozdelat' 'to cultivate'	voz-
vydelat' 'to manufacture'	vy-
dodelat' 'to finish, put finishing touches to'	do-
zadelat' 'to block, wall up'	za-
nadelat' 'to make in great quantities'	na-
obdelat' 'to finish off; shape, set'	ob-
otdelat' 'to finish off, trim, adorn, decorate'	ot-
peredelat' 'to remake, alter'	pere-
poddelat' 'to counterfeit, forge, falsify'	pod-
podelat' 'to do' (also in set expressions)	po-
pridelat' 'to add, attach, join affix'	pri-
prodelat' 'to perform, accomplish'	pro-
razdelat' 'to dress (e.g. fowl); cultivate'	raz-

This is not an isolated example, but entirely typical for most Russian verbs, and we have not even begun to talk of the suffixes which can be added. Aspect in Russian is not just a grammatical matter, it is a lexico-grammatical matter; and there is more to it than imperfective versus perfective, there are numerous additional *Aktionsarten* which need to be taken into account and which Slavicists have barely begun to explore in detail (see also Townsend 1975:118–122; McCoard 1978:21–22).

Aspect in German

German is a useful language to look at because it gives us an additional formal handle on lexical aspect through its versions of the perfect and the passive. Anyone who has done a year or two of German at school will know the rule that most verbs form their perfect with *haben* 'to have', but a small number of verbs, in particular verbs of motion and change of state, form their perfect with *sein* 'to be' (see e.g. Durrell 2002:246–248). But what you probably were not told at school is that this property reflects the lexical aspect of the verb: intransitive verbs which form their perfect with *haben* are durative, whereas verbs which form their perfect with *sein* (all verbs which form their perfect with *sein* are intransitive) are perfective (I use Helbig and Buscha's terms, but one could also characterise the difference as atelic versus telic). So *schlafen* 'to sleep' is durative, but *einschlafen* 'to fall asleep' is perfective:

(8) a. Er hat geschlafen.
          'he has slept'
     b. Er ist eingeschlafen.
          he is fallen asleep
          'he has fallen asleep'   (Helbig & Buscha 1989:75; Duden 1998:121;
                                            Zifonun et al. 1997:1872)[34]

We saw with English the property that some verbs allow their 2nd participle to be used attributively, whilst others do not. Again, anyone who has studied the slightest amount of German will have noticed this construction as being a very German or Germanic construction. You can say in German 'the sitting on the fence bird' (*der auf dem Zaun sitzende Vogel*), which you certainly cannot say in English. But the construction has its restrictions in German, too, and as with English it is the lexical aspect of a verb which determines whether its 2nd participle can be used attributively or not:

(9) a. *das geschlafene Kind
          the slept   child

    b.   das eingeschlafene Kind
        the fallen asleep child
        'the child who has fallen asleep'

Verbs whose 2nd participle can be used attributively, like *einschlafen* 'to fall asleep' in (9b), have the lexical aspect perfective, whilst those whose 2nd participle cannot be used attributively, like *schlafen* 'to sleep' in (9a), have the lexical aspect durative. This property goes hand in hand with perfect with *haben* or *sein*, i.e. if a verb forms its perfect with *sein* its 2nd participle will have an attributive use, and if an intransitive verb forms its perfect with *haben* its 2nd participle will not allow an attributive use (Helbig & Buscha 1989:76).

But what makes the attributive participle in German particularly interesting is that the addition of an adverbial phrase, usually of direction or motion, often renders an ungrammatical attributive phrase grammatical:

(10)   a. *der gelaufene Junge
           the run   boy
       b. der aus dem   Zimmer gelaufene Junge
           the out of the room   run   boy
           'the boy who had run out of the room'   (Helbig & Buscha 1989:76)

This is clearly another example of compositional aspect: the addition of the adverbial changes an expression from durative to perfective (Zifonun et al. 1997:1872–1873).

German has one more piece of formal evidence for lexical aspect which English does not have, and that arises from the fact that German has a statal passive with *sein* 'to be' as well as an actional passive with *werden* 'to become'. As the names imply, the actional passive with *werden* expresses an action,[35] whereas the statal passive with *sein* expresses a state. In essence it is the same actional versus statal passive that English has, but whereas in English it is a subtle semantic distinction in German the difference is realized formally and unambiguously in the auxiliaries *werden* versus *sein*. For a verb to form a statal passive with *sein* it has to be perfective. If a verb does not easily form a statal passive with *sein* it is an indication that the verb is durative:

(11)   a. Die Tür ist geöffnet.
         'the door is opened'
       b. *Der Student ist gelobt.[36]
         the student is praised

Thus *öffnen* 'to open' is revealed in (11a) to be perfective, and *loben* 'to praise' is revealed in (11b) to be durative (Helbig & Buscha 1989: 77).

In sum, there are three formal indicators of a German verb having the lexical aspect perfective as opposed to durative: perfective verbs form their perfect with *sein*, allow an attributive use of their 2nd participle, and readily form a statal passive. Although German, like English, does not have morphologically marked lexical aspect Russian-style, as long as we follow the golden rule that we must have formal – in this case syntactic, i.e. combinatorial – evidence in order to posit a lexical aspect we will not go far wrong, and we can recognise that German, like English, does indeed have lexical aspect.

CHAPTER 3

The passive

We can now turn to a construction which illustrates better than any other the structuralist dictum that form determines meaning, i.e. the idea that grammarians should start with form and ask 'What does this form mean?', rather than starting with meaning. The most widespread analysis of the passive today, in traditional, pedagogical, descriptive, generative and every other kind of grammar, is that passives and actives are (cognitively) synonymous, in line with which passives are derived from their underlying actives. This is the voice analysis of the passive. It will be shown in this chapter, however, that passives and actives are not synonymous – the so-called actional passive has its own independent meaning, viz. the expression of a new state on the subject as the result of a preceding action (hence the subject is patient) – and passives are not derived from an underlying active, rather, they are an aspect of the type Auxiliary + Participle, like the perfect and the progressive in English. Passivizability depends not on transitivity but on the lexical aspect of the verb and the compositional aspect of the sentence. But all that comes in the second half of the chapter. Let us begin with the commonly accepted voice analysis of the passive.

The passive consists in English of *be* + V-*ed*, with *be* an auxiliary and V-*ed* the 2nd participle.[37] An example is given in (12) below:

(12)   The detective was murdered by the butler.

The main problem with the passive is how to explain that in it the subject (*the detective* in (12)) is interpreted as patient, not agent.[38] To that end since time immemorial passives have been 'derived' from an 'underlying' 'active', so that (12) is said to derive from (13):

(13)   The butler murdered the detective.

Sentences (12) and (13) are considered to be synonymous in their basic cognitive or referential meaning,[39] though they differ in respect of theme/rheme.[40] In the process of conversion from active to passive five morpho-syntactic and lexical changes take place. Firstly, the subject of the active sentence (*the butler* in (13)) moves to object of a preposition. Secondly, the object of the active sentence (*the detective* in (13)) moves to the subject position which has just become vacant. Thirdly, the auxiliary *be* is introduced. Fourthly, the finite verb changes to 2nd participle. And finally, the preposition *by* is introduced. The verb is said to have two 'voices', the active voice and the passive voice. Thus we have an explanation for why it is that in the passive the subject is interpreted as patient. The reason is that the subject started out as object of a transitive active sentence, where it was, of course, patient. When it becomes promoted to subject in a passive sentence it retains its original patient meaning. At the same time we obtain a rule for which verbs can form a passive: only transitive verbs can form a passive, because an object is needed (with patient meaning) to be promoted to subject (Quirk et al. 1985: 159–160); on transitivity see Hopper & Thompson 1980.

The voice analysis, i.e. the notion that one should derive passives from actives, is reflected in the name given to the construction *be* + V-*ed*, the 'passive'. It is called 'the passive' because the subject passively 'receives the action of the verb', as school grammar puts it, rather than initiating an action as agent, which is the more usual role of subjects. The point is often reinforced by giving example sentences containing the verb *to hit*.

Be + V-*ed* has two interpretations, one actional,[41] the other statal. The passive sentence (12) is actional, i.e. it expresses an action. (14) below, on the other hand, is a statal passive, i.e. expresses a state:

(14)   The building is already demolished.

In (14) the form *demolished* is more like an adjective – adjectives typically express a state – than a verbal participle. A mark of a statal passive is that it cannot appear with an agentive *by*-phrase.

In (14), because of the context supplied, there is no doubt that it is a statal passive. But often a sentence taken in isolation – and even in actual texts – is ambiguous between an actional reading and a statal reading. Consider, for example, (15):

(15)   The door was closed.

Sentence (15) could mean either the door was closed by the janitor at 6.00 (actional passive), or the door was closed (= shut, not open) when I walked past it at 6.00 (statal passive). Only supplying a further context resolves the ambiguity.

Get is a common alternative to *be* as the passive auxiliary, in addition to which there is *become, grow,* and *seem* (Quirk et al. 1985: 152). Svartvik 1966 further admits *appear, lie, look, seem, stand, feel,* and *rest* as passive auxiliaries.

The agentive *by*-phrase in the passive is optional. In fact, it is rare. According to Quirk et al. (1985: 164–165) approximately four out of five English passive sentences have no expressed agent, usually because the agent is irrelevant or unknown, as in *My house was burgled last night.*[42]

There are also alternatives to the preposition *by* in passives, viz. the prepositions *about, at, over, to,* and *with,* as in *We were all worried about the complication, I was a bit surprised at her behaviour* (Quirk et al. 1985: 169).

Some verbs are transitive in the sense of having a following object but do not passivize. Quirk et al. (1985: 162) give the following six examples:

(16)   They have a nice house.

(17)   He lacks confidence.

(18)   The auditorium holds 5000 people.

(19)   The dress becomes her.

(20)   John resembles his father.

(21)   Will this suit you?

The question of non-passivizable transitive verbs is the most important and most intractable problem of the passive. Most grammars, including Quirk et al. 1985, do not attempt to explain why they exist, but simply note their existence and list them.[43]

A similar problem is presented by prepositional verbs, which are sometimes passivizable and sometimes not. The nearest that grammarians have come to an explanation for this phenomenon within the voice analysis is to say that it depends on whether the sentence produces an observable result (Stein 1979: 80) or a noticeable effect (Bolinger 1974: 223–224). For example, *They wrote on the page* can lead to *The page was written on,* but *They sat on the bench* cannot easily lead to ?*The bench was sat on.* Whilst ?*The bridge was walked under by the dog* sounds strange, *The bridge has been walked under by generations of lovers* sounds acceptable. Attempts have also been made within theme-rheme analysis to explain such examples. But these are vague and intuitive criteria – no one has ever found a grammatical, i.e. morpho-syntactic explanation within the voice analysis for why some prepositional verbs or sentences form a passive and others do not.

The problem of odd passives is not restricted to prepositional verbs, however, it extends much further than that. W. S. Allen (1974: 277) points out that most active sentences are grotesque curiosities when put into the passive, e.g. (22)–(23):

(22) a. John likes girls.
      b. ?Girls are liked by John.

(23) a. Henry can read English and French.
      b. ?English and French can be read by Henry.   (cited by Svartvik 1966:2)

McCawley (1974:83–84) says the same for (24):

(24) a. Hubert loves God.
      b. ?God is loved by Hubert.

The reader can confirm this for himself by taking any text and trying to convert the transitive actives in it into the passive – most of them will not go, or end in 'grotesque curiosities'. The problem becomes even more intriguing when one realises that most odd passives can be made grammatical or normal-sounding with a bit of ingenuity:

(25) a. ?Girls are liked by John.
      b. Girls are liked by most men.

(26) a. ?God is loved by Hubert.
      b. God is loved by everyone.

(27) a. ?A good time was had by James.
      b. A good time was had by all.

(28) a. ?The film was enjoyed by John.
      b. The film was enjoyed by everyone.

(29) a. ?The prize is deserved by Peter.
      b. The prize is deserved by several contestants.

(30) a. ?This was had for twopence at a grocer's.
      b. This may be had for twopence at any grocer's.

(31) a. ?James is liked.
      b. James is well-liked.

Even the resilient *to resemble* can passivize:

(32) a. ?Mary is resembled by Fiona.
      b. Mary isn't resembled by any of her children.
                    (Halliday 1967a:68, quoted in Huddleston 1971:94)

Most of the tinkering with these odd passives involves changing the agent noun phrase from definite to indefinite or from singular to plural. One is led to conclude that passivizability is a property of sentences, not verbs.

That was the voice analysis of the passive form *be* + V-*ed*, i.e. a description of the passive under which passives are derived from an underlying active. Every grammatical description of a given phonological form has three basic aims: to categorise it grammatically or parse it, i.e. to say what category or type of construction it is; to give the syntax of the form, i.e. with which other forms can it combine; and to say what the meaning of the form is. The answer of the voice analysis to these three questions can be summarised as follows:

Voice analysis of *be* + V-*ed*
Category
The form *be* +V-*ed* is derived from an underlying active, thus verbs have two 'voices', active and passive, whereby *be* + V-*ed* is the passive voice.

Syntax
All and only transitive verbs can form a passive.

Meaning
(Actional) passives are cognitively synonymous with their underlying actives.

The voice analysis of the passive brings with it numerous problems and unanswered questions. The most obvious one is that it is hard to believe that a construction can involve five formal changes to no semantic effect. You do not have to be a rabid structuralist waving the banner of 'one form:one meaning' to find that hard to swallow. The object moves, the subject moves, *be* and *by* are introduced, and the verb changes from finite to non-finite, all with no repercussions on meaning (except for theme/rheme)! Unlikely, I think. In effect the voice analysis says that *be* + V-*ed* means nothing, which makes one wonder why it exists at all.[44] So what does *be* + V-*ed* mean?

The statal passive is also a problem. *Be* + V-*ed* normally expresses an action; no state. But sometimes it expresses a state; no action. Something wrong there, I think.

The statistic from corpus analyses that four-fifths of passive sentences in texts occur without the agentive *by*-phrase makes a nonsense out of deriving passives from actives. In the active subjects are obligatory; there can be no active sentences without a subject. So where do all these passives with no agent come from, whereby the agent is unknown? Not from an underlying active, obviously. It is common practice to assume a 'dummy' subject in such cases, equivalent to 'someone', i.e. underlying *My house was burgled* is the sentence *Someone burgled my house*. But that is stretching a point beyond credibility.

Be is a small word, which can slip in quietly in the derivation of passives from actives. But *get* is a bit bigger, and *become*, *grow*, *seem* etc. storm into view with their own full-blown semantics, making it highly implausible that any sentence containing them was derived from an underlying active (see Stein 1979:27). The same argument applies to the numerous alternatives to the preposition *by* in the agentive phrase, viz. *about, at, over, to*, and *with* (Quirk et al. 1985:169). *By* is another small word, and the voice analysis can get away with claiming in effect that it is meaningless, since the NP which *by* governs derives its agentive meaning from the fact that is started out life as the subject of the underlying active. But the prepositions *about, over*, etc. quite obviously have a bigger semantics, and the NP which they govern quite obviously means what it means because of the meaning of *about, over*, etc., not because it started out life as subject in an underlying active sentence.

Quirk et al. attempt to get over this problem by presenting a 'passive gradient' and the notion of semi-passive, exemplified by the following sentences:

(33)   This violin was made by my father.

(34)   This conclusion is hardly justified by the results.

(35)   Coal has been replaced by oil.

(36)   This difficulty can be avoided in several ways

- -

(37)   We are encouraged to go on with the project.

(38)   Leonard was interested in linguistics.

(39)   The building is already demolished.

(40)   The modern world is getting more highly industrialized and mechanized.

(41)   My uncle was/got/seemed tired.

The dotted line indicates the break between real passives and semi-passives. Those above the line are real passives, those below the line are increasingly remote from the ideal passive with a unique active paraphrase, and are not real passives at all – they are semi-passives. Particularly the last one in the gradient, (41), is a Copular + Adjective construction, an analysis which is confirmed by the possibility of inserting the intensifier *very*, a sure sign of an adjective, into the sentence (Quirk et al. 1985:167). But (37) and (38), they go on to say, also display adjectival properties, e.g. the possibility of coordinating the participle with an adjective, or the possibility of modifying the participle with *quite, rather, more*, etc. (Quirk et al. 1985:168). And they might have added the most adjective-like property of all, viz. the occurrence of the participle after the verb *to be* (a property which, of course, applies to all passives). Although the passive gradient does start to address a genuine problem it still begs the question, why? Why does the same form, be + V-*ed*, start off at the top of the passive gradient indicating an action only, and end up at the bottom of the gradient indicating a state only, no action, for state is indeed the meaning of the part of speech Adjective? And why are there intermediate stages, with different mixes of action and state? The problem is similar to that of the statal passive mentioned above, viz. how can the same form express either an action (no state) or a state (no action)?

Another intriguing problem arises from the sentence which Quirk et al. (1985: 167–168) give, presumably based on the corpora which underlie much of that grammar, as being a typical passive sentence, viz. sentence (36) above, *This difficulty can be avoided in several ways*. The sentence which one encounters time and again in discussions of the passive is very different, something like *John was hit by Bill*, with the verb *to hit*, emphasising the fact that John 'receives the action of the verb', i.e. gets hit by Bill. Quirk et al. chose sentence (36) as a typical passive because it has no agentive *by*-phrase realized. But there are other features of the sentence which strike me as being typical as well: an abstract noun as subject, the presence of an adverbial phrase, and the presence of a modal verb which results in the passive verb being in the infinitive form. This is all very different from *John was hit by Bill*, with its singular definite noun phrase as subject, no modal verb, and no adverbial (quite apart from the main difference, i.e. the presence/absence of an agentive *by*-phrase). So why is sentence (36) a typical passive, and not *John was hit by Bill*?

Why is it that some transitive verbs do not form a passive? It is not enough to say that they exist and to list them, we need to know why they exist. And why are odd passives so easy to invent, simply by taking virtually any active sentence in a text and converting it into the passive? And then why can almost any odd passive be rendered grammatical, with sufficient ingenuity? And why is the passive participle also used in the perfect in English, so that in traditional grammar the 2nd participle was known as the perfect passive participle? All these questions are raised by describing be + V-*ed* as derived from an underlying active.

They are answered, however, by recognising that be + V-*ed* is an aspect of the verb, of the type Auxiliary + Participle, like the perfect (*have* + V-*ed*) and the progressive (*be* + V-*ing*) in English.[45] It expresses a new state which arises on the subject as the result of an action – hence the subject is patient (Poupynin 1996: 133; Abraham 2000: 151). And its combinability is determined by the lexical aspect of the verb and the compositional aspect of the sentence: verbs and sentences which are atelic, i.e. which do not potentially contain an end-point such that an action can lead to a resultant state, cannot form a passive (Schoor-lemmer 1995:245–274). For clarity and comparison let us put this analysis on the template of Category-Syntax-Meaning which we used to sum up the voice analysis earlier in this chapter:

Aspect analysis of be + V-ed

Category

The form *be* + V-*ed* is an aspect of the type Auxiliary + Participle (like the perfect and the progressive in English).

Syntax

The occurrence of *be* + V-*ed* is determined by the lexical aspect of the verb and the compositional aspect of the sentence. Only telic verbs or telic sentences can form a passive, whereby the object of a clause usually provides the telic end-point necessary for a passive.[46] Verbs and sentences which do not potentially contain an end-point which can become the state of the 'action + state' meaning of *be* + V-*ed*, i.e. which are atelic, cannot (easily) form a passive.[47]

Meaning

Be + V-*ed* expresses an action and the new state that results from that action. In other words, *be* + V-*ed* means 'action + state'. Since the passive is intransitive, i.e. only has the subject participant, the new state that arises arises on the subject, i.e. the subject undergoes a change of state. If the subject NP undergoes a change of state it is affected by and indeed created by the action of the verb, which is what the patient role is (see fn. 38), usually associated with the object. It is because of this meaning which *be* + V-*ed* has that the subject of passives is interpreted as patient.

Whatever theme-rheme analysis you proposed for the passive under the voice analysis – e.g. the passive exists to make the patient unmarked theme – remains under the aspect analysis, except that instead of saying the passive exists to make the patient unmarked theme we say that in the passive it so happens that the patient is unmarked theme, a fact which comes in handy sometimes in the construction of texts. To justify the very existence of the passive construction by means of theme-rheme analysis is to mix levels in an inappropriate way. Is it likely that such a subtle factor as theme-rheme organization would affect lexico-morpho-syntax so drastically as to produce a whole new construction, the passive, which has less a lexico-morpho-syntactic status than a theme-rheme status? I think not. The passive must have first and foremost a lexico-morpho-syntactic status – and now we know what it is – and its theme-rheme status fits in around that.

Let us exemplify the aspect analysis on sentence (12), repeated here as (42):

(42)   The detective was murdered by the butler.

Under the aspect analysis there is no active structure underlying (42). The subject, *the detective*, is taken from the lexicon, like any other subject. *Was* is an aspectual auxiliary, like *be* of the progressive and *have* of the perfect. It is not necessary to posit a special category called voice, with *be* as a unique passive auxiliary. Instead, we assimilate the passive *be* into a category which already exists, containing perfect *have* and progressive *be*. *Murdered* is an aspectual participle, and is homonymous with the perfect participle because passive and perfect belong to the same category, viz. Auxiliary + Participle aspect, and indeed have a similar meaning (see below). Once again we do not need to leave the passive participle stranded, on its own, the sole member of a one-member category, viz. passive participle. Instead, we see that English has three aspectual participles: the perfect, the progressive, and the passive. Finally, *by the butler* is an ordinary prepositional phrase, in which the preposition *by* has its dictionary meaning of 'through the agency, means or instrumentality of'. Like most prepositional phrases it is optional. Sentence (42) means that an action happened, viz. a murder took place, as a result of which the detective is in a new state, viz. that of being dead, after being murdered. Another way of saying this is that the detective underwent a change of state, from not being murdered to having been murdered. It is for this reason that the subject NP *the detective* in (42) is interpreted as patient.

Thus we see that the categories 'active' and 'voice' were a fiction, postulated specifically to try to explain the passive. But they and their circular definitions noted in fn. 39 are not needed. The category to which the passive belongs already exists in English, it is the category Auxiliary + Participle aspect, which is already recognised in English as containing the perfect and the progressive. The significant formal generalization that linguists have been seeking for aeons with respect to the passive lies here, in the category aspect.

During the many years that I have taught this analysis several students have suggested that I rename the passive in line with the new analysis, perhaps 'the mutative' (cf. Lyons 1968:315). It is a tempting idea, but on balance I think there would be more to lose than to gain by doing that. It is true, as asserted earlier in this chapter, that the term 'passive' is intimately connected with the voice analysis, so much so that it even presupposes it. If one interprets the term 'passive' literally in this way the statement 'the passive is an aspect' is a self-contradiction (in contrast the statement '*be* + V-*ed* is an aspect' is not a self-contradiction). But firstly, as was argued in Chapter 2 on pp.19–20, it is bad practice for any linguist, particularly a structuralist, to name a category after the meaning he thinks it has, for reasons given there, in Chapter 2. Secondly, it seems to me that the term 'passive' is now so well entrenched in the consciousness of linguists that it would be nigh on impossible to replace it, moreover, it is so well entrenched that most linguists are only vaguely aware that it originally meant 'subject receives the action of the verb' anyway, most linguists view it as a technical term referring to a particular construction, whereby the term may or may not be semantically motivated. I therefore propose to keep the term 'passive', but as a historical term, no longer implying what it used to imply, i.e. the voice analysis.

That is the aspect analysis of the passive. All I need to do now is to justify it, i.e. to say why it is correct and better than the voice analysis. The aspect analysis of the passive explains a wide range of problems which are raised by the voice analysis, mentioned earlier in this chapter. Firstly, it explains the great discrepancy between the form of the passive and the form of the active, when the two constructions are supposed to be (cognitively) synonymous: *Five* formal changes and no change in meaning really does not sound credible. The explanation is that the discrepancy is an artefact of an incorrect analysis. Actives and passives are not (cognitively) synonymous, therefore it is not surprising that they differ formally in numerous ways. The true formal simplicity of the passive is shown in the following equation:

be + V-*ed*   (passive)
have + V-*ed* (perfect)
be + V-*ing*   (progressive)

Both parts of the passive re-appear elsewhere in the grammar, the 2nd participle in the perfect,[48] the auxiliary *be* in the progressive. If you think that passives are related to a category which you call 'active' in a category which you call 'voice', then you have made for yourself the problem of explaining how it is that five morpho-syntactic changes lead to no (significant) semantic change. But if you don't, you don't. If instead you recognise that the passive is an aspect, like the perfect and the progressive, with its own meaning, the problem does not arise.

Secondly, the voice analysis raised the question, so what does *be* + V-*ed* mean? The answer which the aspect analysis gives is 'action + state', the expression of a new state which arises on the subject as the result of a preceding action. At the very least this sounds more plausible than saying that *be* + V-*ed* means nothing at all, which is what the voice analysis says. But its plausibility goes much further than that. If you recall from Chapter 2 that a general gloss on the perfect is 'past action with current relevance', and that the main meaning of the perfect is resultative, in which the perfect expresses an action together with the result that ensues from that action, i.e. 'action + result', then one can see that it is entirely natural and logical for the passive, with its meaning of 'action + state', to be formally similar to the perfect. The passive and the perfect are similar in meaning and similar in form.

We can also see now why the statal passive is possible. All that happens is that the statal passive picks up the notion of state already present in the actional passive. Under the voice analysis the state of the statal passive comes from nowhere. In the aspect analysis the state of the statal passive links in with the state of the so-called actional – which is really action + state – passive.

The fact that four-fifths of actually occurring passive sentences in texts occur without an agentive *by*-phrase is also now easily explained. We see that, once again, the problem is an artefact of the incorrect voice analysis. If you think that passives are derived from actives you have made for yourself the problem of explaining how it is that the overwhelming majority of passives appear without the subject from the active, whereby in many cases the subject/agent is not known (and so the active can never have existed!). But if you recognise that the passive is an aspect, and not derived from anything, then it is clear that the *by*-phrase is an ordinary prepositional phrase, optional like most prepositional phrases, in which *by* has its ordinary dictionary meaning of 'through the agency, means or instrumentality of'. The NP in the *by*-phrase of the passive means agent not because it started out as the subject of an underlying active, but because it is governed by the preposition *by*, meaning 'through the agency, means or instrumentality of'. If the agent is known it can be mentioned, if not, not.

We can also see now why it is that plenty of other prepositions are possible in the *by*-phrase, e.g. *about, at, over, to, with*. We no longer need to turn a blind eye to the fact that each of these prepositions brings with it its own meaning into the passive sentence. *By* is an ordinary preposition with its own meaning, and so is *about*, and *at*, and all the rest of them, each of them optional. We no longer need to pretend that *We were all worried about the complication* might come from *The complication worried us all* (Quirk et al. 1985: 169), which it so obviously doesn't.

In a similar vein we can see why there are also numerous alternatives to *be* in the passive, e.g. *get, become, grow, seem*. They are possible because the auxiliary in passives is taken from the lexicon, not from an underlying active, and the range of auxiliaries available is as wide as can be accommodated by the 2nd participle and by the lexical semantics of the verb being passivized. Notice furthermore that at least two of the alternatives to *be* in the passive, viz. *get* and *become*, crop up in the progressive, just like *be*: *to get going*, *it becomes tiring*.[49]

The reason why Quirk et al. 1985's passive gradient, discussed on pp.38–39, exists also becomes clear. The gradation from pure action to pure state (i.e. Copular + Adjective) in the 2nd participle, with all the intermediary stages, is determined by the lexical aspect of the verb. Under the voice analysis the passive gradient is a problem, because one wonders where to make the cut-off point, distinguishing real passives from semi-passives, and one wonders how on earth you get from a true passive to a Copular + Adjective construction using the same form, *be* + V-*ed*. But under the aspect analysis it is natural that different verbs have different lexical aspects, leading to a different mix of action and resultant state in the 2nd participle, even a mix which is so weighted towards state that the form in question is more like an adjective than a passive participle, as in *He was tired*. The argument here is the same as was used above for the statal passive. Under the voice analysis to go from pure action to either a statal passive or a Copular + Adjective construction is a mystery. But if the canonical passive with *be* + V-*ed* already contains an element of state, viz. it means 'action + state', then it is entirely natural for the same form, *be* + V-*ed*, to produce a statal passive like *The door was closed*, a Copular + Adjective construction like *He was tired*, or a half-way house like *Leonard was interested in linguistics*.

But the most convincing proof of the aspect analysis lies in non-passivizable transitive verbs, since the aspect analysis furnishes us with an explanation for those. The aspect analysis claims that for a verb to passivize its lexical aspect must be right, viz. it must be telic, i.e. it must contain an inherent end-point, capable of becoming the end-state of the meaning 'action + state'. No potential end-point, no passive. Let us look again at sentences (16)–(21) on p.35. We see there the six verbs *have*, *lack*, *hold*, *become*, *resemble*, *suit*. None of these verbs contain a potential end-point in their meaning, i.e. they are all atelic. Hence they cannot form a passive, despite being transitive.

Proof? Yes, we need formal proof of that, and here it is. We have already said that the passive, with its meaning 'action + state', is similar in meaning to the resultative perfect, with its meaning 'action + result'. In Chapter 2 on p.22 we pointed out that only telic verbs – verbs with an inherent end-point in their semantics – can form a resultative perfect, atelic verbs form a continuous perfect. Thus the criterion for the formation of a resultative perfect – the verb must be telic – is identical with the criterion for passivizability – again, the verb must be telic. It follows that if a verb cannot form a passive – because it is atelic – it will also not be able to form a resultative perfect, for the same reason. Such verbs will lack a potential end-point capable of becoming either the end-state of a passive or the end-result of a perfect. All we need to do is to test sentences (16)–(21) for their possibility of forming a resultative perfect:

(43)   They have had a nice house.

(44)   He has lacked confidence.

(45)   The auditorium has held 5000 people.

(46)   The dress has become her.

(47)   John has resembled his father.

(48)   This has suited you.

Can (43)–(48) be interpreted as resultative perfects? No, they are at best ex-periential perfects, at worst not possible in the perfect at all, i.e. just plain ungrammatical. What they are certainly not is resultative perfects. Thus we see that the passive and the perfect react in the same way to the same verbs. If a verb is atelic, such that it will not form a resultative perfect, it will also not form a passive, for the same reason, viz. it lacks a potential end-point to become ei-ther the end-result of 'action + result' (perfect) or the end-state of 'action + state' (passive). The passive behaves like the perfect, confirming that it is the same construction as the perfect, viz. an Auxiliary + Participle aspect sensi-tive to lexical aspect. The perfect-passive correlation described here is formal,[50] syntactic[51] proof that non-passivizable transitive verbs do not for ɪ passive because of their lexical aspect, that the lexical aspect in question is ..elic, and that the passive is an aspect of the type Auxiliary + Participle, like the perfect and the progressive in English.[52]

The aspect analysis also explains the phenomenon of odd passives, and why odd passives can be made grammatical with some tinkering and some ingenuity. In general terms the reason is that aspect is not just lexical, it is compositional, i.e. the aspect of a sentence is determined not just by the lexical aspect of the verb but by other constituents, particularly the subject, object, and adverbials as well, as we saw in Chapter 2 on pp.23–25. Thus the aspect analysis predicts that changes to the subject, object, and adverbials in a sen-tence will affect passivizability. In more specific terms, what is happening in sentences (22)–(32) is connected with the mix of action and state conveyed by the 2nd participle. The verbs there (which are all stative) seem to want to form a 2nd participle which is mostly statal but a little bit actional as well, though not too much. Thus, looking at the verb *to like* in (22) and (25), you can't quite say *Girls are liked* because that would be too statal (adjective-like), and you can't say ?*Girls are liked by John*, with a definite agent, because that would be too actional. But to say *Girls are liked by most men* is alright because the indefinite agent leaves the participle mostly statal but a little bit actional as well, though not too much. The same argument applies to the remaining sentences in (22)–(32): you can almost say *God is loved*, but not quite, almost *The film was enjoyed*, but not quite, etc. The NP in the agentive *by*-phrase adjusts the mix of state and action in the 2nd participle to produce a grammatical, odd or ungrammatical sentence accordingly, depending on the particular verb concerned and its lexical aspect as well as on other elements making up the compositional aspect of the sentence.

What we also see in (25)–(32), the odd passives made grammatical by clever tinkering, is features associated with aspect, such as the change from singular to plural ((25), (27), (29), Bolinger's walked-under bridge example), the change from definite to indefinite ((25)–(30), (32), Bolinger's example again), and negation (32). Wilding 1978 found in her corpus an overwhelming tendency for the agentive *by*-phrase to contain an indefinite NP, and Abraham (2000: 146) speaks of the 'deindividualising' of the agent. The total absence of a *by*-phrase, which, as we have seen, is the norm in passives, can be seen as an extreme version of the indefiniteness or deindividualising of the agent. We see some of those same features on Quirk et al. 1985's typical passive sentence *This difficulty can be avoided in several ways*, as opposed to the favourite example of the voice analysis, *John was hit by Bill* (see p.39), viz. indefiniteness (enhanced by the absence of the *by*-phrase), plurality, and probably the passive infinitive as well – note that in sentence (30) the normally non-passivizable *to have* becomes passivizable in the infinitive. It is not by chance that features normally associated with aspect are the ones which render odd passives grammatical – not by chance, but because the passive is itself an aspect.

The passive in Russian

In our exposition of the aspectual analysis of the passive we have concentrated so far on English. Time, now, to have a brief look at the passive in Russian and German. Russian has two constructions traditionally called passive, one consisting of *byt'* 'be' + passive participle, the other formed from the reflexive suffix *-sja* '-self'. The two types are exemplified in (49) and (50) below:[53]

(49) a. Izvestnyj inžener   postroil most.
          famous   engineer built-PF bridge
          'a famous engineer built the bridge'
      b. Most byl postroen izvestnym   inženerom.
          bridge was built-PF famous-INSTR engineer-INSTR
          'the bridge was built by a famous engineer'

(50) a. Izvestnyj inžener   stroil   most.
          famous   engineer built-IMPF bridge
          'a famous engineer built the bridge'
      b. Most stroilsja   izvestnym   inženerom.
          bridge built-itself-IMPF famous-INSTR engineer-INSTR
          'the bridge was built by a famous engineer'

A well-known rule of Russian grammar is that the two passive types are largely restricted to a particular aspect: the participial *byt'* passive tends to occur only on the perfective verb, whilst the reflexive *-sja* passive tends to occur only on the imperfective verb, as shown in examples (49) and (50) above, where (49) is the participial passive of a perfective verb, and (50) is the reflexive *-sja* passive of an imperfective verb (Русская грамматика 1980:615–616; Isačenko 1962:449–450; Wade 1992:325, 374). The voice analysis cannot begin to say why, hence the question is never asked, but we are in a position to ask why. Why is the participial *byt'* passive confined on the whole to perfective verbs, and the reflexive *-sja* passive to imperfective verbs? Given the aspect analysis of the passive the answer is clear.[54] Recall the difference in meaning between the imperfective and perfective aspect in Russian: the imperfective aspect views an action from within, as on-going; the perfective aspect, on the other hand, views an action from outside, as a whole, from its beginning to its end. The participial *byt'* passive in Russian, like the passive *be* + V-*ed* in English, expresses an action and the state that results from it, i.e. it means 'action + state'. The *-sja* passive does not mean that, it has a 'receptive' (subject = patient)[55] meaning which arises from the basic meaning of reflexivity, whatever that basic meaning is (this is not the place to go into the basic meaning of reflexives in Russian, but it is clearly congenial to the interpretation of the subject as patient). Only the perfective verb is compatible with the *byt'* passive, because only the perfective aspect encompasses the end of an action, since it views an action from its beginning to its end.[56] In other words, only the perfective aspect is telic. The possibility of expressing the end of an action is a pre-requisite for compatibility with the passive, because it is the end of the action which becomes the end-state of the passive meaning 'action + state'. Without that end-state a *byt'* passive cannot be formed. In other words, in the same way that the English passive with *be* + V-*ed* requires a telic lexical aspect for a passive to be formed, the Russian *byt'* passive also requires a telic lexical aspect, which in Russian is the perfective, for it to be formed. The imperfective verb cannot express the end of an action, and hence it is incompatible with the *byt'* passive. The imperfective verb, however, is compatible with the reflexive -*sja* passive, because the -*sja* passive does not mean 'action + state'; it has a meaning connected with reflexivity, having nothing to do with end-states.[57]

Thus we have the same analysis for the (participial) passive in both English and Russian. In both languages the passive – in English *be* + V-*ed*, in Russian *byt'* + passive participle – is an aspect of the type Auxiliary + Participle, meaning 'action + state', whose occurrence is dependent on a particular lexical and compositional aspect, called telic, i.e. one containing a potential end-point (which becomes the end-state of the meaning 'action + state' – without that potential end-point no passive with the meaning 'action + state' is possible). The voice analysis missed this common factor between the passive in the two languages. Under the voice analysis transitivity determined passivizability in English ('all and only transitive verbs form a passive'), whilst in Russian the aspect of the verb determined it ('only the perfective verb, usually, forms a participial passive). But what is the common factor between the two? The answer is telicity: in both languages telic aspect determines passivizability. In English (and German) telicity replaces transitivity as the criterion for passivizability, in Russian it replaces perfectivity. The barriers between the Germanic languages – we will see in the next sub-section that German fits into the same pattern – and the Slav languages are coming down. What we thought was a difference in structure is not there at all, we mistakenly imposed that difference on the two language families. In truth the passive in both languages, English and Russian, is the same construction, with the same meaning, with the same conditions of occurrence.

The passive in German

German has a passive construction very similar to English, but with the difference that, whereas in English the distinction between the actional passive and the statal passive is a subtle semantic one, i.e. they are both realized by *be* + V-*ed*, in German the distinction is formally realized in the choice of auxiliary: *werden* 'become' + *ge*-V-*t* is the actional passive, whilst *sein* 'be' + *ge*-V-*t* is the statal passive, as exemplified in (51) (actional passive with *werden*) and (52) (statal passive with *sein*) below, where both translate into English as 'the door was closed':

(51)   Die Tür   wurde   geschlossen.
      the   door   became   closed
      'the door was closed'

(52)   Die Tür   war   geschlossen.
      the   door   was   closed
      'the door was closed'

(on the passive in German see Helbig & Buscha 1989:161–188; Duden 1998:172–186; Zifonun et al. 1997:1788–1858; Durrell 2002:307–322).

The aspect analysis of the passive given above for English and Russian applies *mutatis mutandis* to German. The passive *werden/sein* + 2nd participle *ge-V-t* is an aspect of the type Auxiliary + Participle, like the German perfect. The actional *werden*-passive means 'action + state'[58] – hence the subject is patient – and its occurrence is determined by the lexical aspect of the verb and the compositional aspect of the sentence, whereby either the verb or the sentence have to be telic, i.e. they must contain an inherent or potential end-point, capable of becoming the end-state of the meaning 'action + state'.

Many of the arguments given above for English apply also to German. However, German offers some formal structures which English does not have which support the case for the aspect analysis of the passive still further. For one thing, the auxiliary which German happens to use in the actional passive, viz. *werden*, means 'to become' when *werden* is used as a full lexical verb, i.e. it expresses a change of state. If the full verb *werden* means a change of state, it is no surprise to find that the passive, which uses *werden* as an auxiliary, also expresses a change of state, in the meaning 'action + state'.

The perfect in German is formed with *haben* or *sein* + 2nd participle – thus one of the passive auxiliaries, *sein*, crops up again in the perfect. This is no surprise if the passive is the same construction as the perfect, viz. an aspect of the type Auxiliary + Participle (cf. Zifonun et al. 1997:1876–1877; Andersen 1989, 1991; Klein 2000; Abraham 2000). However, there is not just a formal similarity between the statal passive and the perfect with *sein*, there is a semantic similarity as well:

(53)   Die Frucht ist gereift.
      'the fruit has ripened'

(54)   Das Fenster ist geöffnet.
      'the window is opened'

In both cases, the perfect (53) and the passive (54), the sentences are partly verbal and partly adjectival, in which an adjective can be substituted for the participle without much change in meaning: *reif* 'ripe' for *gereift* and *offen* 'open' for *geöffnet*. This formal and semantic parallel is entirely understandable and predictable within the aspect analysis but an anomaly or a fluke within the voice analysis of the passive (cf. Helbig & Buscha 1989: 176–177; Bartsch 1969: 100–101).

In our discussion of English above we saw that the English passive has various adjectival qualities. A further adjectival quality that the German ac-tional *werden*-passive has is that the passive participle takes adjective endings in attributive position, as shown in (55), where the adjective ending -*e* is italicised:

(55)   der von ihm geschrieben*e*   Brief
       the by him written-ADJ.ENDING letter
       'the letter written by him'

The presence of the agentive phrase *von ihm* confirms that (55) is an actional passive, not a statal passive. So, given the fact that adjectives typically express a state, what is an adjective ending doing on a word-form which is supposed to express action only, not a state, according to the voice analysis? The answer is that the so-called 'actional' passive does express a state, it expresses a state which arises as the result of a preceding action. Hence it is entirely natural and logical for the attributive passive participle to appear with adjective endings, giving formal expression to that statal element of its meaning.

German has a passive construction which, if the voice analysis is to be believed, should not exist, and that is the passive of intransitive verbs, as shown in (56):

(56)   Es wurde getanzt.
       it was   danced
       'there was dancing'

(The *es* is a place-filler, not the personal pronoun *es*, cf. *Gestern wurde getanzt* 'yesterday there was dancing'). *Tanzen* 'to dance' is an intransitive verb. But the voice analysis requires an object for it to work, an object which is promoted to subject position, and consequently asserts that only transitive verbs form a passive. Under the voice analysis sentences like (56) are an anomaly. But the aspect analysis says that the lexical aspect of the verb determines passivizability, so that in principle the passive of intransitive verbs is not excluded. As long as the lexical aspect of a verb is right, whether it is transitive or intransitive it can form a passive.[59]

It is already well recognised in German grammar that the occurrence of the statal passive with *sein* is determined by the lexical aspect of the verb: only verbs with the lexical aspect 'perfective' (e.g. *öffnen* 'to open', *vernichten* 'to destroy') form a statal passive, durative verbs (e.g. *fragen* 'to ask', *loben* 'to praise') do not (see Helbig & Buscha 1989:77; Zifonun et al. 1997:1813–1814, where they show how telicity plays a role). This fact alone carries with it the implication that the statal passive in German is an aspect, of the type Auxiliary + Participle, for it to be sensitive to lexical aspect. But it also renders the idea unsurprising that the *werden*-passive is also sensitive to a lexical aspect, viz. a verb has to have the lexical aspect telic in order to form a *werden*-passive.

Indeed, it is already known that intransitive verbs which form their perfect with *sein* do not normally form a *werden*-passive (Duden 1998:180; *Grundzüge einer deutschen Grammatik* 1980:550–551). But verbs which form their perfect with *sein* have the lexical aspect perfective (Helbig & Buscha 1989:75). So once again we already have evidence in the standard grammars of German that passivizability is determined by lexical aspect, and that could only happen if the passive were itself an aspect, of the type Auxiliary + Participle (see also Abraham 1984).

As was said earlier many of the arguments given above for English apply also to German. Of these the most important is the perfect-passive correlation based on non-passivizable transitive verbs, and it is so important that it is worth going into in some detail for German. Sentences (57)–(79) below, containing non-passivizable transitive verbs, have been culled from the major grammars of German, viz. Helbig and Buscha 1989:170–173; *Grundzüge einer deutschen Grammatik* 1984:334–336, 549–551; Duden-*Grammatik* 1998:179–180; Zifonun et al. 1997:1796–1808, 1816–1817. The a sentences present the verbs in an active sentence which is grammatically correct. The b sentences show that they do not form a *werden*-passsive. If the aspect analysis of the passive applies also to German they will not form a resultative perfect. The c sentences reproduce the a sentences in the perfect. Although German does have a recognised resultative perfect (see e.g. Helbig & Buscha 1989:151–152) it is harder to get hold of than in English, because the first meaning of the German perfect is synonymous with the preterit. For example, *Er hat einen neuen Hut gekauft* can mean either 'he bought a new hat' (perhaps last year, and may have lost it since then, i.e. synonymous with the preterit, and one can say in German, unlike in English, *Er hat letztes Jahr einen neuen Hut gekauft* lit. he has bought a new hat last year 'he bought a new hat last year'), or else 'he has bought a new hat' (and is now the proud owner of a new hat, i.e. resultative perfect). However, one can isolate and guarantee a resultative meaning by beginning the sentence with *jetzt* 'now' (Gelhaus & Latzel 1974: 228–229), so that *Jetzt hat er einen neuen Hut gekauft* could only be interpreted as a resultative – 'now he has bought a new hat', not as equivalent to a preterit. If one examines the c sentences in (57)–(79) and asks, using the *jetzt* construction as an aid, can they be interpreted as resultative perfects, the answer in 21 out of the 23 cases (= 91%) is no, they cannot be interpreted as resultative perfects (the exceptions are *bekommen* in (59c) and *ergeben* in (60c)):[60]

(57) a. Sie haben einen Garten.
          'they have a garden'
      b. *Ein Garten wird von ihnen gehabt.
          a garden is had by them
      c. Sie haben einen Garten gehabt.
          'they have had a garden'

(58) a. Ihr Freund besitzt schon ein Auto.
          'her friend possesses a car already'
      b. *Ein Auto wird schon von ihrem Freund besessen.
          a car is possessed by her friend already
      c. Ihr Freund hat schon ein Auto besessen.
          'her friend has possessed a car already'

(59) a. Er bekam den Brief.
          'he received the letter'
      b. *Der Brief wurde von ihm bekommen.
          the letter was received by him
      c. Er hat den Brief bekommen.
          'he has received the letter'

(60) a. Der Versuch ergab ein positives Resultat.
          'the experiment produced a positive result'
      b. ?Ein positives Resultat wurde von dem Versuch ergeben.
          a positive result was produced by the experiment
      c. Der Versuch hat ein positives Resultat ergeben.
          'the experiment has produced a positive result'

(61) a. Das Heft kostet einen Groschen.
          'the booklet costs 10 pfennigs'
      b. *Ein Groschen wird von dem Heft gekostet.
          10 pfennigs are cost by the booklet
      c. Das Heft hat einen Groschen gekostet.
          'the booklet has cost 10 pfennigs'

(62)   a.   Der Sack wiegt einen Zentner.
            'the bag weighs a hundredweight'
       b.   *Ein Zentner wird vom Sack gewogen.
            a hundredweight is weighed by the bag
       c.   Der Sack hat einen Zentner gewogen.
            'the bag has weighed a hundredweight'

(63)   a.   Die Kiste enthält Bücher.
            'the crate contains books'
       b.   *Bücher werden von der Kiste enthalten.
            books are contained by the crate
       c.   Die Kiste hat Bücher enthalten.
            'the crate has contained books'

(64)   a.   Der Saal fasst 1000 Menschen.
            'the room holds 1000 people'
       b.   *1000 Menschen werden vom Saal gefasst.
            1000 people are held by the room
       c.   Der Saal hat 1000 Menschen gefasst.
            'the room has held 1000 people'

(65)   a.   Er ähnelt seinem Vater.
            'he resembles his father'
       b.   *Seinem Vater wird von ihm geähnelt.
            his father is resembled by him
       c.   Er hat seinem Vater geähnelt.
            'he has resembled his father'

(66)   a.   Der Lebensstandard hängt von der Arbeitsproduktivität ab.
            'living standards depend on labour productivity'
       b.   *Von der Arbeitsproduktivität wird vom Lebensstandard abgehangen.
            labour productivity is depended on by living standards
       c.   Der Lebensstandard hat von der Arbeitsproduktivität abgehangen.
            'living standards have depended on labour productivity'

(67)   a.   Er verdankt seinen Lehrern viel.
            'he owes his teachers a lot'
       b.   *Viel wird von ihm seinen Lehrern verdankt.
            a lot is owed by him to his teachers
       c.   Er hat seinen Lehrern viel verdankt.
            'he has owed his teachers a lot'

(68)   a.   Klaus weiß die Verkehrsregeln.
            'Klaus knows the Highway Code'

    b. ?Die Verkehrsregeln werden von Klaus gewusst.
       the Highway Code is known by Klaus

    c. Klaus hat die Verkehrsregeln gewusst.
       'Klaus has known the Highway Code'

(69) a. Er kannte das Buch nicht.
       'he did not know the book'

    b. ?Das Buch wurde von ihm nicht gekannt.
       the book was not known by him

    c. Er hat das Buch nicht gekannt.
       'he has not known the book'

(70) a. Alle Tänzer beherrschen noch nicht diesen Schritt.
       all the dancers control   not yet this   step
       'not all the dancers have mastered this step yet'

    b. ?Dieser Schritt wird noch nicht von allen Tänzern beherrscht.
       this step is not yet controlled by all the dancers

    c. Alle Tänzer haben diesen Schritt noch nicht beherrscht.
       all the dancers have this step not yet controlled
       'not all the dancers have mastered this step yet'

(71) a. Der Fuß schmerzt ihn.
       the foot hurts   him
       'his foot hurts'

    b. *Er wird von dem Fuß geschmerzt.
       he is hurt by the foot

    c. Der Fuß hat ihn geschmerzt.[61]
       'his foot has hurt'

(72) a. Sein Verhalten wundert mich.
       'his behaviour surprises me'

    b. *Ich werde von seinem Verhalten gewundert.
       I am surprised by his behaviour

    c. Sein Verhalten hat mich gewundert.
       'his behaviour has surprised me'

(73) a. Das Geschenk freut   mich sehr.
       the present   pleases me   greatly
       'I am delighted with the present'

    b. *Ich werde von dem Geschenk sehr gefreut.
       I am greatly pleased by the present

    c. Das Geschenk hat mich sehr gefreut.
       'I have been delighted with the present'

(74) a. Der hässliche Fleck in der Mitte ärgerte ihn sehr.
         'the ugly stain in the middle annoyed him greatly'

      b. ?Er wurde von dem/durch den hässlichen Fleck in der Mitte sehr geärgert.
         he was greatly annoyed by the ugly stain in the middle

      c. Der hässliche Fleck in der Mitte hat ihn sehr geärgert.
         'the ugly stain in the middle has annoyed him greatly'

(75) a. Wir wähnten ihn gesund und wohlbehalten.
         'we believed him [mistakenly] to be safe and well'

      b. *Er wurde gesund und wohlbehalten gewähnt.
         he was believed [mistakenly] to be safe and well

      c. Wir haben ihn gesund und wohlbehalten gewähnt.
         'we have believed him [mistakenly] to be safe and well'

(76) a. Es friert   mich.
         it freezes me
         'I am freezing'

      b. *Ich werde gefroren.
         I   am   frozen

      c. Es hat mich gefroren.
         'I have been freezing'

(77) a. Es hungert mich.
         it hungers me
         'I am hungry'

      b. *Ich werde davon gehungert.
         I   am   by it hungered

      c. Es hat mich gehungert.
         'I have been hungry'

(78) a. Es graut   mir.
         it terrifies me
         'I dread it'

      b. *Mir wird gegraut.
         I am terrified by it

      c. Es hat mir gegraut.
         'I have dreaded it'

(79) a. Es gibt viele Tierarten.
         it gives a lot of animal species
         'there are a lot of animal species'

      b. *Viele Tierarten werden gegeben.
         a lot of animal species are given

    c.   Es hat viele Tierarten gegeben.
        'there have been a lot of animal species'

Grammars of German explain the above non-passivizable transitive verbs by a variety of exclusively semantic means. They say that verbs of possession, psychological verbs, relational verbs, verbs without a proper object, verbs without a proper agent, etc., etc., cannot form a *werden*-passive; whilst recognising that it is far from being the case that all such semantically defined verbs are precluded from a *werden*-passive. But we see in (57)–(79) a single formal-syntactic[62] explanation for all those semantically diverse groups of verbs: almost none of them can form a resultative perfect. This is what is meant when descriptive grammarians talk about searching for a (single) formal generalization which can capture a large amount of (differentiated) data.[63] This formal-syntactic[64] generalization, viz. the fact that most transitive non-passivizable verbs also cannot form a resultative perfect, reveals that the passive behaves like an aspect – like the perfect – in being sensitive to and incompatible with roughly the same verbs as the resultative perfect. Moreover, it shows that the *werden*-passive has a similar meaning – action + state – to the perfect's action + result, since whatever it is that prevents those verbs from forming a resultative perfect also prevents them from forming a *werden*-passive. The thing about these German verbs that prevents them from forming either a resultative perfect or a passive is the same as we saw above for English: they are atelic, i.e. they lack an inherent end-point in their meaning capable of becoming either the end-state of the passive's 'action + state' meaning or the end-result of the perfect's 'action + result' meaning. Once again, we are faced with persuasive evidence that the actional *werden*-passive in German is an aspect of the type Auxiliary + Participle, with its own meaning, viz. action followed by the resultant new state on the subject, leading to the subject having the semantic role of patient.

Methodological implications

The aspectual analysis of the passive has several methodological implications for linguistics and structuralism. Linguists and laymen alike are inclined to view the analyses of traditional grammar, e.g. the voice analysis of the passive (i.e. the practice of deriving passives from actives), as statements of obvious fact. This attitude is taken to extremes in generative grammar, where the active-passive relationship is taken as data, and the task of the linguist is seen as that of constructing a formal grammar or theory which accounts for and explains *inter alia* that relationship. But we have seen that the voice analysis was wrong, and that the passive is an aspect.[65] The first point to note from this is that the analysis under which passives are derived from actives is not data, but theory – it is based on one way, but not the only way, of analysing *be* + V-*ed*. In general the analyses of traditional grammar – be it an account of the Latin noun which posits five declensions, an account of tense formation in English which leaves approx. 200 verbs as irregular exceptions, a description of French nouns which has two genders, a description of German noun plurals which leaves most of them as lexical idiosyncrasies, etc. etc. – are theories or hypotheses, they are not statements of obvious fact, irrefutable and to be held for all time.

Furthermore, the aspectual analysis of the passive confirms the structuralist idea that form determines meaning. To see this one must distinguish between the real or actual level of form and the level of scientific analysis. *Be* + V-*ed* is a phonological form which has a meaning in the real or actual structure of English, and as scientists we do our best to analyse the form and its concomitant meaning in a scientific analysis. Presumably we will never reach the real level of language – if we do our scientific discipline will disappear, because we will have solved all the problems in it, and we can all go home – but in the meantime we provide the best analysis/description we can manage at the time. Either way form determines meaning, whether at the real level of language or at the level of scientific analysis. To claim that *be* + V-*ed* is a voice of the verb entails the belief that actives and passives are synonymous (because the meaning of an item is determined by its place in the system). To claim, on the other hand, that *be* + V-*ed* is an aspect of the verb entails the belief that *be* + V-*ed* means action followed by resultant state, i.e. actives and passives are not synonymous (again, because the meaning of an item is determined by its place in the system). It would be very odd if someone were to mix the two, and to claim, for example, that *be* + V-*ed* meant 'action + state' and yet cling to the belief that passives are derived from actives.[66] In both cases, the voice analysis and the aspect analysis, form determines meaning. The formal category or construction that you believe as a linguist a given phonological sequence belongs to determines what you are going to say about the meaning of that phonological sequence. In other words form determines meaning, at the level of scientific analysis as it does at the real level of language structure.

One must also distinguish between at the level of language the subconscious semantic intuitions which speakers of a language have and at the level of scientific analysis the semantic intuitions which people have when they intellectualise about language forms and engage in scientific analysis, be they professional linguists or the layman talking about language on the basis of what he was taught at school as a child. When speakers use the passive construction they know intuitively what it means – that is part of 'knowing' and 'speaking' a language. But the grammarian's semantic intuitions – be he a professional or an amateur – about a given form are different, they are conscious and intellectual, based on what he was taught at school if he is an amateur or on his scientific research if he is a professional. If you are familiar only with the voice analysis you will look at passive forms and intuit a meaning in which they are synonymous with an underlying active; and this will approximate with what speakers 'know' (in that special sense of knowing a language) the passive means. If you are familiar with the aspect analysis you will intuit the meaning 'action + state' on the passive; and this again will approximate – more closely, I have argued in this book – with what speakers 'know' the passive means. The subconscious semantic intuitions of the speaker and the conscious semantic intuitions of the grammarian are different, but they are both based ultimately on a formal-grammatical analysis.

It follows that Tobin is right to describe linguistics as a search for meanings (see p.6). In terms of the great debate as to whether to go from form to meaning or from meaning to form, it is the people who go from form to meaning who have got it right. If we had started with meaning, viz. the idea that actives and passives are synonymous, we would have been stuck with that meaning for ever. We would never have contemplated the notion that *be* + V-*ed* might mean something else, such as action followed by state.

Under the voice analysis *be* + V-*ed* is considered meaningless – all attention is on the movement of the NPs, especially in generative accounts. How many other meaningless forms in language can we uncover meanings for? Ablaut and the -*en* ending of the strong verbs in English? The gender system of nouns? The plural system of German nouns? The syncretisms of inflectional paradigms?

We also have confirmation from the aspect analysis of what is known in philosophy as subjective idealism, viz. the idea that reality – not just as we perceive it but as it is – is a construct of the perceiver and her perceptual apparatus, as discussed at the end of Chapter 1. Grammarians looked at the sentence *John was hit by Bill* and felt intuitively that it is synonymous with *Bill hit John*. But they were looking at it through voice-coloured spectacles. The bit of the universe designated by a synonymous-with-the-active passive is not objectively there, it is created by the voice analysis, which acts as a perceptual apparatus through which we see it. If it weren't for the voice analysis we would not see it. It's not just that it is there all along, but we need that angle, the voice analysis, to see it. Rather, without the voice analysis it is not there: the voice analysis creates that bit of the universe. Anyone who has studied and understood the aspect analysis looks at the sentence *My house was burgled last night* and sees it through aspect-coloured spectacles, they feel – also intuitively – that it expresses an action followed by the resulting state. But the 'action + state' that one sees is also not objectively there, it too is created, this time by the aspect analysis, which again acts as a perceptual apparatus through which we see it. Again, if it weren't for the aspect analysis we would not see it. And again, it's not just that the 'action + state' bit of reality is there all along, but we need that angle, the aspect analysis, to see it. Rather, without the aspect analysis it is not there, the aspect analysis creates that bit of the universe. The particular formal-grammatical analysis that you are committed to creates the meaning that you see.[67] The same principle applies to our perception of the universe generally. The things and actions, houses and trees, love and hate, beauty and ugliness that we see in the universe are not objectively there, they are created by the perceptual apparatus which we bring to bear in seeing them: by mind, language, the five senses, plus other biological and physical properties which humans happen to possess. Here again, it's not just that the things and actions, houses and trees, love and hate, beauty and ugliness are there all along, in objective reality, but we need our perceptual apparatus in order to see them. Rather, our perceptual apparatus creates them – without our perceptual apparatus, i.e. without us, they are not there. They are no more there objectively than is the bit of reality designated by a synonymous-with-the-active passive, or the 'action + state' bit of reality designated by an aspectual passive. The formal-grammatical analysis that you hold and the perceptual apparatus that you have create reality for you.

The aspect analysis confirms not only the interdependence of form and meaning, as we have just seen, but the interdependence of form, meaning, and syntax (syntax in the sense of combinatorial possibilities). This comes to light through the template of Category-Syntax-Meaning given for the voice analysis on p.37 and for the aspect analysis on p.40. The voice analysis says that the grammatical form of the passive (or category to which it belongs) is a voice of the verb, that only transitive verbs form a passive, and that actives and passives are synonymous. The three things go together, they are inextricably linked. The aspect analysis says something different for all three things. It claims that the grammatical form or category of the passive is aspect, that only telic verbs and sentences form a passive, and that the passive *be* + V-*ed* means 'action + state'. But again, the three things go together, they are inextricably linked. It would be odd if someone were to mix them up and claim, for example, that the passive is a voice of the verb and only telic verbs form a passive (but see fn. 66). Form, meaning and syntax are inextricably linked.

Moreover, out of the three it is syntax which is primary. The idea that the passive might be an aspect of the verb came to me whilst I was researching into non-passivizable transitive verbs for my Ph.D. in 1976–1979. Transitive verbs are part of the syntax of the passive, i.e. if one asks which verbs does the passive combine with the answer traditionally given is transitive verbs. Non-passivizable transitive verbs are the unexplained exceptions to that transitive rule of the passive. It was only when I spotted that most of the non-passivizable transitive verbs also do not form a resultative perfect[68] that the thought came to me that the passive might be the same construction as the perfect, i.e. an aspect of the type Auxiliary + Participle. And it was only then that I started to see that the passive expresses an action and the new state which arises on the subject from that action. Out of form-meaning-syntax it is syntax (in the sense of combinatorial possibilities) which is the primary, determining factor.[69]

We have also seen that what appeared to be irregularity – the non-passivizable transitive verbs – was not irregularity at all in the actual structure of the languages concerned, but an artificial by-product of an incorrect analysis. Analyse *be* + V-*ed* as a voice of the verb and you get irregular exceptions – analyse it as an aspect of the verb and you don't. Irregularity in language turned out to have been introduced artificially into what we thought was the structure of language. How many other such instances are there? Can the same thing be done for irregular verbs? We will look in Chapter 5 at how feasible that is and what progress has been made in that direction.

Finally, the aspect analysis of the passive brings with it the method of lexical exceptions. As was asserted two paragraphs above, it was research into non-passivizable transitive verbs which led me to the aspect analysis of the passive. Non-passivizable transitive verbs are unexplained exceptions to the voice-based rule that all transitive verbs are capable of forming a passive. Since using unexplained lexical exceptions to arrive at a new analysis of the passive in 1979 I have tried to use the method again, on strong or irregular verbs such as *drink-drank-drunk*, and to develop the method generally into one which could be used by other linguists on other areas of grammar in other languages. The final chapter of this book, Chapter 7, is devoted to that topic, but for the moment let us note that it was transitive verbs which do not form a passive, i.e. unexplained lexical exceptions to a grammatical rule, which led to the aspect analysis of the passive.

CHAPTER 4

Generative grammar

The passive was and still is *the* most important construction in the development of generative grammar, and we will use the insights of the previous chapter as we now look at the generative way of analysing language. If you have an aversion to formalisms, and have seen enough of generative grammar to know that you do not want to analyse language the generative way, you may skip this chapter (the students are saying: 'Great, this is my kind of book, you only have to read half of it!'). The rest of you – read on!

Linguistics today is divided into two camps, descriptive and generative. Not that you would know it to look at the literature, with the generativists ignoring the descriptive approach, pretending it does not exist, and the descriptivists banished to the nether regions of text grammar, pragmatics, applied linguistics and sociolinguistics. But the division is still there. I am a descriptivist, and this book is descriptive, but we need to examine and understand generative grammar, i.e. its failings, because generative grammar still dominates theoretical linguistics today.

Descriptive linguistics is traditional and pedagogical grammar, i.e. the kind of grammar that one encounters at school, particularly when learning a foreign language, imbued with the insights of structuralism; plus other advances made in our understanding of language in the course of the 20th century and up to the present day, such as text and corpus linguistics, sociolinguistics, language and politics, speech act theory, etc. The term 'descriptive' is misleading, because it can be taken to imply a taxonomic, merely labelling, non-explanatory approach, and generative grammar in its inception accused descriptive grammar of being just that and hence we needed generative grammar. However, descriptive grammar is not merely descriptive, it provides analyses, theories, and explanations, as can hopefully be seen in this book. Perhaps, yet again, we should change the name to reflect the nature of the object? But perhaps not, since the proof of the pudding is in the eating anyway, i.e. if descriptive grammar is understood correctly it will be seen to be explanatory anyway, no matter what it is called. At most one might use the term 'theoretical-descriptive linguistics', whereby 'theoretical' is meant here in a pre-Chomskyan, pre-model-building sense.

Generative grammar is an approach to language which was initiated by Noam Chomsky, Department of Linguistics and Philosophy, Massachusetts Institute of Technology (MIT), Boston, USA, with the publication of Chomsky 1957 and 1965.[70] It is particularly wide-spread in the United States of America, though less so in Europe and elsewhere in the world. Irrespective of numerically how many or how few adherents it has, generative grammar towers over the scene in linguistics like a colossus, its supporters would say because it works, its critics would say not least because English, the native language of Chomsky and most of his followers and the language on which most generative work has been done, happens to be the dominant world language. Generative grammar is considered by its practitioners to be a revolutionary new way of analysing language, and the only truly scientific approach to language study, with Chomsky being described in print as a genius. It is difficult to get a job in core linguistics (i.e. grammar), publish in core linguistics, or even give a paper at a conference on core linguistics without being to some extent generative, at least in the English-speaking world.

Generative grammarians believe that it is the job of the linguist to construct formal models/theories/grammars of language which explain how it is that speakers produce grammatically correct sentences, how they interpret sentences correctly, and how children acquire language so rapidly and efficiently. In this chapter I will first make an honest attempt to play devil's advocate and present generative grammar as Chomsky and the generativists see it. I will then present a critique of the generative approach, showing why it is wrong and misguided. The critique rests on two related points, firstly, that formalization generative-style, i.e. notationalism, is not in itself explanatory or scientific, but trivial; and secondly, that the mainstay of the generative technique is to make assumptions or postulations, not as a means to an end but as an end in itself. The assumptions are made to look real by presenting them in a formal notation. But assumptions, even 'formalized' ones, are not explanations, they are quite simply nothing more than assumptions. If generative assumptions were of the kind that could be empirically tested we could say fine, maybe they are right, one day we will find out, when an experimentalist eventually gets round to testing their hypotheses, their models. But the assumptions are not testable. Generative assumptions are of a kind which can never, ever be tested. All that happens is that they eventually get replaced by another set of assumptions, as the models evolve over time or as new models appear. But, to repeat, assumptions – even formalized ones – are not explanations.

4.1 Minimalism

We will illustrate the generative method initially by looking at Chomsky's latest model publicly available at the time of writing, Minimalism (see Chomsky 1995; Martin et al. (Eds.) 2000; Radford 1997). Minimalism is the latest stage in a series of changes made to the original models of Chomsky 1957 and 1965, and incorporates a number of additions and adjustments which have been made on the way, such as X' (pronounced X-bar) syntax, traces, government and binding theory, principles and parameters, and the θ-criterion (theta-criterion). The name Minimalism expresses Chomsky's desire to have as few categories and principles as possible, in keeping both with a general scientific aim of covering as much data as possible with as few statements as possible, and with the specific rationale of generative grammar that the child is born with the template of language, known as Universal Grammar or UG for short, in its head, i.e. language is innate, and the simpler or more minimal the grammar is the closer it is likely to be to UG. Radford 1997 is a lucid and highly readable account of Minimalism, and we will draw mainly on that book in our presentation here. Obviously we cannot cover the whole of the model, but will select the most important points in it in order to illustrate this particular model and the generative method in general.

Let us start with X' syntax. It is a fundamental fact of both descriptive and generative grammar that words in sentences go together to form phrases or constituents. Take, for example, the sentence given in (80) below:

(80)   The opposition will vote against privatization.

The words *the* and *opposition* form a phrase, called in the Minimalist model a determiner phrase (DP) because the most important or head word in it, *the*, is a determiner. The words *against privatization* form a prepositional phrase (PP), whose head word, *against*, is a preposition. Phrase structure is shown in tree diagrams – the tree diagram for sentence (80) is given in (81) below:

(81)

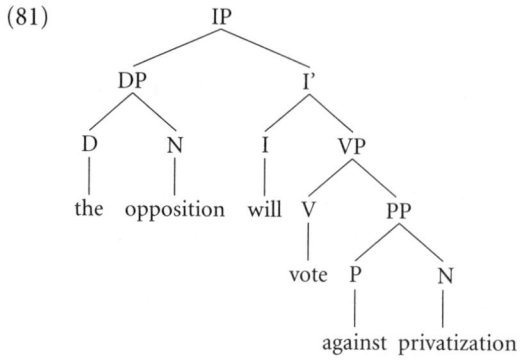

(Radford 1997:97)

In this model auxiliaries like *will* are subsumed along with the tense and agreement endings *-ed* and *-s* under the same overarching category, called Inflection, or I for short (Radford 1997:49–54). Syntactic constituents are said to be 'projections' of their head word, so that for example the NP *students of linguistics* is a projection of its head noun, *students*; in the sentence *They will help you* the phase *help you* is a VP which is a projection of its head word, the verb *help*. A minimal projection is a constituent which is not a projection of some other constituent, hence heads (i.e. words) are minimal projections. A maximal projection is a constituent which is not contained within any larger constituent with the same head, so that in (81) the VP *vote against privatization* is a maximal projection. An intermediate projection is a constituent which is larger than a word but smaller than a phrase. Intermediate projections are indicated by a ´ after the relevant symbol (or a horizontal line above the symbol): in (81) the constituent *will vote against privatization* is an I' (pronounced I-bar), which merges with the DP *the opposition* to form the IP (inflected phrase, i.e. sentence) *The opposition will vote against privatization*.

Phrases or projections such as NP, VP, AP, PP have a special property in common, viz. that they all contain a head word. This property is expressed in symbols by the expression XP (X-phrase), in which X stands for noun, verb, adjective, etc. Thus it can be seen that X' syntax derives its name from capturing and formalizing two important generalizations, the notion of head word, and the notion of intermediate level of structure.

The expression following a head word is called its complement, e.g. in the NP *students of linguistics* the expression *of linguistics* is the complement of the head noun *students*. In English head words precede their complements, in contrast to for example Korean, where heads follow their complements: English is known as a head-first language, whereas Korean is a head-last language

(Radford 1997:18–19). The expression preceding (in English) a head word is called its specifier, e.g. if we expand the NP *plans to privatize hospitals* by adding the word *government* to its beginning, giving the NP *government plans to privatize hospitals*, the word *government* is the specifier of the NP *plans to privatize hospitals* (because it specifies who has devised the plans). In the Minimalist model subjects are considered to be the specifier of a VP, and objects the complement of a VP; moreover, specifiers are considered to be sisters of an intermediate (X') projection, whereas complements are sisters to a head, which can be seen in (81), where the complement PP *against privatization* is sister to the head verb *vote*, but the specifier DP *the opposition* (here a subject) is sister to an intermediate projection, here an I' (Radford 1997:89–93). This view of subjects and objects is also expressed by saying that objects are internal to the VP, but subjects are external to the VP.

Let us now turn briefly to trace theory. The Minimalist model assumes that all sentences have a complementizer such as *that* or *if* in underlying structure, even if the complementizer is not realized in surface structure. For example, the underlying structure of the sentence *Money can buy happiness* is considered to be (82):

(82)

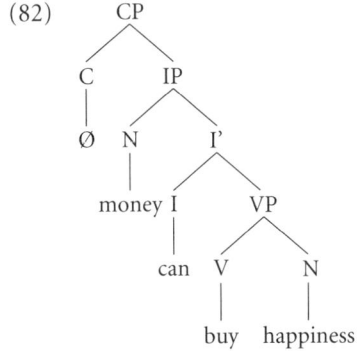

Here the sentence *Money can buy happiness* is shown to have a null complementizer, C, as part of a clause called a Complementizer Phrase, CP. There is not the space here to review the arguments in support of this assumption, but let us just say that it is as if the sentence were *that money can buy happiness*, as in *He thinks that money can buy happiness* and its alternative *He thinks money can buy happiness*, with the *that* deleted (Radford 1997:147–151).

Questions in English are considered to start out in underlying structure as assertions, as shown in (83) below:

(83)

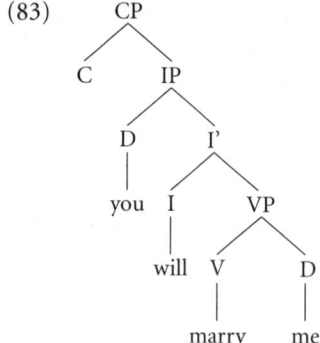

The assumption is made that the auxiliary *will* moves from the head position of the I' to head of CP, as shown in (84) below:

(84)

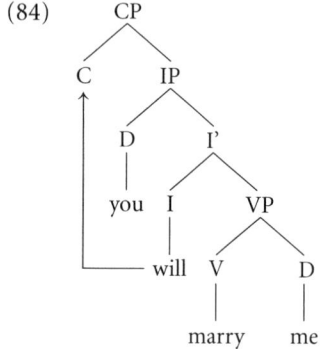

In doing so it leaves behind a trace of itself, symbolized as *t*, as shown in (85):

(85)

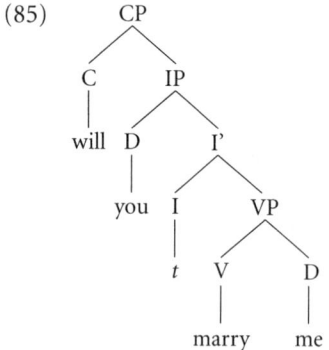

A moved constituent and its trace form together what is called a (movement) 'chain' (Radford 1997: 216–222).

As well as null complementizers English has null subjects. Consider (86):

(86)   a.   We would like [you to stay].
       b.   We would like [to stay].

In the Minimalist model the *you* in the bracketed infinitive complement clause of (86a) is considered to be the subject of that clause. In (86b), on the other hand, the bracketed infinitive complement clause has no subject; and yet somehow the sentence manages to mean that 'we' do the staying. How does it do that? The Minimalist answer is to assume that the clause in question has a null subject, called PRO (because it shares certain properties with pronouns). Given this assumption the sentences in (86) have a very similar structure, the difference between them being that whilst (86a) has an overt subject, (86b) has a covert subject, shown in (87):

(87)

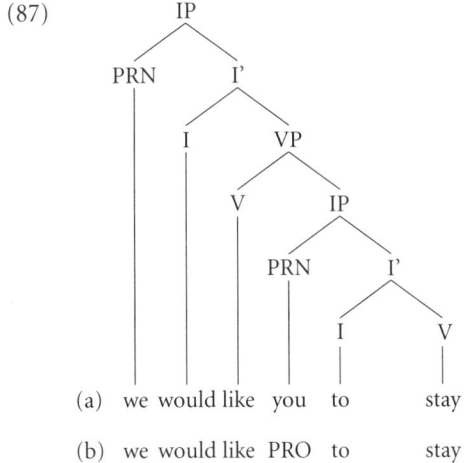

(a)   we would like   you   to   stay

(b)   we would like   PRO   to   stay

The subject *we* in the b sentence is said to 'control' the null subject PRO, or to be its antecedent, such that PRO refers back to it; *we* is the controller of PRO. Verbs such as *like* which behave in this way are called control predicates (Radford 1997: 131–132).

Control predicates are to be distinguished from raising predicates. The verb *to seem* is a raising predicate – cf. (88):

(88)   a.   It seems [that he understands her].
       b.   He seems [to understand her].

In (88) we see a similar problem to that of (86): in (88b) the complement clause has no subject, and yet semantically it is the subject *he* of the matrix clause

(= main clause) which does the understanding. How does that work? It works by a movement rule called 'raising', which operates cyclically and which we will illustrate on the basis of sentence (89):

(89)   The men do seem to understand the situation.

Supporters of the Minimalist model adduce arguments which there is not the space to go into here but which suggest that in (89) *the men* starts out as the subject of *understand the situation*, is raised to subject of *to understand the situation*, is then raised again to subject of *seem to understand the situation*, and finally is raised again to subject of *do seem to understand the situation*, in cyclical fashion, each time leaving a trace *t* of itself behind, as shown in (90) (in which TP is a tense phrase, i.e. a phrase headed by an abstract tense morpheme T):

(90)

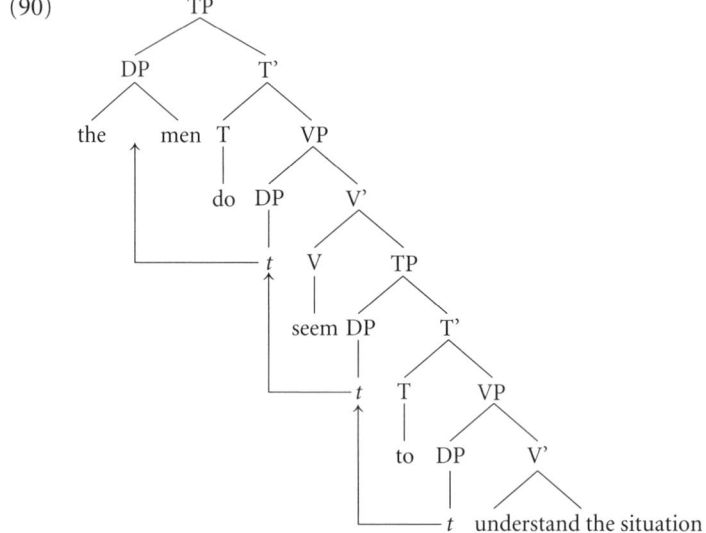

Thus the verb *to seem* is a raising predicate (Radford 1997: 334–337).

Let us now examine the θ-criterion (theta-criterion). The noun phrases in sentences can be ascribed semantic roles, such as agent, patient, experiencer, etc. Some examples are given below, in which the noun phrases in question are italicised:

Theme (or **patient**): an entity undergoing the effect of some action:

(91)   The FBI arrested *Larry Luckless*.

(92)   *Mary* fell over

(93)   *The president* went to Boston.

Agent: the causer or instigator of some action:

(94)   *John* killed Harry.

Experiencer: an entity experiencing some psychological state:

(95)   *John* felt happy.

Recipient/possessor: an entity receiving/possessing some entity:

(96)   John got *Mary* a present.

(97)   The *suspect* received a caution.

Goal: entity towards which something moves:

(98)   John went *home*.

Because generativists consider theme to be the most important semantic role they call semantic roles 'thematic roles'; and because the Greek letter θ (theta) begins with a *th-*, the initial consonant of the term 'theme', they also call them θ-roles (Radford 1997:326). So at least they have a sense of humour! To return to control predicates versus raising predicates, another difference between them is that whilst control predicates like *to try* θ-mark their subjects, raising predicates like *to seem* do not θ-mark their subjects. Consider the following sentences:

(99)   a.   John tried to understand the problem.
       b.   ?My goldfish tried to understand the problem.
       c.   *Your kettle is trying to boil over.

Here we see that the verb *to try* requires an agent subject, i.e. it θ-marks it subject for agent, such that only (99a) is grammatical – (99b) and (99c) are ungrammatical. Now consider the sentences in (100):

(100)   a.   John seemed to understand the problem.
       b.   My goldfish seems to have escaped.
       c.   Your kettle seems to be boiling over.

All three sentences in (100) are grammatical. No matter what thematic role the subject of *seem* appears to be the sentence is grammatical. Chomsky concludes from this that the verb *to seem* does not θ-mark its subject, i.e. it does not require its subject to have a given semantic role.

    The distribution of thematic roles over the arguments of verbs is determined by the θ-criterion, which is given in (101) below:

(101)   θ-criterion
        Each argument bears one and only one θ-role, and each θ-role is assigned
        to one and only one argument.

The constraint is illustrated by the examples in (102) below:

(102)   a.   Percy Peabrain admires himself.
        b.   *Percy Peabrain admires.

In (102a) the subject Percy Peabrain is experiencer, and the reflexive object
himself is theme, thus each argument is assigned one θ-role and the θ-criterion
is satisfied. In (102b), on the other hand, it looks as though either the subject
Percy Peabrain has been assigned two θ-roles, experiencer and theme, thus violating the θ-criterion, in which case the derivation crashes at LF (logical form –
i.e. the semantic interpretation does not work), or else the theme role associated with the verb *to admire* has not been assigned, thus again violating the
θ-criterion and again the derivation crashes at LF (Radford 1997:339).

Let us now see how Minimalism deals with passives. It is an important
test, since, as already mentioned, the passive has always been crucial in the
development of generative grammar. Consider the passive sentences in (103)
and the active sentences in (104):

(103)   a.   The students were arrested.
        b.   ?The camels were arrested.
        c.   ??The flowers were arrested.
(104)   a.   They arrested the students.
        b.   ?They arrested the camels.
        c.   ??They arrested the flowers.

In (103) the a sentence is fine, the b sentence odd, and the c sentence odder
still. In (104) the same thing applies. How can we account for these facts?
Minimalism does it by assuming that UG correlates thematic structure with
syntactic structure in a uniform fashion, a hypothesis known as the 'uniform
theta assignment hypothesis' or UTAH. If we adopt UTAH it follows that passive subjects must originate in the same position as active complements. Since
the students in (103a) is theme of the verb *to arrest* and is subject of *to arrest*,
and *the students* in (104a) is again theme of *to arrest* but this time its complement, it is natural to suppose that the subject *the students* in the passive (103a)
started out as the complement of *to arrest*, as in (104a). But if so, how does *the
students* end up as subject of *were*?

The answer in the Minimalist model is that the DP *the students*, starting out as complement of the passive participle *arrested*, undergoes passivization, i.e. is moved from being complement of the passive participle *arrested* to become its subject, and then undergoes raising, i.e. is moved from being subject of *arrested* to subject of *were*, as shown in (105) below:

(105)

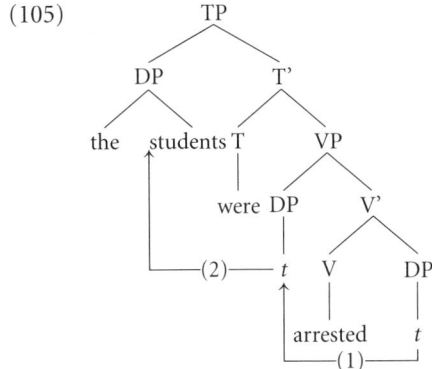

In this way the subject of passives acquires the same θ-role, viz. theme (or patient), as the complement (or object) of the active verb (Radford 1997:341–342).

4.2 Critique of Minimalism and generative grammar

Our necessarily brief account of the basics of generative grammar, using Chomsky's Minimalist model by way of illustration, is now complete. So what exactly is wrong with generative grammar? It is important to get the criticism right. Ever since its inception numerous linguists – indeed, the overwhelming majority of linguists – have sensed that something is wrong with the generative method but have been unable to put their finger on it and say why it is wrong. Let me say immediately that two criticisms which one encounters frequently are in my opinion not correct. Firstly, it is wrong to criticise Chomsky for his adherence to competence or I-language (internalised language) – the language of the idealised native speaker, ignoring slips of the tongue, etc. – as opposed to performance or E-language (externalised language). Competence, like Saussure's *langue*, is simply part of sentence-grammar (as opposed to text grammar), and we do not want to throw out the baby with the bath water. People who criticise Chomsky on account of competence are in effect arguing for performance or *parole* or text grammar to replace sentence-grammar, and that is not something which I would argue for (see Chapter 6), and it certainly does not address the error of the generative method.

The second incorrect criticism of generative grammar concerns the innateness hypothesis. One frequently encounters the view that generative grammar is wrong because language is not innate, it is learned. But the innateness hypothesis came late to generative grammar, after 1957, in Chomsky 1959 and 1962, when the essence of the generative method – to assume or postulate formal devices which serve as explanations of sentence structure – was already well established, i.e. in Chomsky (1957). Indeed, there is a whole group of generativists working within computational linguistics who explicitly, even vehemently deny the relevance of the innateness hypothesis to the generative method, e.g. Gerald Gazdar and his GPSG model (Generalized Phrase Structure Grammar):

> In view of the fact that the packaging and public relations of much recent linguistic theory involves constant reference to questions of psychology, particularly in association with language acquisition, it is appropriate for us to make a few remarks about the connections between the claims we make and issues in the psychology of language. We make no claims . . . that our grammatical theory is *eo ipso* a psychological theory. . . . Our general linguistic theory is not a theory of how a child abstracts from the surrounding hubbub of linguistic and nonlinguistic noises enough evidence to gain a mental grasp of the structure of a natural language. Nor is it a biological theory of the structure of an as-yet-unidentified mental organ.
>
> Thus we feel it is possible, and arguably proper, for a linguist (*qua* linguist) to ignore matters of psychology. . . . The most useful course of action . . . is probably not to engage in further programmatic posturing and self-congratulatory rhetoric of the sort that has characterized much linguistic work in recent years, but rather to attempt to fulfill some of the commitments made by generative grammar in respect of the provision of fully specified and precise theories of the nature of the languages that humans employ.
>
> (Gazdar et al. 1985: 5)

So some linguists practise generative grammar deliberately and almost crusadingly without the innateness hypothesis. Clearly, then, the innateness hypothesis is not essential to the generative method. The debate about the extent to which language is innate and the extent to which it is learned, like sin, will always be with us. Much of the evidence cited in the debate can be used by both sides to justify their view; how you interpret it and which side you are on is determined largely by where you are coming from and what political and methodological axes you have to grind. But it all has very little to do with the day-to-day construction of formal models which explain syntactic structure, except perhaps as a means of adding some plausibility to the procedure. The innateness hypothesis and the plausibility which it may or may not bring is very much in the background; to refute it certainly does not begin to address the problems inherent to the generative method. An indication of criticism of generative grammar based on competence/performance and the innateness hypothesis being wrong is the fact that after 45 years of such criticism generative grammar survives almost unscathed.

The best way to see the error of the generative method is to examine its treatment of the passive, undeniably the most important construction in the history of generative grammar, in the light of the discovery that the passive is an aspect of the verb, not a voice of the verb, as we saw in Chapter 3. Look again at the Minimalist account of the passive given above (pp. 70–71). It is obvious that that account is actually based on the view from traditional grammar that passives are derived from actives, and that the subject of the passive is equivalent to the object of the corresponding active sentence.[71] Chomsky, I am sure, would have no difficulty in admitting this, indeed, he has stated openly that traditional grammars are implicit generative grammars, and conversely generative grammars are an explication – a formal explication – of traditional grammar:

> It would not be inaccurate to regard the transformational model as a formalization of features implicit in traditional grammars, and to regard these grammars as inexplicit transformational generative grammars.
>
> (Chomsky 1964:918, quoted in Růžička 1967:1709)

Let us recap on how we came to the view in Chapter 3 that the passive is an aspect of the verb, not a voice of the verb (i.e. not derived from an underlying active). The problem which both descriptivists and generativists face with the passive is as follows. In English there is a construction which, formally speaking, is as given in (106) below:

(106)   NP – *be* V-*ed* (*by* NP)

It consists of a subject, an auxiliary, a participle, and an optional *by*-phrase, all formally defined. That is the form of the passive. Let us now turn to its semantics, its meaning. In semantic terms what is special about the passive is that in it the subject is patient. This is unusual, since most subjects in English are agents. The question is, how do we explain the fact that in passives the subject is patient, not agent?

Chomsky knows that language is a formal entity, and any explanation we give will need to be a formal one, in keeping with the formal nature of language; and I agree with him on that. But how does Chomsky arrive at a formal explanation? He says there must be a formal structure or structures behind the passive, or else how could speakers use it and interpret it correctly (and how could children acquire it so quickly and effortlessly if the formal structures underlying the passive were not already in the child's head, pre-programmed). There must be something there, so in the absence of any better solution, let us suppose that the passive subject starts out in the same position as an active complement, and then is moved by one movement rule called passivization and another movement rule called raising, each of them leaving a trace of the moved NP, to end up in its final position as subject of the sentence, where it is interpreted as theme/patient because of the traces it left behind in the course of its journey. I admit, says Chomsky, that this is only a hypothesis, but all the elements of the derivation of passives are independently justified (except for the movement rule 'passivization'), i.e. they are needed in the grammar elsewhere to do other jobs, and until someone comes up with a better idea, i.e. a better hypothesis, at least we have an explanation, albeit a tentative one, and we can work on it to develop one day, hopefully, a better solution. So Chomsky's solution consists of assuming or postulating several formal structures or devices to explain the passive, in other words he constructs a formal model.

But recall the solution we found in Chapter 3, in particular the formal nature of that solution. Our solution – that the passive is an aspect – was based on the observation that the passive (*be* + V-*ed*) is excluded from roughly the same transitive verbs as the resultative perfect (*have* + V-*ed*), i.e. from *resemble*, *lack*, *suit*, etc. This is a formal (not semantic) observation, based on the combinatorial possibilities (the syntax) of the passive, *be* + V-*ed*. On the basis of this formal observation and analysis it becomes clear that the passive, as an aspect, expresses a new state which arises on the subject as the result of a preceding action, and hence the subject is patient. There are two things which distinguish this solution from Chomsky's solution. Firstly, it is a discovery, not a hypothesis: the discovery can be confirmed or refuted by someone else repeating the experiment under which roughly the same transitive verbs were found to be excluded from both the actional passive and the resultative perfect. And secondly, it does not involve a notation: the analysis can be presented in plain English, or plain any other language, without the need of a notation (we use abbreviations such as NP, V, Aux, etc., but there is no claim that such abbreviations constitute an explanatory formal notation).

Where does this leave Chomsky's account of the passive in his Minimalist model, particularly his technique of making assumptions in a hypothesis which he formalizes in a notation? What it does is to expose his assumptions as fictions and inventions, and his use of a notation as merely notational, not formal, as trivial, not explanatory. 'Formal' in descriptive grammar means 'not semantic', it does not mean notational. Form arises through contrast in a substance, and there are three ways in which form manifests itself in natural language: by word order (syntax), by phonological shape (morphology), and by combinatorial possibilities (also known as syntax, sometimes known as syntagmatics). No mention here, in form understood descriptively, of notations. Notation has nothing to do with form in natural language. All the Minimalist account achieves is to express in a notation, together with some assumptions, an ancient but incorrect analysis, viz. the voice analysis of the passive, i.e. the idea that the passive is derived from an underlying active. But we saw in Chapter 3 that the voice analysis of the passive from traditional grammar is itself a hypothesis, and one which we showed to be false: the passive is not a voice of the verb, it is an aspect of the verb, of the type Auxiliary + Participle, like the perfect, with its own meaning, viz. 'action + state, i.e. passives and actives are not synonymous after all. You can formalize in a notation the voice analysis of the passive as much as you like, but it won't change the fact that the passive is not a voice of the verb, it is an aspect of the verb. Chomsky's 'formal' syntax is not formal at all, it is notational; and his assumptions are not a revolutionary new way of doing science, far from it, they are ad hoc and meaningless. One is forced to agree with Lamb (1967) that generative grammar is pretentious nonsense which is its own self-parody, and with Hall (1987) that it is a pseudo-science.

It is possible to identify the exact moment when Chomsky mistook notation for form. In a chapter entitled 'Limitations of phrase structure description' Chomsky (1957:39) wrote the following rule:

(107) $Aux \rightarrow C(M)$ $(have + en)$ $(be + ing)$ $(be + en)$

Here we see that Chomsky has spotted the formal similarity between perfect, progressive, and passive. One can imagine him looking at the three syntagms and saying, 'Why? Why are they so similar in form? There must be a formal way to explain it, there must be a formal way, there is a formal way, here it is:'

(108) $NP_1 - Aux - V - NP_2 \Rightarrow NP_2 - Aux + be + en - V - by + NP_1$

(adapted from Chomsky 1957:43)

This was the world's first Transformation. This was the moment when Chomsky slipped from form to notation, from science to pseudo-science, between pages 39 and 43 of *Syntactic Structures*. Talk about forcing your data to fit a preconceived theory – Chomsky redefined what theory is, to make it fit the data! Rule (107) is formal – it is based on the formal (in the descriptive sense) similarity between *have + V-ed, be + V-ed,* and *be + V-ing.* But rule (108) is not formal in the descriptive sense, it is at best formal in a quasi-mathematical sense, but even that would be an insult to mathematics, it is quite simply notational, and nothing more than that. In effect Chomsky was saying, if we assume a transformational rule of passive, and we write it as '⇒', then '⇒' is formal. It looks just like 'NP', 'V', etc., and they are formal, so '⇒' must be formal, too. And if '⇒' is formal, then the entity behind '⇒', i.e. the Transformation, must also exist, just as the entities behind 'NP' and 'V' exist, i.e. nouns and verbs.

But '⇒' is not formal, it is notational; and Transformations (and their analogues in post *Syntactic Structures* models) do not exist in the way that nouns and verbs exist, they were something which Chomsky assumed/postulated in his imagination. Those who have read Chapter 3 of this book know the formal solution to Chomsky's dilemma in confronting (107). The three syntagms are formally similar because they all belong to the same category, aspect, of the type Auxiliary + Participle; the passive is there because, like the perfect and the progressive, it reacts to the lexical aspect of the verb and the compositional aspect of the sentence, and it has an aspectual-style meaning, too, viz. 'action + state'. If only Chomsky had known that in 1957 he might never have embarked upon the generative enterprise. But what's the use, let's not get depressed, he didn't know it and he did embark upon it.

The point about assumptions not being explanations and notational not being formal becomes even clearer when one looks at other solutions to the passive which Chomsky has proposed in the past. For example, in the Government-Binding (GB) model of the 1980's he proposed for sentence (109a) the underlying or D-structure (109b) and the surface or S-structure (109c):

(109)   a.   John was killed.
       b. $[_{NP}e]$ INFL be $[_{VP}[_{V}kill][_{NP}John]]$
       c. $[_{NP}John]$ $[_{VP}was\ killed\ t]$

In this model the NP *John* starts out in D-structure in object position after the verb. An affixation rule adds the passive morpheme *-en* to *kill,* forming *kill-en.* The passive morpheme has two special properties. One is that it absorbs the Case-assigning function of the verb, so that the Objective Case of *John* in (109b) is absorbed by *kill-en. John* is thus left without Case, which is a violation of the Case Filter (the Case Filter states that every phonetically realized NP must be assigned (abstract) Case). Another property of the passive morpheme is that it prevents the assignment of a θ-role to the subject $_{NP}e.$ This is necessary to prevent the assignment of two θ-roles to $_{NP}e,$ which, were it to happen, would be a violation of the θ-criterion. The NP *John* is moved to the empty subject position, $_{NP}e$, where it receives Nominative Case to satisfy the Case Filter, leaving behind a trace *t* in S-structure, to indicate its original object position. In this way John is interpreted as object of *killed*, even though in S-structure it appears as subject (Chomsky 1986:73–74, 118, 157, 209; Cook 1988:121–125).

Here we see some assumptions which made it through to Minimalism, and some which didn't. The ones which didn't are the Case Filter, and the idea that the passive morpheme *-en* absorbs the Objective case of the object and prevents the assignment of a θ-role to the subject $_{NP}e$. Otherwise the analysis is similar to Minimalism, e.g. the use of traces, raising, and an empty subject position; and most importantly of all, the idea that passives and actives are synonymous and that the subject of passives is equivalent to the object of a corresponding active. But Chomsky's GB account of the passive is just as misguided as his Minimalist account, for the same reasons: all he does is to formalize in notation the incorrect voice analysis of the passive from traditional grammar, using some assumptions which are simply ad hoc to the GB analysis. But the passive is not a voice of the verb (derived from an underlying active), it is an aspect of the verb, with its own meaning.

One can do this for all of Chomsky's accounts of the passive, running back in time through REST (Revised Extended Standard Theory), EST (Extended Standard Theory) and ST (Standard Theory), i.e. the Aspects model of 1965. I will spare you the gory details. Suffice it to say that the ST hypothesis was never tested, nor was the EST hypothesis, nor the REST hypothesis. None of Chomsky's hypotheses, i.e. models, have ever been tested, and none of them ever will be tested, because they cannot be tested and are not meant to be tested. They are not hypotheses at all in the scientific sense of that term, i.e. a theory which gets tested in practice to see if it is correct, and if experiments confirm the theory the hypothesis has been shown to be correct and is accepted, and if experiments refute the theory the hypothesis has been shown to be false and is rejected. Rather, Chomsky's hypotheses are an end in themselves, not a means to an end. They can never be falsified, because the method of generative grammar works by constructing a hypothesis whose only *raison d'être* is to be eventually replaced by another hypothesis, and that one by another one, and again by another one, *ad infinitum*, till the cows come home. To put it in Herbert Dingle's terms (see the quotation from Dingle below on p.102), science has gone from examining nature to assuming that mathematical truths may be found in nature to assuming that mathematical truths are necessarily found in nature to assuming that the referents of *quasi*-mathematical statements are necessarily found in nature. It is not science, it is pseudo-science. The fictional devices of generative grammar bear a greater resemblance ontologically to the postulates of religions – angels with wings flying about the place, cloven-hoofed devils with horns sticking out of their heads – or to the postulates of folklore – fairies, hobgoblins, and leprechauns – than they do to scientific concepts. Watching two generative grammarians discuss language is like watching a conversation between two lunatics, one of whom believes passionately in the existence of fairies but definitely not leprechauns, the other of whom believes passionately in the existence of leprechauns but definitely not fairies. Each lunatic describes in great detail, using mathematical formulae, the appearance of his fairy tale creature. University departments are founded, journals are initiated, scientific books are written, conferences are held, and there is a heated scientific debate between the two sides over whether it is fairies that exist or leprechauns. If you go up to the two lunatics and say ahem, excuse me, actually neither fairies nor leprechauns exist, though dogs and cats exist, they look at you as though you were mad, unable to comprehend or engage with what you are saying, muttering how do we know that dogs and cats exist.

To adopt a different analogy, generative grammar is shadow-boxing. Generative grammarians are like people who have read how science is done, and go through the motions of doing science in a mime, but never actually do it.

Generativists claim that they do test their hypotheses/models, and it works like this. They run the rules of the model, and if the rules generate the correct sentences the model has been tested and has been shown to work. But this is not a genuine testing of a hypothesis. The generativist starts off with a piece of data – a given construction, a given set of sentences – and constructs his model to generate those sentences, to cover that data. Of course the model generates those sentences, that is why it was constructed! Testing of a model in this way is, of course, circular and vacuous.

D–n and blast, we are not geniuses after all! Scientists have the same thought processes, use the same logic, and have the same rationality as everyone else. It is important that descriptivists, agnostics and other undecideds grasp this point and do not allow themselves to be blinded by pseudo-science. Generative grammar is wrong not because of competence versus performance, not because of the innateness hypothesis, but because its formalness is not formal but notational, and its analyses are untestable assumptions, not explanations. It would not matter if generative grammar and the model-builders were a minor sect somewhere, which the rest of us could ignore, but they are not. They have hijacked and taken over core linguistics completely, and they do not tolerate dissent. But we must fight back, for the sake of the discipline. There will be no progress in core linguistics until the generative cuckoo is ousted from the nest.

4.3 The equivocation of form and notation

So far we have looked at two generative accounts of the passive – in Minimalism and GB theory – and compared them to a descriptive account of the passive – the aspectual analysis – in order to see how the two methodologies, generative and descriptive, differ from one another. Let us now look more specifically at the treatment of non-passivizable transitive verbs in generative and descriptive grammar, to see how that comparison can help shed light on the difference between the two approaches, particularly regarding their different understanding of 'form' and 'formal'. Non-passivizable transitive verbs are verbs which are transitive and therefore one would expect to form a passive but which do not form a passive, e.g. *have, resemble, cost*. The task is to explain that fact. In a book written by one of the major early practitioners of generative grammar G. Lakoff (1970) said that non-passivizable transitive verbs are exceptions to the rule of passive and should be registered as such in the lexicon. He suggested that this might happen in two stages. First, a lexical item is registered as reacting in a non-normal (marked) way to a rule **i**:

(110) [m R(i)]

where **m** stands for 'marked' and **R** for 'rule'. Secondly, a further rule specifies that lexical items marked for a rule **i** cannot undergo **i**:

(111) [m R(i)] → [-R(i)]

where '-' means 'cannot undergo' (G. Lakoff 1970: 19–20, 24–25).

Wilkins (1980) proposed a very different solution. In keeping with the Extended Standard Theory of the time she assumed that passives are derived by a single rule of NP-preposing, symbolized as:

(112) $\Delta - V - NP \Rightarrow NP - V - \emptyset$

In line with (112) transitive verbs are marked in the lexicon as having optional subjects (i.e. in the active), as shown in (113):

(113) +(NP) –

where the brackets around NP indicate optionality. Thus the NP of (113) (the active subject) can be omitted, in order to allow the NP of (112) (the object) to occur in its place, becoming the passive subject. Non-passivizable transitive verbs like *resemble* are excluded from the passive by marking them in the lexicon as taking an obligatory (active) subject, as shown in (114):

(114)   +NP –

where the absence of brackets indicates obligatoriness. Since the active subject of *resemble* cannot be omitted, the rule of NP-preposing cannot apply to replace it by an object NP (Wilkins 1980: 722–723).

Those are two generative explanations of non-passivizable transitive verbs. Recall now the explanation given in Chapter 3 within descriptive grammar of the same verbs. In Chapter 3 we said that the passive with *be* + V-*ed* is an aspect of the type Auxiliary + Participle, meaning 'action + state'. It is well known that aspects of the type Auxiliary + Participle react to lexical aspect, e.g. stative verbs do not form a progressive with *be* + V-*ing* in English. In order to form a passive a verb must have the lexical aspect telic, i.e. it must have a potential end-point, which can become the end-state of the meaning 'action + state'. Thus verbs which are atelic – such as *resemble, suit, cost* – cannot form a passive (because they lack the necessary potential end-point). This analysis is confirmed by the fact that most non-passivizable transitive verbs also cannot form a resultative perfect,[72] and indeed it was the discovery by experiment of this perfect-passive correlation which led us to see that the passive is an aspect in the first place. Thus it is seen that the existence of non-passivizable transitive verbs is an artefact of an incorrect analysis, the voice analysis, and that if the passive is seen in its true light, as an aspect, then the oddity of non-passivizable transitive verbs does not arise. The aspectual analysis of the passive is a formal-syntactic analysis in the descriptive sense: formal, because it is based on the perfect-passive correlation and relies for its evidence on things such as the formal similarity between the passive, the perfect, and the progressive in English (*be* + V-*ed*; *have* + V-*ed*; *be* + V-*ing*); and syntactic (syntax in the sense of combinatorial possibilities, not word order) again because it is based on the perfect-passive correlation. To say that it is formal, however, does not entail that we ignore meaning altogether, since the sign is bilateral: the aspectual passive does have a meaning, viz. 'action + state', but it is a meaning which we were led to by new formal observations, discoveries, and data.

That is a descriptive explanation of non-passivizable transitive verbs. We now have two sets of explanations for the same phenomenon, one generative, the other descriptive, side by side. What is the difference between them? The two approaches could hardly be more different, and the differences between them are very clear. The two generative explanations we looked at take it as read that non-passivizable transitive verbs are exceptions to the rule of passive for-mation, and attempt to provide a formal explanation in a formal meta-system which they themselves construct. But the meta-system which they construct is not formal, it is notational; and by the technique of generative grammar they are allowed to construct/assume/postulate virtually any device or struc-ture they like, and invent virtually any notation they like in which to express their assumptions as they go along. Generative grammarians subsume formal in the descriptive sense and notational under one heading, which they call 'for-mal'. But theirs is an equivocation with the term 'formal': sometimes they use the term 'formal' correctly, in a descriptive sense, but other times they use it to mean notational. The result is a methodology which is so unconstrained as to be meaningless, and which is neither explanatory nor scientific.

The descriptive explanation we looked at, on the other hand, does not use a notation and does not need a notation to be understood. And yet it is formal: it is formal in the descriptive sense of that term. Moreover, it does not consist of assumptions/postulations/hypotheses (which are nothing of the sort anyway, because they are not testable), rather, it re-locates non-passivizable transitive verbs within familiar and well-established descriptive categories such as perfect and telic, and meaning components such as actions and states. Furthermore, it can be tested by another scholar examining transitive verbs to see if the same subset is precluded both from the passive and the resultative perfect. The de-scriptive explanation is empirically based, genuinely explanatory, and testable, whereas the generative explanations are invented, trivial, and not testable. Strip away the notation and the ad hoc assumptions from the generative accounts and you are left with the descriptive observations which you started out with in the first place. The notation is nothing more than a code, hiding a descriptive analysis beneath it. Formalization in linguistics is obfuscation, not explication.

Most of the key terms in generative grammar are used ambiguously, in the way that we have seen for the term 'formal', and indeed many critics of generative grammar have spoken of a 'systematic ambiguity' that one finds in Chomsky's writings. Some examples are the terms 'theory', 'explain', 'grammar', 'syntax', 'language', 'structure'. All of these terms are used by generativists some-times in a descriptive sense, sometimes in a generative sense. For example, the statement 'A formal grammar is a theory of language which explains syntac-tic structure' can be understood in a descriptive sense or in a generative sense. It is this systematic ambiguity which has misled many descriptively-oriented linguists into accepting generative grammar as valid.

4.4 Lexical-Functional Grammar

So far we have concentrated on Chomsky's models, but there have been break-away movements within generativism and we should look at some of those to see if the failings which we have found in Chomsky's models apply equally to them. Let us start with Joan Bresnan's Lexical-Functional Grammar (LFG), as presented in Bresnan (2001). Bresnan criticises what she calls the serial approach in Chomsky's work, by which one starts with a deep structure and applies transformations to it to arrive at a surface structure. LFG, in contrast, has three parallel structures: argument structure (e.g. agent, patient), functional structure (e.g. subject, object), and categorial structure (e.g. noun phrase, verb phrase). The relations between the three types of structure are made explicit in what is called a relational design of the model. The relational design of LFG implies that argument structure, functional structure, and categorial structure are equally important in how language works, in contrast to Chomsky's configurational and serial approach, which implies that categorial structure, being at a deeper level, is more important. Bresnan (2001: 19–20) illustrates the relational design or architecture of LFG as shown in (115):

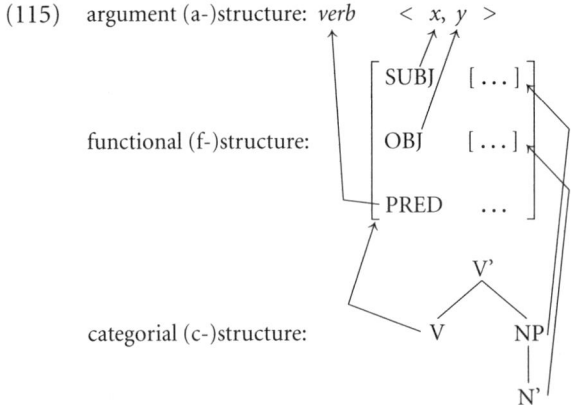

(115)   argument (a-)structure: *verb* $< x, y >$

functional (f-)structure:

categorial (c-)structure:

In LFG subject and object are primitives and hence appear directly in the model, in contrast to Chomsky's configurational models, where they are not primitives but derived, derived from constituent structure. The advantage of having subject and object as primitives is that it allows one to cover what the generativists call 'non-configurational' languages, i.e. highly inflecting languages with little syntax (Bresnan 2001:6). The three structures of LFG are linked by 'principles of functional correspondence', shown by the arrows in (115).

The passive was one of the main motivating factors behind the initiation of LFG in the first place (Bresnan 2001:25), and it is therefore particularly appropriate that we look at how LFG analyses the passive. Bresnan notes that whilst in the active the subject is agent, in the passive the subject is patient, with the agent expressed in an optional prepositional phrase. In Chomsky's configurational design of universal grammar this remapping of roles to functions is carried out by movement rules, which we showed above in (105). In the relational design of universal grammar, on the other hand, the remapping of predication relations is characterized as follows:

(116)   active   passive

R < x y >   ⇔   R < x y >
        | | | |
        s   o   (OBL)   s

Bresnan writes quite coherently (for someone writing within an incoherent paradigm), and we can give her gloss on (116) verbatim:

> Here the active and passive verb forms share the same predicate argument structure (with roles indicated by variables x, y), and the roles are lexically associated with, or mapped to, alternative sets of grammatical functions, s (subject) and o (object). This characterization abstracts away from the language particular realizations of subject, object, and oblique (OBL) relations, which may be configurational or nonconfigurational.
>
>   In LFG, relation changes are thus lexical alternations in predicate-function mappings.
>   (Bresnan 2001:26)

She first gives an LFG-analysis of a sentence in Malayalam (a non-configurational language), a Dravidian language spoken in southern India. She then gives an LFG-analysis of the translation of that sentence into English (a configurational language). The sentence is *The elephant was worshipped by the child*, and is analysed as follows, first the active version, then the passive sentence:

(117)

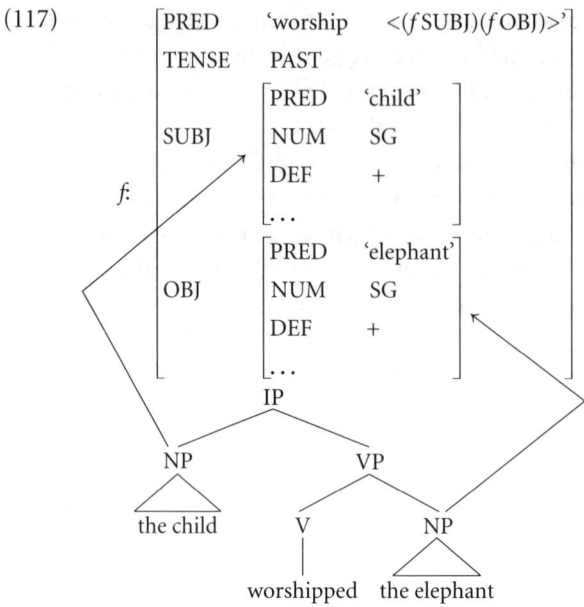

(118)

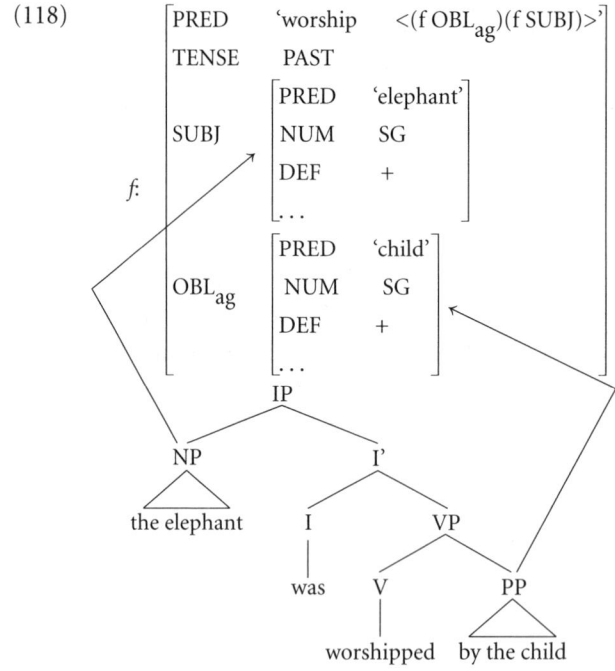

(Bresnan 2001:29)

The key difference between this analysis and Chomsky's is that it sees the passive as a lexical rule, not a syntactic rule. Verbs can appear in an active form, or alternately in a passive form. If they appear in the active the verb form itself inflects for tense. If they appear in the passive the past participle is used. Since the past participle cannot be inflected for tense, another form is used – tense-bearing verbs that can take participial complements – such as *get* (*John just got handed a can of worms*), *have* (*We had the agents sent phony passports*), *keep* (*She keeps her library painted a dark burgundy colour*), or *be* (*John was handed a book*). There is no movement involved, instead an association between different roles and functions:

> The argument role which is associated with the object function in the active lexical form of the verb will be associated with the subject function in the passive lexical form of the verb. Since the object NP follows the verb, and the subject NP precedes the verb, the NP expressing this role will appear to shift positions from the active to the passive. (Bresnan 2001:28)

The evidence in LFG that passivization is a lexical relation change, not involving syntactic transformations, is that passivization is input to lexical processes of derivational morphology such as nominalization, adjective formation, and compounding. Some examples of adjective formation from passive participles are *an opened can, hard-fought battles, my broken heart, You can ignore any recently gone over accounts*. A syntactic rule of passive has lexical items as input to it, and once passivization has happened it is not possible to go back and subject the lexical items in the newly formed passive sentence to lexical processes such as adjective formation (Bresnan 2001:30–32). The conversion of passive participles to adjectives is possible because:

> Adjective conversion in general denotes a state derived from the semantics of the base verb. .... The state denoted by the adjective appears to be the result state of the eventuality denoted by the past participle (Langacker 1991:202–203; Parsons 1990:236; Levin & Rappaport 1989). ... Because the activity of running lacks an inherent result state, it is strange to say *a run child*. But when the goal is supplied to the activity, a result state is defined, and now conversion is possible (*a run-away child*). (Bresnan 2001:34–35)

Let us now turn to our critique of LFG, in our attempt to understand the wider generative method. First the bad news. Like the Chomskyan models we looked at earlier LFG confuses notation with form: Bresnan seems to believe that the mere act of expressing something in a notation renders it formal. But of course it doesn't. For example, the notion of subject is a grammatical function which can be defined formally – 'the subject is the first item in a stylistically neutral sentence', or semantically – 'the subject is usually agent'. But to write subject as SUBJ does not make it suddenly formal or change it in any way whatsoever. Subject continues to be subject, a formal and semantic entity, no matter in what notation you write it, no matter how you 'formalize' it, as the generativists say. Thus, looking at the LFG analysis of the passive in (116)–(118), once you strip away the notation and decode it you are left with the familiar active-passive relationship or voice analysis of the passive from traditional grammar, and nothing else. The notation adds nothing to our understanding of the passive, it merely gets in the way.

Moreover Bresnan, like Chomsky, has formalized the wrong descriptive analysis. She has formalized the voice analysis of the passive, i.e. the idea that passives are derived from an underlying active. In the Chomskyan manner she has treated the active-passive relationship as data, and built up a 'theory' around it. But the active-passive relationship is not data, it is itself a hypothesis, a hypothesis which in Chapter 3 we showed to be false: passives are not derived from actives, for the passive is an aspect, with its own meaning, 'action + state'. As with Chomsky's models, it is plain that what Bresnan thinks is formal is not formal but notational: formal is what the aspect analysis is. To recast the familiar voice analysis of the passive in formal symbols is notational and trivial; to have shown that the passive is an aspect is formal and explanatory.

Now the good news. The good news is that Bresnan, like most generativists, works in a way which is a mixture of descriptive and generative,[73] and her examples and descriptive observations are extremely interesting. Indeed, the points she makes about passive participles being adjectives and adjectival passives expressing 'a result state of the eventuality denoted by the past participle' are exactly in line with and reminiscent of the aspectual analysis of the passive presented in Chapter 3. This is the tragedy of generative grammar. What will become of Bresnan's valid and interesting descriptive observations? Are they destined to be known only to supporters of the LFG model, or will they make it into the wider community? I would like to talk to Bresnan about the descriptive elements of her work, but I don't want to swear an oath of allegiance to LFG and adopt its idiosyncratic assumptions and notation in order to do so. Maaike Schoorlemmer's book on the Russian passive, Schoorlemmer (1995), is another example of this phenomenon. Schoorlemmer (1995) was written within the Government-Binding and Minimalist models. Buried deep within it, submerged beneath a morass of formalisms and generative-style assumptions, is the valid and descriptive observation that imperfective verbs in Russian tend not to form a participial passive with *byt'* 'to be' because the participial passive in Russian expresses a resultant state – Schoorlemmer calls it 'the Perfect Effect' – and only the perfective aspect in Russian is capable of expressing a resultant state. This is an observation which I very much agree with – see pp.47–48 – and again, I would like to discuss it with Schoorlemmer. But not if I have to learn and adopt the idiosyncratic assumptions and notation of Government-Binding theory of the 1980s and Minimalism of the 1990s in order to do so (see Beedham 1998a, 2001). If I am going to join a fan-club I would rather support a football team than a linguistics model. What will happen to Schoorlemmer's descriptive insights? Are they only for the eyes and ears of GB-theorists and Minimalists of that period? Who is going to take the time and trouble to decipher that particular code to get at the descriptive insights it conceals (I did it in Beedham 1998a, but I had special reasons to, nobody else will)? Will Schoorlemmer and Bresnan talk to each other about their similar insights? If they try will they be able to, across models?

How many models of language are there? One of the leading early generativists called his book *Thirty Million Theories of Grammar* (McCawley 1982). Many a true word spoken in jest. We have not reached that number yet, but there are dozens of models around, each with its own assumptions and notation, and most of them containing data and descriptive observations which are valid and which ought to be accessible to everyone. But they aren't, you have to learn the notation and the idiosyncratic assumptions of each model in order to get at them. Apart from being theoretically and methodologically flawed the models approach to studying language does not work from a purely practical point of view. It prevents linguists from talking to each other and from having proper access to each other's work.

This criticism applies also to descriptively oriented models such as Stratificational Grammar (Lamb 1966), Systemic Grammar (Halliday & Matthiessen 2004; Bloor & Bloor 2003), and Cognitive Grammar (Langacker 1987, 1991; Janssen & Redeker (Eds.) 1999).[74] Bloomfield's dislike of 'schools' in science is aptly conveyed by Fries (1961:196):

> The subject title of this chapter would have made Bloomfield very unhappy. He despised 'schools', insisting that the usual attitude of the adherents of a 'school' strikes at the very foundation of all sound science. Science, he believed, must be cumulative and impersonal. It cannot rest on private theories. To Bloomfield one of the most important outcomes of the first twenty-one years of the Linguistic Society of America was that it has 'saved us from the blight of the odium theologicum and the postulation of "schools"'.

The models approach has done untold damage to linguistics; we need to return to a mainstream again. The true test of the validity of a new grammatical analysis is whether it makes it into pedagogical grammars, particularly grammars for foreign learners but also grammars for native speakers. It is, of course, well known and widely accepted that generative grammar is not applicable in foreign language teaching (Lamendella 1969). But in general the whole schools and models approach to language analysis is not applicable in foreign language teaching. In a linguistics dominated by generative grammar writers of pedagogical grammars face an impossible task in having to understand and decode the innumerable models in order to get at any descriptive sense which may lie buried beneath the notations and model-specific terminology. Thus the link between theoretical linguistics and applied linguistics has been severed (Beedham 2002b). In my own case it was my experience as a student of German and Russian, trying to get to grips from a purely practical point of view with the passive and irregular verbs in those languages, which led me to tackle those areas of grammar in those languages and thence in my native language, English, from a theoretical point of view, arriving at the analyses presented in this book. Thus pedagogical grammar plays a crucial role in the beginning and the end phases of theoretical grammar, in presenting us in a clear manner with the problems and anomalies which need to be overcome and explained, and in confirming that we have indeed explained them if our theoretical analyses are taken up by applied linguists and included in their pedagogical grammars. I have to confess that the aspectual analysis of the passive has not yet been taken up in pedagogical grammars, but I would venture to suggest that if the model-building approach had not broken the link between theoretical and applied linguistics it would have been by now, and I still hope and believe that it will be eventually. It is foreign language learning and teaching which has always provided the best inspiration to theoretical linguistics, and it is time we recognised this and returned to that firm and familiar foundation to our discipline. The best kind of (theoretical) linguistics is that which is a mixture of theory and practice – an equivalent in the natural sciences would be someone who was both a (theoretical) physicist and an engineer. It is an approach which is common in Eastern Europe, fairly widespread in western Europe, but rare now in the Anglo-American world.

4.5 Head-Driven Phrase Structure Grammar (HPSG)

Generative grammar has its origins in the theory of mathematical languages. *Syntactic Structures* (Chomsky 1957), the slim volume which initiated the generative enterprise, was written for students of computer science, not linguists

(Chomsky 1986:49).[75] The innateness hypothesis, the psychological reality of linguistic theories, and the relevance of grammars to the mind/brain was added later, but there is a group of generativists within computational linguistics who trace their work back specifically to Chomsky 1957, not Chomsky 1965. The group includes Gerald Gazdar and his Generalized Phrase Structure Grammar (GPSG – see Gazdar et al. 1985), as already mentioned above, and Pollard and Sag with their Head-Driven Phrase Structure Grammar (HPSG – see Pollard & Sag 1987, 1994). Such linguists openly proclaim their debt to computer science and the theory of computer programming languages, and openly and explicitly borrow formalisms from computer programming languages, citing works such as Pereira and Shieber (1987), or Carpenter (1992). Ironically from the perspective of a descriptivist, for this group of generativists Chomsky, in abandoning the computational approach, has abandoned formalization:

> We emphatically reject the currently widespread view which holds that linguistic theory need not be formalized. Rather, our position is the same as the one advocated by Chomsky (1957).   (Pollard & Sag 1994:7)

HPSG has certain properties in common with LFG, in particular a belief in the sharing of certain subparts of levels rather than in transformational operations between levels, and the belief that passive is a lexical rule, not a syntactic rule. HPSG subcategorizes verbs for the NPs that can occur with them in a feature called SUBCAT. Pollard and Sag (1994:153) give passivization as a lexical rule which cyclically permutes SUBCAT lists, as illustrated in (119):

(119)   *read, devour, ...*:
      SUBCAT $<NP_1, NP_2> \rightarrow$ SUBCAT $<NP_2, PP\ [by]_1>$
      give, donate, ...:
      SUBCAT $<NP_1, NP_2, PP\ [to]_3> \rightarrow$ SUBCAT $<NP_2, PP[to]_3, PP[by]_1>$

The Passive Lexical Rule is given by Pollard and Sag (1987:215) as in (120) below:

(120)   PASSIVE:

$$
\text{base} \wedge \text{trans} \begin{bmatrix} \text{PHON} & \boxed{1} \\ \text{PAST-PART} & \boxed{2} \\ \text{SYN} \,|\, \text{LOC} \,|\, \text{SUBCAT} & <...,[\ ]\,\boxed{3}\,,[\ ]\,\boxed{4}> \\ \text{SEM} \,|\, \text{CONT} & \boxed{5} \end{bmatrix} \rightarrow
$$

$$
\text{passive} \begin{bmatrix} \text{PHON} & f_{\text{PSP}} \ (\,\boxed{1}\,,\boxed{2}\,) \\ \text{SEM} \,|\, \text{LOC} \,|\, \text{SUBCAT} & <(\text{PP[BY]}\,\boxed{4}\,),...,[\ ]\,\boxed{3}> \\ \text{SEM} \,|\, \text{CONT} & \boxed{5} \end{bmatrix}
$$

The overall effect is given by Pollard and Sag (1987:216) as in (121) below:

(121)

$$
\text{base} \wedge \text{strict-trans} \begin{bmatrix} \text{PHON see} \\ \text{PAST-PART seen} \\ \text{SYN} \,|\, \text{LOC} \,|\, \text{SUBCAT} <\text{NP}\,\boxed{2}\,,\text{NP}\,\boxed{1}> \\ \text{SEM} \,|\, \text{CONT} \begin{bmatrix} \text{RELN SEE} \\ \text{SEER}\ \boxed{1} \\ \text{SEEN}\ \boxed{2} \end{bmatrix} \end{bmatrix} \rightarrow
$$

$$
\text{passive} \begin{bmatrix} \text{PHON seen} \\ \text{SYN} \,|\, \text{LOC} \,|\, \text{SUBCAT} <(\text{PP[BY]}\,\boxed{1}\,),\text{NP}\,\boxed{2}> \\ \text{SEM} \,|\, \text{CONT} \begin{bmatrix} \text{RELN SEE} \\ \text{SEER}\ \boxed{1} \\ \text{SEEN}\ \boxed{2} \end{bmatrix} \end{bmatrix}
$$

There is not the space here to go into the details of (119)–(121), but it is obvious that HPSG, like the other generative models we have looked at, bases its passive rule on the voice analysis of the passive familiar to us from traditional grammar. But again, we showed in Chapter 3 that the passive is an aspect, and is not derived from an underlying active. Like Chomsky and Bresnan, Pollard and Sag have formalized the wrong descriptive analysis of the passive. They think they have explained the passive with a formal solution, but all they have done is to maintain the old problems raised by the voice analysis of the passive in their own special notation. How long can the generativists go on re-casting the voice analysis of the passive – the active-passive relationship – in different notations? If McCawley 1982 is right there will be 30 million theories of grammar and 30 million ways of formalizing the voice analysis, an analysis which is wrong!

But that argument aside, what is gained by presenting the active-passive relationship as in (119)–(121), in HPSG? To some extent it depends on what you do with it. HPSG-ers are to be praised for stating frankly that their source of formalisms is computer programming languages, displaying more openness than some generativists I could mention. But it does raise the question, is an HPSG-grammar meant to be implementable on a computer? If so, I think we should be told. If so, then that is what you have achieved – you have achieved a grammar which can be implemented on a computer. Very worthy, very practical, and at least it is something. But does that make it a theory of grammar? Obviously not – many things can be implemented on a computer, but that does not make them theories. If HPSG is computer-implementable Pollard and Sag may be good programmers, but does that make them theoretical linguists? I think not.

Or perhaps an HPSG grammar is not really meant to be implemented on a computer, they just use the symbols from programming languages. This is what Maurice Gross had to say about generative grammarians adopting the formalisms of computer programmers:

> The formal mechanisms used by theoreticians are simply (within terminological changes) those used by professional programmers who specialize in the treatment of non-numerical data. For example, the dummy symbol Δ is essentially a reserved memory whose content is specified by program: the trace symbol t is an address pointer: the bar notation is an indexing device for the number of times a loop is entered, etc. Arguments about these mechanisms of abstract grammar are then isomorphic to those involved in optimization of the programming of any algorithm. The choice between two theories, e.g. between 'generative' and 'interpretative', is analogous to the choice between SNOBOL and PL 1 for a given program – with the operational difference that a programmer for whom the result would be sufficiently important can always program his algorithm in both languages, and choose according to the performance of the program in each language. In the same situation, generative linguists have not succeeded in exhibiting any experimental clues favoring the superiority of one system over another. One more difference between linguists and programmers is that the latter are of necessity more rigorous because they are limited by convention to certain well-defined languages. Linguists, on the contrary, tend to believe that introducing new formal devices constitutes an original and creative contribution to the field. Lack of scientific culture prevents them from seeing that this activity is in general trivial, and that numerous mechanisms (together with variants) can often be proposed by professional programmers. Such mechanisms would be those that linguists pompously call 'alternative

theories', and which they praise for 'empirical adequacy' and 'explanatory
power'.   (Gross 1979:874–875)

So if HPSG is not meant to be computer-implementable it reduces it to the
same status as Chomsky's and all the other generative models: a bizarre reformulation in code or notation of certain well-known descriptive facts and
observations. Not formal, not explanatory, and not scientific. In sum, HPSG-
ers, GPSG-ers, and other generativists within computational linguistics are
either good computer programmers or are engaged in just as trivial and eccen-
tric an activity as Chomsky and all the other generativists. Either way they are
not theoretical linguists in a meaningful sense, producing theories of natural
language which explain sentence structure.

How did it happen? How could it have happened that people thought that
rendering a sentence of English in the formalisms of a programming language
constitutes an explanation of that sentence? Presumably it happened because
in the 1950s, when generative grammar first emerged, programming languages
were new and little understood and people were amazed at the seemingly mag-
ical powers of computers. It was a genuine mistake, and with hindsight one can
see how it happened. But in the light of the experience of the last 50 years it is
time now to recognise and to admit to ourselves that it was and is a mistake.

So what happens to the generative grammarians now? What do you do
if you are a generativist and you suddenly recognise the error of your ways?
Many generativists have a large dose of data-orientation and descriptivism in
their work, and will be able to adjust fairly easily to a descriptive approach.
Some generativists, on the other hand, are more mathematically and com-
puter-programming inclined, and they will have to move fully into either computers or logic or mathematics. That is their business, not mine. But one thing
is certain: they must stop the nonsense of generative grammar.

4.6 Formal semantics

Formal semantics is based on an even more disastrous equivocation of form
and notation, as well as on a complete misunderstanding of the relationship
between form and meaning. It takes meanings and 'formalizes' them, i.e. expresses them in a notation. In doing so it is aware that form and meaning are
inextricably linked, but it believes that by expressing meanings in a notation it
has captured those meanings formally and thus explained them scientifically. It
is, of course, sheer folly. Notations are not forms, they are mere notations; and

the relationship between form and meaning in natural language is that form creates meaning – natural language is itself a formalization of the universe. The meanings we perceive are determined by the forms through which we see them. And by scrutinising those forms carefully and scientifically we can gain greater insight into the meanings which they create/express. But to translate meanings into a notation is a trivial and senseless activity.

Let us take two examples to illustrate formal semantics, generative semantics and Montague Grammar. Starting with the former, McCawley (1968) analysed the English verb *to kill* as given in (122) (Newmeyer 1986:93):

(122)

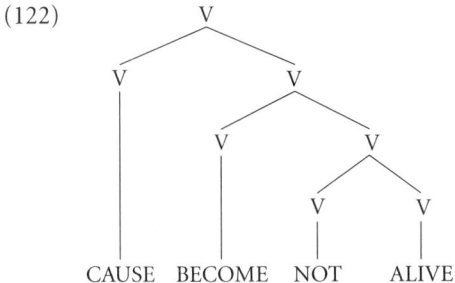

Here we see that McCawley has decomposed *kill* into semantic components, written them in upper case letters, and put them on a tree diagram. They called it 'abstract syntax', but it is neither syntax nor abstract. It is a trivial reformulation of a word's meaning in a particular notation.

Dowty (1991:202) translates *kill* into Montague Grammar as given in (123) below:

(123)   λΦλxΦ{ŷ[∨P[P{x} CAUSE BECOME ¬**alive**′(y)]]}

This is not the place to delve into the intricacies of Montague Grammar or formal logic in general.[76] But there is one simple point which I would like to make. The propositional calculus of formal logic does not formalize the meaning of the English word *and*, it formalizes logical conjunction; it does not formalize the meaning of the English word *or*, it formalizes logical disjunction; and it does not formalize the meaning of the English phrase *if…, then…*, it formalizes logical conditionals. The meaning of the English word *and* is determined by its place in the system of English, similarly for *or* and *if…, then…*. In fact, the Saussurean dictum that the meaning of a word is determined by its place in the system applies equally well to formal logic as it does to natural language: the meanings of the logical symbols &, v, ∼, → are determined by their place in the system of propositional calculus. Of course, the meanings of the logical symbols can be given a gloss in a natural language, e.g. English, Russian, He-brew, etc., but that does not mean that the logical symbol '&' is a formalization of (the meaning of) the English word *and*. Russian has two words which cor-respond to the English word *and*, *i* and *a*. *I* means roughly 'and', but *a* means 'and' with an element of 'but' thrown in, and is often translated as 'but'. But there are not two propositional logics, one for English and one for Russian. & means & in propositional calculus quite independently of how we render that meaning in English or Russian or any other natural language.

The conclusion to be drawn from this with regard to the translation of the English verb *to kill* into Montague Grammar, as given in (123), is that it may be good logic – I leave that to the logicians to say – but it does not tell us anything about the place of the verb *to kill* in the lexical and grammatical system of English, and that is what counts if we want to get at the meaning of the English verb *to kill*. Formal logics are a formal semantics of that bit of the universe which they cover, but they are not a formal semantics of the natural language in which you happen to gloss their statements.

Whereas generative grammar confuses form with notation, the use of for-mal logic in linguistics confuses linguistic form with logical form. English (or German, or Russian, or any other natural language) is a formal system, yes, but its forms are determined by their place in the system of English (or German, or Russian, etc.), not by their place in some system of formal logic. The use of logic in linguistics has the virtue that at least formal logic is a valid (and indeed genuinely mathematical) subject in its own right, unlike generative grammar which, being notational not formal, is not. But the criticism still remains that to translate a sentence of English into a statement of formal logic is not to give a formal explanation of the English lexico-grammatical forms in that sentence – only a form-oriented descriptive linguistics can deliver that – but to capture the meaning of the sentence in formal-logical terms. There is nothing wrong in that, that's fine, let there be logic. But it is logic, not linguistics. And whilst it may be explanatory in a logical sense – again, I leave that to the logicians to judge – it is not explanatory in a linguistic sense.

4.7 Connectionism

Parallel Distributed Processing (PDP), or connectionism, is a technique for writing computer programs which is more efficient than traditional meth-ods, and claims to imitate the way the human brain works. In psychology it has been applied to motor control, perception, memory and language

(McClelland, Rumelhart, & Hinton 1986:13), and in a more practical vein is used in electrical appliances such as washing machines and rice cookers (Pinker 1999:104). The major work of connectionism is Rumelhart and McClelland (Eds.) 1986a/McClelland and Rumelhart (Eds.) 1986, which consists of 26 papers by a number of 'cognitive psychologists' trained in physics, mathematics, neuroscience, molecular biology, computer science, and psychology (Rumelhart & McClelland (Eds.) 1986a:xi), including a paper entitled 'On Learning the Past Tenses of English Verbs' by the editors of the whole work, Rumelhart and McClelland. In its application to language connectionism claims to be an alternative to Chomsky's Language Acquisition Device (the LAD), which "hypothesizes explicit inaccessible rules" (Rumelhart & McClelland 1986b:217):

> Put succinctly, our claim is that PDP models provide an alternative to the explicit but inaccessible rules account of implicit knowledge of rules.
>
> (Rumelhart & McClelland 1986b:218)

Amidst great acclaim connectionism was heralded as a revolution in science. In a review in the journal *Language* Geoffrey Sampson wrote:

> Linguists remember 1957 as the publication year of Noam Chomsky's *Syntactic structures* .... In decades to come, perhaps 1986 will be remembered by academics as the year of publication of the pair of volumes reviewed here: they constitute the first large-scale public statement of an intellectual paradigm fully as revolutionary as the generative paradigm ever was.
>
> (Sampson 1987:871)
>
> ...
>
> Rules ... may more or less accurately DESCRIBE the output behavior of this model; but nothing corresponding to such rules exists within the model: the rules in no sense EXPLAIN its behavior. What causes that behavior is a large set of numerical weights associated with the various connections.
>
> (Sampson 1987:876)

In a review headed 'A turning point in linguistics' which appeared in the *Times Literary Supplement* a reviewer said: "to continue teaching [linguistics] in the orthodox style[77] would be like keeping alchemy alive" (Pinker 1999:104).

In order to see how connectionism works let us examine Rumelhart and McClelland's article, "On Learning the Past Tenses of English Verbs" (Rumelhart and McClelland 1986b; see also Pinker 1999:103–109). In the paper the authors describe a project in which they programmed a computer to produce the correct past tenses of English verbs, both regular and irregular. The program they wrote works by using 'units' and connections between the units. The computer is 'trained' to produce the right result – the correct past tense form of

English verbs, especially irregular verbs – in several run-throughs by strengthening the connections between the appropriate units when it gets the answer right, and by weakening those connections when it gets it wrong. The architecture of the program simulates, it is claimed, the architecture of the brain. The brain has neurons and synapses connecting them: PDP programs have units and connections between them. Moreover, PDP programs simulate the way the human brain works by having parallel processing in them: it is unlikely that the brain works in a serial or sequential manner, rather, it works by addressing a problem on several fronts simultaneously. PDP programs, with their parallel architecture, work in a similar manner:

> PDP models appeal to us for psychological and computational reasons. They hold out the hope of offering computationally sufficient and psychologically accurate mechanistic accounts of the phenomena of human cognition which have eluded successful explication in conventional computational formalisms; and they have radically altered the way we think about the time-course of processing, the nature of representations, and the mechanisms of learning.
> (McClelland, Rumelhart, & Hinton 1986: 11)

The computer was 'trained' to produce the correct past tense forms of English verbs in the following way. The base forms (present tense) of 420 English verbs, some regular, some irregular, were entered into the computer, together with their past tense forms (i.e. together with the right answer). The verbs were entered in the form of 'Wickelphones'. Wickelphones, named after Wickelgren (1969), are a way of registering the phonemes of a word in terms of a given phoneme's following phoneme, the preceding phoneme, and the word boundaries. For example, using the symbol # to indicate word boundary, the word *cat* consists of the Wickelphones $_\#k_a$, $_ka_t$, and $_at_\#$, where, as can be seen, the phonemes/word boundary either side of a given phoneme are represented as subscripts of that phoneme (Rumelhart & McClelland 1986b: 233–234). In addition to being entered into the computer in terms of their Wickelphones, the verbs were entered in terms of associations between Wickelphones. The computer was then asked to produce the past tense of a given verb. If it got it right the associations between (the Wickelphones of) that verb and (the Wickelphones of) its past tense form were strengthened, if it got it wrong the associations were weakened. After 200 run-throughs or trials the computer was getting it right over 90% of the time, correctly converting *look* to *looked*, *hit* to *hit*, *sing* to *sang*, and even *go* to *went* (the program does not distinguish between regular and irregular verbs, it simply produces a past tense form on the basis of the weighted connections between Wickelphones, irrespective of whether the

verb is regular or irregular). That may not be surprising, after all that train-
ing, but what was surprising was that when the computer was presented with
86 new verbs (72 regular and 14 irregular) on which it had not been trained
it got the past tense right for 91% of the verbs overall, and for 84% of the irregular verbs (Rumelhart & McClelland 1986b: 261). Moreover, for those few
mistakes that it did make many of them were of the kind that children make as
they go through their stages of learning the irregular verbs. Bybee and Slobin
(1982) found that children make different mistakes on different classes of irregular verb at different stages in their learning. Rumelhart and McClelland's
computer was reproducing the same kind of differentiated mistake, depending
on the class of verb and the stage of learning it was at (Rumelhart & McClelland
1986b: 245–260).

Two questions arise in respect of PDP programs in general:

(i)   Is PDP a more efficient way of programming a computer to perform
      certain tasks?
(ii) Do PDP programs simulate the working of the human brain?

And three further questions arise out of the use of a PDP program to get a
computer to produce the correct past tense forms of irregular verbs:

(iii) What is the relevance of the PDP type of computer program to the learn-
      ing of irregular verbs by children, and for psycholinguistics in general?
(iv) What is the relevance of PDP programming to generative grammar?
(v)   What is the relevance of the PDP type of program for core descriptive
      linguistics (lexico-morpho-syntax), specifically to the past tense forms of
      English verbs?

As regards the first question I leave it to computer programmers and other
computer experts to decide. As regards the second question, I leave that one
to AI (Artificial Intelligence) experts and psychologists to answer. The third
question I leave to psycholinguists to settle. On the fourth question I do have
something to say. Before I answer it let us recap on what we have learnt about
generative grammar in this chapter so far. We have seen that the generative
method consists of constructing a set of assumptions which one formalizes in
a formal notation – the 'model'. The model, it is claimed, explains the syntactic
structure of sentences of natural language, both their form (how they are constructed) and their meaning. We saw that the factor that language is innate and
how children learn a language was a *post factum* add-on to the methodology,
to bolster its plausibility, but is by no means a necessary part of the method,
as confirmed by HPSG, GPSG, and other generativists working in the tradi-

tion of computational linguistics. We learnt that Chomsky (1957), the seminal work of generative grammar, was written for computer science students, not linguists; that many generativists borrow formalisms from programming languages without letting on that that is where they are from; that Chomsky has since abandoned such programming formalisms (though he still uses other formalisms); that some generativists, viz. HPSG-ers and GPSG-ers, consider such abandonment a betrayal of the ideals of generative grammar and indeed tantamount to an abandonment of formalization altogether; and that the formal models of generative grammar are untestable assumptions not explanations, which are notational in a trivial sense not formal in an explanatory sense, and that the generative method is therefore completely and utterly, irredeemably and catastrophically, misguided. Now to the fourth question. What connectionism does is to pick up two elements of generative grammar, one of which – language learning in children and the place of grammar in the mind/brain – is considered irrelevant to generative grammar by one group of generativists (GPSG and HPSG), the other of which – the implementability of grammars on a computer – is considered irrelevant to generative grammar by another group of generativists, notably by Chomsky himself. In doing so connectionism ignores completely the central core of generative grammar, i.e. the construction of formal models which purport to explain sentence structure. The answer to the fourth question, therefore, by dint of connectionism's double misinterpretation of the already misguided generative method, is that connectionism is of no relevance to generative grammar whatsoever. Ironically and unintentionally but to its credit, the claim of connectionism to compete with generative grammar is false.

Let us now turn to the fifth question: What is the relevance of connectionism to core descriptive linguistics (lexico-morpho-syntax), specifically to the past tense forms of English verbs? To answer this question we must split connectionism up into two parts, the programming part on the one hand, and the part concerned with a description of the English past tense forms and their investigation in experimental psycholinguistics on the other. As regards the former part, my answer is that the fact that a program can be written to implement the verbal system of English on a computer is irrelevant to the key and standard questions of (descriptive) core linguistics. Many things can be implemented on a computer: PDP models are no more a theory and explanation of linguistic structure than they are a theory and explanation of washing machines and rice cookers. As regards the second part I have a more optimistic answer. To a (descriptive) grammarian searching for patterns in the verbal system of English the data accumulated and observations made by psycholinguists observing the way children acquire the past tense forms of irregular verbs are interesting and valuable. The concept of Wickelphone is particularly interesting, since it leads to the vowel + consonant sequences (VCs) and consonant + vowel sequences (CVs) of the irregular verbs being singled out for attention, as, for example, in the *-ing* → *-ang* class of irregular verb (*sing sang*) (Rumelhart & McClelland 1986b: 234), or the negative association of *dr-* with *-nked* and *-ink* with *-nked*, inhibiting the incorrect past tense form *drinked* (Pinker 1999: 108). In the next chapter, in an entirely descriptive vein, we will see how the VCs and CVs of the irregular verbs serve as phonotactic markers of irregular conjugation. In sum, then, the descriptive and experimental-psycholinguistic part of connectionism is of interest to descriptive linguists, but the computer programming part is not of direct interest or relevance.

4.8 Steven Pinker as a descriptivist

In 1994 the best introduction to descriptive linguistics ever written, *The Language Instinct* by Steven Pinker, then in the Department of Brain and Cognitive Sciences, MIT, was published by Penguin, and rightly made a huge impact on linguistics, related disciplines, and the general public. But why do I say "to descriptive linguistics"? Surely Pinker is a Chomskyan, *vide* the fact that by the 'language instinct' Pinker means what Chomsky calls Universal Grammar, as he tells us in Pinker (1999: 197), *vide* numerous laudatory mentions of Chomsky in *The Language Instinct*, and not least *vide* Pinker (1984)? The reason I say to descriptive linguistics is that in all the 494 pages of *The Language Instinct* there is only one chapter which indulges in the practice of constructing hypotheses and formalizing them in a notation, and that is the chapter specifically devoted to generative grammar, Chapter 4 'How Language Works', and even there Pinker succeeds in extracting primarily the descriptive and the sensible from the generative paradigm. All the rest of the book is pristinely, impeccably, indubitably descriptive, and a joy to read. Moreover, Pinker's subsequent book, *Words and Rules*, on irregular verbs, is entirely and completely 100% descriptive, with not a hint of an untestable assumption dressed up in a formalism in sight. And it, too, like its predecessor, is lucid, erudite, incisive and hilarious, all at the same time. So why does everyone think Pinker is a Chomskyan? Oh, and by the way, why does Pinker himself think he is a Chomskyan?

The answer is because Pinker, as a psycholinguist, is a Chomskyan from the peripheral angle of the innateness hypothesis, but when it comes to the hard core of the Chomskyan method – constructing assumptions in a notation and claiming that they are explanations – Pinker is nowhere to be seen (at least not in Pinker 1994 and 1999). The innateness hypothesis was added after Chomsky (1957), in Chomsky (1959 and 1962), when the quasi-mathematical model-building technique was already established, as is loudly proclaimed by GPSG and HPSG, as we have seen. It was added to give plausibility to an implausible method. It is significant that in *The Language Instinct* Pinker dates the beginning of generative grammar to 1959, not 1957. He has latched on to the innateness hypothesis in Chomsky's work, but not to the quasi-mathematical model-building side. *The Language Instinct* is almost entirely descriptive, and *Words and Rules* is entirely descriptive, and contains some extremely interesting observations on 'families' of irregular verbs, based on the vowels and consonants which they contain, which I will cite in the next chapter as corroboration for my own work on the VCs and CVs of the irregular verbs. It is vital that people grasp this point. It is a tragedy that the brilliance of Pinker's *The Language Instinct* has been attributed to 'the new linguistics', i.e. generative grammar, when in fact it is a brilliant book precisely because it is not generative, it is descriptive (see Beedham 2002a).

The situation is both tragic and ironic. A group of psycholinguists has emerged who proclaim themselves to be Chomskyans, but who do not use the Chomskyan method. I, on the other hand, reject the Chomskyan method but because I am a grammarian am expected to use it. To this group of confused psycholinguists I say: If the generative method is so good you use it! I don't want it, here, you have it!

4.9 The mathematical, model-building approach in other disciplines: Physics

Linguists are entitled to ask, if the mathematical, model-building approach doesn't work in linguistics, what about other disciplines, especially physics? Does it not work there?[78] The answer is that the mathematical, model-building approach is also controversial in physics, and rejected by some experimental physicists, notably by Dingle 1972 (see also Theocharis and Psimopoulos 1987; Nordenson 1969; Essen 1971). Dingle says that the problem with theoretical physics is that it assumes that everything which is mathematically valid will be found in nature. But that is manifestly not the case. Many things are mathematically true which are not to be found in nature. In mathematics $1 + 1 = 2$, and it is indeed sometimes the case that in nature the addition of one object to another object results in two objects, e.g. if the objects are apples. But if the objects are drops of water the addition of one drop of water to another drop of water does not lead to two drops of water, it leads to one drop of water. Sometimes the addition of one man to one woman leads to three people. Somebody once added one rabbit to another rabbit in Australia and the result was several million rabbits. Sometimes mathematical truths are to be found in nature and sometimes they are not – it depends on the physical, chemical, and biological properties of the objects concerned (Dingle 1972:125). Consequently, when theoretical physicists construct elegant and precise mathematical theories or models, which, for example, predict the existence of a sub-atomic particle, and experimental physicists try to detect that particle in a particle accelerator, if the particle really does exist it would be a fluke, just as when in nature 1 + 1 = 2 it is an accidental consequence of the properties of the objects being added together. Dingle goes on to say:[79]

> So it is with other operations of mathematics. In algebra, if a = b, then 2a = 2b. This was applied in the Middle Ages to prove the immortality of the soul. To be half dead was the same as to be half alive: double both, and it follows that to be dead is to be alive. This particular argument would carry little weight now, but equally naïve applications to experience of mathematical truths do flourish. Not long ago the mathematical fact that log 1 = 0 was applied to prove that there was no difference between something and nothing. The late Professor E. A. Milne proposed a theory called *kinematical relativity*, according to which it was equally legitimate to represent the measurement of time by a certain symbol and by its logarithm. It was a short step from this to the conclusion that the question whether a distant nebula was moving rapidly away from us or remaining at the same distance was a 'no-question'; the two processes were the same, since the only difference lay in our free choice of the way of measuring time, and we could equally well measure it directly or logarithmically. When it was pointed out that, if this were true, the principle could be applied equally well to a stone that is thrown at you, so that whether you would experience the impact or not would depend on what kind of watch you carried, Milne refused to consider the physical application of the mathematics. On one scale of time the stone hit you a few seconds after being thrown; on the other an infinite time would elapse; this was mathematically certain, and therefore the two cases were equivalent.   (Dingle 1972:125–126)

There has been a steady decline over the centuries, says Dingle, from science based on observation and experiment to a situation in the 20th century where hypotheses are taken in themselves as absolute truths. He quotes an earlier statement of his on this point from a book he published in 1931:

I will give three quotations from representative scientists, covering the period from Newton to the present time and separated by roughly equal intervals. The first is from Newton himself (1687): 'I frame no hypotheses. For whatever is not deduc'd from the phaenomena, is to be called an hypothesis; and hypotheses, whether metaphysical or physical, whether of occult qualities or mechanical, have no place in experimental philosophy.' The second is from Laplace, referring to his famous 'nebular hypothesis' (1796): 'I will suggest an hypothesis which appears to me to result with a great degree of probability, from the preceding phenomena, which, however, I present with that diffidence, which ought always to attach to whatever is not the result of observation and computation.' The third is from Eddington (1926): Care is taken to provide "macroscopic" equations for the human scale of appreciation of phenomena as well as "microscopic" equations for the microbe. But there is a difference in the attitude of the physicist towards these results; for him the macroscopic equations – the large-scale results – are just useful tools for scientific and practical progress; the microscopic view contains the real truth as to what is actually occurring.' The course of development is from a categorical rejection of hypotheses of any kind whatever, through a diffident presentation of one which results 'with a great degree of probability' from phenomena, to the confident assertion that a hypothesis contains 'real truth' and phenomena are just 'useful tools.' The question of the validity of this process is the most vital question, both for the philosophy of Science and for the application of scientific ideas to other departments of thought, at the present time.

(Dingle 1931:44, quoted in Dingle 1972:27–28)

The situation has deteriorated still further, asserts Dingle, to the point where *any* (mathematical) hypothesis is *necessarily* true. He goes on to ridicule the 'discovery' of neutrinos and radio galaxies, experiments to try to observe 'tachyons', hypothetical particles that travel faster than light, and a discussion in the journal *Nature* on whether an effect can precede its cause (Dingle 1972:28).

Returning to the question of geniuses, the western world's best known scientific genius is Albert Einstein, with his Relativity Theory. But not everyone is so enamoured of Relativity Theory; there are plenty of experimental physicists who consider it to be nonsense and folly. Nordenson 1969 claims that the Theory of Relativity is dependent for its validity on a new meaning of the word 'time' which Einstein introduces, a meaning which is elusive and questionable:

> *The Einstein time concept is and will therefore remain a phantom, an arbitrary mathematical symbol without known physical meaning.* ... Neither in the Special nor in the General Theory can we say if in principle the new symbols attained with the fundamental equations *have* a physical meaning and in that

case *what* their physical meaning is. *They are in principle only the result of mathematical constructions.*   (Nordenson 1969: 196)

Nordenson refuses to accept the famous twins paradox as a paradox, but says it is a blatant contradiction which refutes the Theory of Relativity, exposing the latter as nonsense:

> The Einstein extension of the classical Principle of Relativity to electro-magnetic phenomena thus either puts us face to face with contradiction or leads us to an ambiguous use of words and concepts, which results in statements that lack all meaning. We are therefore in principle obliged to go back to prerelativistic views. As a consequence we state that the vast amount of relativistic literature with its beautiful and complicated formulae but lacking all known physical meaning can be totally disregarded and deleted.
>
> Many of the most sensational consequences drawn from the formulae, such as the idea that a travelling person ages more slowly than one remaining at rest, is due to the attribution of two different meanings to the word 'time', and must be treated as mere nonsense. ...
>
> I do not hesitate to declare as a result of my investigation the opinion that Einstein's Theory of Relativity is not only among the most sensational fancies, but also one of the most serious logical incoherencies in the history of science.
>   (Nordenson 1969: 197–198)

The fiercest contemporary critic of modern theoretical physics is T. Theocharis. In an article in *Nature* in 1987 entitled "Where science has gone wrong" Theocharis and Psimopoulos attack the basic methodology of theoretical physics under which 'anything goes'. I recommend this article strongly to linguists, because reading it you realise that much of what they say could be applied with almost no change in formulation to theoretical linguistics. For example, they – like Dingle – lament the move from experiment and observation to hypothesis construction:

> If verifiability and falsifiability are not the criteria, then what makes a proposition scientific? ... [The] answer is more obvious in Thomas Kuhn's writings: a proposition is scientific if it is sanctioned by the scientific establishment. (Example: if the scientific establishment decrees that "fairies exist", then this would be scientific indeed.)   (Theocharis & Psimopoulos 1987: 596)

They regret that science is no longer about the discovery of truth and reality, and ridicule the fact that it is acceptable in a student textbook on the philosophy of science, viz. Chalmers (1976), for the author to say in his Introduction: "We start off confused and end up confused on a higher level" (Theocharis & Psimopoulos 1987: 597). Science is reduced to a meaningless game:

> By denying truth and reality, the [theoretical approach] reduces science to a pointless, if entertaining game; a meaningless, if exacting, exercise; and a destinationless, if enjoyable, journey. The aim of the game is just to play; the object of the exercise is merely to keep one busy; and the purpose of the journey is but aimless wandering.   (Theocharis & Psimopoulos 1987:597)

You have to pinch yourself to remember that they are talking about physics here, not generative grammar.

In fact, theoretical physics is not as bad as generative grammar, since the physicists can at least say that for the most part their mathematics is impeccable – it is just in its application to nature that problems arise. But we have seen in this chapter that generative grammar, despite the bombastic claims of the generativists, is not a precise, mathematical subject at all – they borrow symbols from other disciplines, especially computer science, usually without acknowledgement, symbols which, when removed from their home context, become meaningless, mere notations, as Gross (1979) has shown. So the generativists cannot say that their mathematics is impeccable; there is that difference between the two disciplines. Moreover, there is a recognized, distinguishable stage in the physicist's work when a different set of people, experimental physicists, come along and test out the theoreticians' mathematical models; in generative grammar there is no such distinguishable experimental stage, carried out by a different set of people, experimental linguists. So here again, theoretical linguistics is worse off than theoretical physics; another difference between the two disciplines. Nevertheless, generative grammar shares with theoretical physics the misapprehension that any (quasi-)mathematical hypothesis is necessarily true or valid.

It was not my purpose in this subsection to rebut theoretical physics, since I am not qualified to attempt such a thing, I am not a physicist. Rather, I wanted simply to show that descriptive linguists opposed to and indeed appalled by the generative method can take comfort in and derive confidence from the knowledge that we have a counterpart in experimental physicists who are equally opposed to the methods of modern theoretical physics.

4.10 Labelling the product

The term 'linguistics' is seriously and misleadingly ambiguous. The difference between for example the descriptive linguistics of the modern language,[80] generative model-building linguistics, and, to return to a theme from Chapter 1, historical linguistics is huge and fundamental. The problem is graphically illustrated by final year students wanting to do postgraduate work in linguistics, either research or taught courses. They go on the web, and read the University prospectuses, and what do they find? They find the term 'linguistics' everywhere, but it takes a lot of further effort and nous to realise for example that by 'linguistics' is meant in one programme generative grammar, and in another philology, when what they want is the descriptive linguistics of the modern language. I realise that since the funding reforms of the 1990s British universities sell science and education like soap powder, but it is ironic that we of all people, linguists of all people, label our product misleadingly. It is time we put our house in order, and ended the ambiguity and prevarication of the term 'linguistics'.

CHAPTER 5

Tense and irregular verbs

We return now to descriptive linguistics and our exploration of language and meaning. Tense is another grammatical category replete with controversy about its meaning. Let us recap on what was said about tense at the start of Chapter 2 'Aspect'. Many grammarians today think it best to confine the notion of tense to inflected forms only, which leaves English having two tenses only, the past tense, formed from adding the grammatical ending -*ed* to the verb, e.g. *worked*, and the present tense, formed from adding the grammatical ending -*s* to the 3rd pers. sing. of the verb and ∅ to all other persons, e.g. *he/she/it walks, I/you/we/they walk*. Under this view the future 'tense', e.g. *She will walk*, is a modal construction, not a tense, formed using the modal verb *will* followed by the infinitive without *to*.

So much for the form of tense; now to its meaning. The commonly accepted view is that tense locates an event in time relative to the moment of speech, i.e. relative to the time at which an utterance is made. The accepted wisdom is that the past tense refers to past time relative to the moment of speech – see (124) below, the present tense refers to present time – see (125), and the future tense – be it a tense or a modal construction – refers to future time – see (126):[81]

(124)   Freda started school last year.

(125)   He is reading the newspaper.

(126)   He will be here in half an hour.

Indeed, following common practice in grammar, as we have already discussed at some length, the tenses are named after their supposed meanings.

However, there is a substantial body of opinion in linguistics which holds that tense does not refer to time. Tobin (1989:62) writes:

> A supposed 1:1 causal connection between time and tense has *never* stood up to the objective scrutiny of actual language data ... many scholars have pointed out the oftentimes loose and questionable connection between time and tense.

The most striking examples of a mismatch between tense and time are those instances in which the present tense refers to something other than present time, the past tense to something other than past time, and the future tense to something other than future time. Tobin (1989:83) hit the mark when he wrote:

> Linguists have traditionally related time to tense and ... this hypothesis appears to work much of the time. However, we still are left with the basic question: what about those familiar, frequent and well-known uses of the verb tense system in which there is no match between the time of the event and the choice of tense used to communicate it? These 'exceptional' uses of verb tense system obviously propose a serious threat to the view that tense is motivated by time. These 'problematic' exploitations of tense morphology have long been recognised and even have been given categorical labels such as 'the historical present', 'the narrative present', 'the timeless present', etc.

Let us now look at some examples of mismatches between tenses and times. The present tense, in addition to referring to present time, can refer to future time, as in (127) and the verb *pay* in (128):

(127)   The plane leaves for Ankara at eight o'clock tonight.

(128)   He'll do it if you pay him.

In fact, it may well be considered that future time reference as in (127) is the most common way of using the so-called present tense. At which point let us return to the view mentioned above that the basic meaning of the present tense is to refer to present time, as in (125). Doubtless the astute reader – and I am sure that all my readers who have made it this far are astute – was not fooled by example (125) for a second. Example (125) is not in the (simple) present tense at all, it is in the present progressive, i.e. it is only in combination with the progressive aspect *be* + V-*ing* that the present tense can refer to present time (R. L. Allen 1966:48).[82] If we take examples of the present tense by itself, without the progressive, i.e. in simple aspect, we get a very different picture. The nearest the present tense alone gets to expressing an action simultaneous with the moment of speech is in special situations such as commentaries, demonstrations, exclamatory sentences and performatives, as exemplified in (129)–(132):

(129)   Beckham passes the ball to Ronaldo ... Ronaldo shoots!

(130)   Now I put the cake-mixture into this bowl and add a drop of vanilla essence. (Leech 1971:3; see also R. L. Allen 1966:186–187, Miyahara Ms)

(131)   Here comes the winner! Up you go.

(132)   I advise you to withdraw.

However, as Leech (1971:3) and Miyahara Ms point out, the actions referred to in commentaries and demonstrations such as (129) and (130) do not occur exactly simultaneously with the moment of speech, but just before or just after it. Thus the so-called present tense not only does not have present time reference as a basic meaning (except on the verb *to be*) it is barely capable of referring to present time, i.e. an action co-temporaneous with the moment of speech, at all. If anything, the basic meaning of the English (simple) present tense is future time reference, or else its generic/habitual meaning, as exemplified in (137) and (138) below.

The present tense can also refer to past time, as in (133), in which the present tense is used for a livelier and more animated story telling (historic present); as in newspaper headlines, e.g. (134); and as in the communication verb *tells* in (135):

(133)   I couldn't believe it! Just as we arrived, up comes Ben and slaps me on the back as if we're life-long friends.

(134)   Seven Spanish agents die in Iraq attack on convoy.

(135)   Martin tells me the Smiths are moving from No.20.

It can also refer to an imagined time, when used as an alternative   the past tense in fictional narrative, as in (136):

(136)   The crowd swarms around the gateway, and seethes with delighted anticipation.

Finally, it can refer to no time at all, in an atemporal use, in eternal truths – (137), the habitual present – (138), and in the text attached to a drawing – (139):

(137)   Water consists of hydrogen and oxygen.

(138)   We go to Brussels every year.

(139)   St George slays the dragon.   (Dahl 1987:493)

In sum, the so-called present tense cannot by itself refer to the present, but it can and does refer to the past, the future, an imagined time, and to no time at all.

The past tense, in addition to referring to past time, can also refer to future time, the very opposite, as it were – see the verb *left* in (140):

(140)   It's time I left.   (see Jespersen 1924:56, 1933:258)

The past tense can refer to present time, in indirect speech, e.g. the verb *was* in (141) and the verb *had* in (142); and in polite use (143):

(141)   How did you know I was a Dane.   (Jespersen 1924:56)

(142)   Did you say you had no money?

(143)   Did you want to see me now?   (see also R. L. Allen 1966:174)

One of the most important meanings of the past tense is to refer to an imagined time, which it does in fictional narrative, i.e. the past tense is the tense used for story telling in literature. It also refers to an imagined time in a hypothetical and imaginative use – see the verb *had* in (144) and again *had* in (145):

(144)   If I had the money I would pay you.

(145)   I wish I had a memory like yours.

In sum, in addition to referring to past time the past tense can refer to the future, the present, and an imagined time.

The future tense, in addition to referring to future time, can refer to the present, as in (146), uttered by someone on hearing the doorbell ring:

(146)   That will be the postman.

Sentence (146) means 'that must be the postman', i.e. *will* here is equivalent to *must* in the 'logical necessity' sense. The future tense also has an atemporal use in eternal truths, as in (147), and to express the characteristic behaviour of someone, as in (148), said of a chatterbox:

(147)   Oil will float on water.

(148)   He'll talk for hours, if you let him.

I have to confess that I have been unable to find an instance of the future tense referring to past time (no doubt due to the fact that the English future is not a tense at all in the sense of an inflected form, but a modal construction using a modal verb, as we have said already, i.e. it consists of full-blown lexical items, not grammatical endings)!

Summarising now for all three tenses, the present tense can refer to future time, past time, an imagined time, and no time at all; it cannot refer to present time. The past tense can refer to future time, present time, and imagined time, in addition to its supposed basic meaning of past time. And the future tense can refer to present time and no time at all, in addition to its supposed basic meaning of future time. Thus it can be seen that the time-based theory of tense could hardly be more wrong – the only contradictory use that we have not found is the future tense used to mean past time. All the other theoretically possible uses which might contradict a time-based analysis of tense have been shown to exist: the present tense referring to the past and future, the past tense referring to the present and the future, the future tense referring to the present. A categorisation of the English tenses based on time gives us not a system but absolute chaos.

But tense-time mismatches are not the only contradiction in widely accepted analyses of tense. Irregular verbs are another striking anomaly in the system.[83] Most English verbs – the regular or 'weak' verbs – form their preterit and 2nd participle by adding the ending -ed, e.g. *walk walked walked*.[84] But a substantial minority of English verbs – the approx. 170 irregular or 'strong' verbs – form their preterit with ablaut and a ∅ ending, and their 2nd participle with ablaut and the ending -en, e.g. *break broke broken*. Given the fact that language is a (Saussurean) system, and that forms always carry meanings (even when some people don't expect them to), as we have seen frequently in this book so far, two questions arise. Can rules be found for the formation of the strong verbs? And what do ablaut, the ∅ ending, and the ending -en mean?

These two questions are not usually asked. Most linguists, and indeed most laymen, assume that strong verbs are a historical vestige from an earlier stage of the language, as mentioned in Chapter 1, and are learned exceptions without their own meanings, i.e. speakers learn that the preterit of *break* is *broke* rather like they learn vocabulary, almost as if *broke* were a new word which they have to learn. But this ancient view does not stand up to closer scrutiny. Let us examine first of all the historical point. It is interesting to realise that the strong verbs were there in English long before the weak verbs. The strong verbs are the original verbs of Indo-European: the dental preterit with -t -, from which the English preterit with -ed emerged, was a Germanic innovation which came later, after the strong verbs, it came in with Gothic (the earliest known form of Germanic), which is dated from about 100 AD (Keller 1978: 26, 48–49; see also Watkins 1962). Historical linguists cannot be certain about the exact dates, but Indo-European is usually dated at around 3,500 BC (Gamkrelidze & Ivanov 1995; Pinker 1994: 251–255). That means that the strong verbs of modern English are over 5000 years old. It is obvious that the 170 strong verbs of modern English could never have survived 5000 years of linguistic change if they were meaningless exceptions, learned by rote like vocabulary items. They would have all died out long ago if that were the case. They could only have survived so long if they were meaningful and rule-governed.

It is true that the number of strong verbs has shrunk over time, as verbs have crossed over from strong to weak: Old English had just over 300 strong verbs, reduced now to about 170 (Baugh & Cable 2002:60; Pinker 1999:80), whilst Middle High German had 339 strong verbs, reducing also to around 200 in modern German (Bittner 1996:143, 166). But at one point in the history of German the number of strong verbs rose: according to Bittner (1996:138, 142), Augst (1975b:249, 254–255), Hempen (1988:194–200), and Durrell (2001:11–12, 14) in the transition from Old High German to Middle High German there was an increase in the number of strong verbs, i.e. the strong verbs were productive during this period. And in general the traffic has not all been one-way, hundreds of verbs have crossed over in the other direction, and have changed from weak to strong, e.g. in English *ring rang, dig dug, stick stuck, wear wore, show shown, fling flung, sling slung, light lit, creep crept, kneel knelt, catch caught, quit quit, dive dove* (American only), *sneak snuck* (American mainly);[85] and some strong verbs have switched from one strong class to another strong class, e.g. *slay slew, draw drew* (Pinker 1999:84). In German the following verbs are strong in modern German which used to be weak: *preisen pries gepriesen* 'to praise', *weisen wies gewiesen* 'to show', *gleichen glich geglichen* 'to resemble', *stecken stak* 'to be', *dingen dang gedungen* 'to hire', *schinden geschunden* 'to maltreat' (Waterman 1966:106; Bittner 1996:110).[86] Furthermore, dialects are full of their own idiosyncratic strong forms, in which speakers have used their intuition and creativity either to create their own version of a strong verb or else to maintain a strong verb which has become weak in the standard language, e.g. in American dialects *help holp, tell tole, melt molt, climb clumb, drive druv* (Pinker 1999:70, 76, 84). Steven Pinker followed up his classic book, *The Language Instinct*, with a book on irregular verbs, *Words and Rules*, which demonstrates convincingly – and entertainingly, in the style of *The Language Instinct* – that the irregular verbs survive because they have patterns and elements of regularity:

> The irregular patterns refuse to die. Irregular verbs are supposed to be a list of arbitrary words memorized by rote, just like *duck* and *walk*, with only a trace of patterning left behind by long-defunct rules. Instead, people extract the patterns and extend them to new words .... (Pinker 1999:87)

Irregular verbs are a historical vestige, but so are the regular verbs (so is everything in language), that does not stop the irregular verbs from being rule-governed and meaningful synchronically, if we can only find the rule(s) and the meaning(s).

It is frequently said that there are only a small number of irregular verbs, and they tend to be the most common, making them easier to remember (Pinker 1999:123–128). But this view also does not stand up to closer scrutiny.

The view is based on the premise that we compare the irregular verbs with all the many thousands of regular verbs, so that speakers only have to remember about 0.1% of verbs as being irregular, which is perhaps feasible, or at least plausible. But that is not a sensible comparison. Irregularity in English verbs applies to the root of a verb – once a verb is irregular it is irregular in all its prefixed forms, e.g. *shine shone shone, outshine outshone outshone; do did done, overdo overdid overdone*, etc. Therefore if we are to compare like with like we should restrict the comparison to simplex verbs only. Having done that it is noticeable that all the irregular simplex verbs in English bar one – *to begin* – are monosyllabic, e.g. *eat, take, run*, etc. What we see here is the first structural marker of irregular conjugation: if a simplex verb is monosyllabic there is a chance that it will be irregular, if a simplex verb is polysyllabic there is almost no chance that it will be irregular and the question of remembering forms therefore does not arise (for those polysyllabic verbs). There is nothing for speakers to remember in the case of polysyllabic verbs, since they know on the basis of a verb's polysyllabicity that it will not be irregular. Once again, if we are to compare like with like we should compare irregular verbs with monosyllabic regular verbs only. Using the *Oxford Advanced Learner's Dictionary of Current English* (henceforth abbreviated as the OALD) as a representative source, that dictionary lists precisely 1,768 regular monosyllabic simplex verbs. These are the verbs which are on the face of it structurally identical with and therefore comparable with the irregular verbs, and if we are going to ask any questions about speakers remembering forms it is relative to these verbs that the question should be asked. 170 English irregular verbs set against 1,768 regular verbs gives a percentage of nearly 7% irregular. The analogous comparison and calculation made for German delivers a percentage of 10% irregular (Beedham 1995–1996: 143–144). To claim that speakers can learn off by heart the irregular preterits and 2nd participles of 0.1% of all verbs is one thing. But to claim that they learn those forms off by heart for 7% or 10% of the relevant verbs is not plausible, and stretches the bounds of credibility. It is too big a proportion of the relevant verbs.

It is true that most of the irregular verbs are common, e.g. *make, buy, go*. But many of them are not so common, e.g. *bid, dwell, grind, seek, strive, tread, wet*, etc.. Plausibly we remember *do did done* through hearing it and using it a lot, but that cannot be said of *grind ground ground*, etc.. Most of us rarely hear or use the verb *to grind*, and yet when we do have to use it we all get it right all of the time, no adult speaker of standard English today would come up with **grinded*. We don't hesitate, and say, now what is the past tense of that verb, I can't quite remember it.[87] Why, if we hardly ever hear or use it? Because there is a rule and a meaning behind it, if we could only discover them.

It is often said by linguists and laymen alike that children's errors with irregular verbs indicate that they are learned exceptions, doomed to extinction sooner rather than later. Children sometimes overgeneralize the *-ed* rule for preterit formation, and say *singed* instead of *sang*, *comed* instead of *came*, etc., which might be thought to presage the end of those irregular forms. But how often do they get it wrong? Steven Pinker and Gary Marcus examined a corpus of the spontaneous speech of 83 children, and found that they got it right 96% of the time. Only in 4% of cases did they produce the incorrect form (Pinker 1999:198–199). We notice children's overgeneralizations a lot because they are cute, but in fact the number of such mistakes is tiny. This result indicates that even in the language of small children the irregular verb-forms are not learnt by rote, they are rule-governed and meaningful.

But the most convincing argument of all that the strong or irregular verb-forms of English must be rule-governed and meaningful comes from Saussurean structuralism. Structuralism tells us that a language is a system whose units are determined by their place in the system. It is for this reason that language works by rules, and that forms have meanings – the linguistic sign, consisting of *signifiant* (form) and *signifié* (meaning), is indivisible. Structuralism does not allow for some forms to exist outside the system, meaningless and not part of the rules of the game. All linguistic forms must fit into the system somehow, and they all must have a meaning, it is simply a case of working out how they fit in and what the meaning is. That is the linguist's job. At the moment we do not know how the strong verbs fit in, by what rules the strong verb-forms are produced and what meaning they have which is different from that of the regular verbs. But meaning they must have, and rules they must have. It is up to us to find them.

What kind of meaning might it be? Tobin (1993:327) claims that the English irregular verbs are resultative, in contrast to a process orientation of the regular verbs.[88] Quirk (1970) and Quirk et al. (1985:106) claim that the irregular *burnt*, *smellt*, *dreamt* etc. are perfective, whilst the regular *burned*, *smelled*, *dreamed* etc. are durative, based on informants' reactions to these forms in perfective-type and durative-type contexts.[89] These two accounts by two scholars working completely independently are very close to each other, whereby resultative = perfective, and process-oriented = durative. Both scholars claim that the semantic difference between strong and weak verbs is of an aspectual nature, and I believe they are right. But we need proof of any meaning we might suppose is there, formal proof from *langue*, i.e. sentence-grammar. We need morpho-phonemic or morphological or syntactic or phonotactic proof of our semantic claims, because that is where the meaning comes from in the first place – every form has a meaning, and form determines meaning.

What kind of rules might they be underlying the irregular verbs? They will be the rules which furnish us with the proof of meaning mentioned in the preceding paragraph. I.e. we will discover the two things simultaneously, both the rules for the formation of the strong verb-forms and the meaning of the strong verb-forms. Again, simply because the linguistic sign, consisting of *signifiant* and *signifié*, is indivisible.

And what are the rules and the accompanying meaning(s)? I am not yet in a position to give a meaning or meanings and a definitive set of rules for the formation of the strong verbs. However, I have uncovered some regularities of a phonotactic nature which point us in a certain direction, viz. that of phonotactics, where we might find some rules and a meaning or meanings after further research. In 1992, with the help of Uwe Junghanns, I carried out an experiment in which an exhaustive list of English irregular verbs was compared with an exhaustive list of structurally identical and therefore comparable regular verbs. 'Structurally comparable', as was adumbrated above, meant simplex verbs only, because once a verb is strong it is strong in all its derived forms. And it meant monosyllabic verbs only, because all the simplex strong verbs bar one – *to begin* – are monosyllabic. The OALD was used as a reference source, and a trawl through that dictionary produced exactly 1,768 monosyllabic simplex regular verbs, as mentioned above, from *ache act add* to *zip zone zoom*. In the irregular list only verbs with both an irregular preterit and an irregular 2nd participle were included, so that e.g. *mow mowed mown* was dropped, to ensure that the list was as purely irregular as possible; and archaic and regional forms were also dropped for the sake of consistency, i.e. we were looking at irregular verbs in modern standard English, not certain dialects of English. The pruning process left 126 strong verbs, from *be bear beat* to *wind wring write*. Thus the ratio of weak verbs to strong was 14:1, i.e. there were 14 times as many weak verbs as strong. If the experiment was to work it was absolutely crucial that both lists were exhaustive, i.e. that every (structurally defined) irregular verb and every (structurally comparable) regular verb was included. We did not want our data tainted, either by the presence of a wrong verb in the wrong list or by omissions. It was then simply a case of looking at the two lists and playing the game of spot the difference. What was it about the verbs in the irregular list that made them different from those in the regular list? There had to be something, because in language *tout se tient* 'everything hangs together': there must be consequences of the strong verbs' irregularity elsewhere in the grammar of

English, a knock-on effect, something with which it hangs together. There had to be some structural indicator of a verb's irregular conjugation, or else how would speakers know that *be bear beat* etc. conjugate irregularly, whereas *ache act add* etc. conjugate regularly?

At first we looked at the vowels, to see if there was a difference in that respect between the two lists. Maybe one list contained a preponderance of front vowels, the other a preponderance of back vowels? But nothing, no difference. Then we looked at consonants: maybe one list contained more voiced consonants than the other? But again nothing, no difference in respect of consonants was to be seen. Then we looked at sequences of vowels and consonants/consonant clusters, e.g. in *sing* the vowel + consonant sequence (VC) [ɪŋ] and the consonant + vowel sequence (CV) [sɪ], and here at last a difference between the two lists became apparent.[90] We noticed that the VCs and CVs in the strong verb list had a low rate of occurrence in the weak verb list. This was surprising, because, given that there were 14 times as many weak verbs as strong, you would expect a VC or CV, if it occurs once in the shorter strong verb list, to occur 14 times in the longer weak verb list, assuming a random distribution of vowels and consonants. Or you would expect it to appear a lot, anyway. But that did not happen. In fact, the reverse happened. If a VC or CV appeared in the strong verb list it tended to appear in the weak verb list in very low numbers, and sometimes not at all! It was as if the VCs and CVs of the strong verbs were suppressing the possibility of their appearing on the weak verbs. That was on the basis of the strong verb infinitives alone. We then went on to check the VCs and CVs of the strong verb preterits and 2nd participles, e.g. in *sang* [æŋ] and [sæ], in *sung* [ʌŋ] and [sʌ], and found the same thing there. They, too, had an unexpectedly low rate of occurrence in the weak verb list.

This phenomenon is shown for VCs in Table 1. The left-hand column shows the VCs, and the first column to the right of it shows the number of weak verbs with a given VC. The next three columns show the number of strong verb-forms – infinitive, preterit, 2nd participle – with that VC. It is noticeable that in many cases if a number appears in one or more of the three right-hand columns, the number in the left-hand column under 'weak verbs' either goes down or is far less than one would expect. But it should go up, because there are 14 times as many weak verbs as strong. For example, looking at the row with the VC [ɛd] there are 3 strong infinitives, 9 strong preterits and 9 strong 2nd participles (they are *shed spread tread bled bred fed fled led read said shed spread*), giving a total of 21 strong verb forms, or 12 if one counts the homonymous preterits and 2nd participles once only. Given that there are 14 times as many weak verbs as strong in our lists, and assuming a random distribution of

Table 1. English VC sequences: statistics of weak versus strong verbs (extract from complete data) NB: zero is indicated by a gap in a cell

VC sequence	weak verbs	strong verbs		
		infinitive	preterit	2nd participle
æp	20			
æv		1		
æm	13		1	
æŋ	6	1	3	
æŋk	15		4	
ait	11	3		
aik	5	1		
ain	9	1		
aʊn	6			
ɛd	6	3	9	9
ɛnd	8	4		
ɛl	7	3	1	
ɛlt	4		4	4
ɛɪv	11		1	
ɪŋ	4	11		
ɪld	1	1		
i:tʃ	8	1		
ɔd	4		1	1
ɔf	3			
ɔz			1	
ɔ:l	16	1		1
ʊd			1	1
ʌk	12		2	2
ʌg	11		1	1
ʌm	11	1		2
ʌŋ	1		8	11
u:t	13	1		
u:z	5	2		
ɜ:l	7			
...				
TOTALS	1,768	126	126	126

vowels and consonants, one would expect 294 (i.e. 21 x 14) weak verbs to have [ɛd], or else 168 (i.e. 12 x 14), or at least a large number. But there aren't, in fact only 6 weak verbs have [ɛd], as the table shows (they are, incidentally, *bed dread head shred thread wed*). The same pattern is to be observed in most of the rows in Table 1, which is an extract from my data which reflects the pattern observed in the complete data.

Table 2a. CVs which are unique to the English strong verbs, i.e. which do not occur on a single structurally comparable weak verb (complete list from our data)

blǝʊ	θru:	spǝʊ	stʊ	swʌ	wǝʊ
tɛǝ	θrǝʊ	splɪ	strai	ʃræ	wʌ
tʊ	θrʌ	spræ	strʌ	hɪǝ	
dwɛ	spɛ	sprɛ	swɛǝ	nju:	
frǝʊ	spi:	sprʌ	swi:	wɛǝ	

Table 2b. English strong verb forms containing CVs unique to the strong verbs, i.e. containing CVs which do not occur on a single structurally comparable weak verb (complete list from our data)

infinitives	preterits	2nd participles
blow	dwelt	blown
dwell	froze	dwelt
hear	knew	frozen
speak	shrank	spent
spend	spent	split
split	split	spoken
spread	spoke	spread
strike	sprang	sprung
strive	spread	struck
swear	struck	strung
sweep	strung	swum
tear	swung	swung
throw	threw	thrown
thrust	thrust	thrust
wear	took	woken
	woke	won
	won	

Table 1 shows 3 VCs which occur on strong verb forms and which do not occur on a single weak verb. They are [æv] as in *have*, [ɔz] as in *was*, and [ʊd] as in *stood*. These VCs are unique to the strong verbs, and do not occur on any structurally comparable weak verbs at all. Turning to CVs, Table 2a shows 27 CVs which occur only on the strong verbs, on not a single weak verb in our data; Table 2b shows the 48 strong verb forms on which those CVs appear.

Let us now inspect more closely those few weak verbs which have a VC or a CV which occurs predominantly on the strong verbs. Most of them have the striking property that they are derived verbs (synchronically, not etymologically), usually from a noun, sometimes from an adjective.[91] In contrast most of the strong verbs – at least 86.5%, more depending on how you count them –

are base verbs, not derived. For example, looking at [ɪŋ] in Table 1, we see there that there are 11 strong verb infinitives with [ɪŋ] – *bring cling fling ring sing sling spring sting string swing wring* – and 4 weak verbs with [ɪŋ] – *ping ring ting wing*. All of the strong verbs except one (*string*) are base verbs, not derived, but all of the weak verbs are derived according to the OALD, derived from a noun: *to ping* from the noun *ping*, *to ring* (meaning 'put a ring on') from the noun *ring*, *to ting* from the noun *ting*, and *to wing* from the noun *wing*. Thus we see a structural difference and peculiarity about those few weak verbs with a strong verb VC or CV, viz. they are derived. In fact, it is only because they are derived from a noun that they exist at all as weak verbs with a strong verb VC or CV. If it weren't for the special circumstances of being derived from a noun these 4 verbs would not exist, and Table 1 would show a gap in the left-hand column alongside [ɪŋ], providing another VC which would be unique to the strong verbs. As it is there are weak verbs with [ɪŋ], but their number is low, only 4 verbs, and they differ structurally from the strong verbs in being derived as opposed to base verbs. This is a pattern which fits many of the weak verbs with a strong verb VC or CV in our data.

Some weak verbs with a strong verb VC or CV are not derived, but have other special properties. For example, looking at [ɪld] on Table 1 we see that there is one strong verb (*build*) and one weak verb (*gild*). The verb *to gild* in English is rare. Looking at [ɛlt] on Table 1, we see that there are 4 strong preterits, 4 strong 2nd participles (*dealt dwelt felt knelt*), and 4 weak verbs. One of the weak verbs is *smelt*, which is a specialist term restricted to a specialised register. Another of the weak verbs is *pelt*, which is slang (the other two weak verbs are *belt* – derived from the noun *belt* – and *melt*). Many of the weak verbs with a strong verb VC or CV are colloquial, slang, or vulgar, e.g. *fuck wank pee chuck booze swot kid*. I would speculate that these verbs have that playful and mischievous quality which we all sense in their sound alone – quite apart from what they denote – precisely because they contain VCs or CVs which they are not meant to contain, i.e. the VCs and CVs which are actually the preserve of the strong verbs. They are verbs with forbidden meanings and forbidden sounds.

Another special feature present on many of the weak verbs having a strong verb VC or CV is phonaesthesia (on phonaesthemes see Bolinger 1975:24–25, 218–220; Marchand 1969:397–428; Blust 1988; Hinton et al. (Eds.) 1994; Bergen 2004; Gamkrelidze 2006). For example, under [æŋ] in Table 1 there is one strong verb infinitive and 3 preterits (*hang rang sang sprang*), and 6 weak verbs (*bang clang gang prang slang twang*). 4 of these 6 weak verbs are phonaesthetic or quasi-onomatopoeic sound verbs – *bang clang prang twang* – verbs whose phonology imitates the sound they denote. Other examples from our data are *slam cry sigh yell blare shriek screech wheeze*. Sound verbs are allowed to exist as weak verbs with a strong verb VC or CV because they could not possibly undergo ablaut, since they have to retain the same sound in order to function as quasi-onomatopoeic sound verbs.

The notion of phonaestheme and sound symbolism extends from onomatopoeia to situations where the sound of a word symbolises or is associated with its denotation even where the denoted object is not a sound – it is often a movement described in a special way – and there are many such examples in our data. For example, Table 1 under [ɔd] shows one strong verb preterit, one strong verb 2nd participle (*trod*), and 4 weak verbs (*nod plod prod sod*). 3 of these 4 weak verbs are phonaesthetic verbs: *to prod* indicates a single, quick, action, *to nod* means to move the head up and down quickly or once, *to plod* means to move slowly. Other examples from our data our *blink tweak snatch kick pat swat skim peep peek ooze bound*. Here again, these verbs are precluded from the possibility of ablaut, since they have to maintain the same sound associated with their meaning, and hence are tolerated by the system of English as weak verbs with a strong verb VC or CV.

Thus we see that, whilst the numbers of weak verbs having the VCs and CVs of the strong verbs are surprisingly low, as shown in Table 1, they would be even lower were it not for special circumstances such as a verb being derived from a noun or adjective, being rare or specialist terminology, or containing phonaesthemes. Were it not for these special factors there would be far more gaps indicating zero in the column headed 'weak verbs' in Table 1, and it would be even more obvious that the strong verbs of English have a set of VCs and CVs which are peculiar to themselves.

So what does it all mean? It means that we have found a phonological – or to be precise, a phonotactic – marker of strong conjugation in English, i.e. the VCs and CVs of the verb. To the question, how do speakers of English know when a verb is strong, the answer is that if a verb is a polysyllabic simplex it is weak, and if it is a monosyllabic simplex it depends on its VC and CV: if it has one of a particular set of VCs/CVs it is weak, if one of another set it is strong.

This result is corroborated by Pinker (1999). There Pinker speaks of 'families' of irregular verb depending on the vowels and consonants in them:

(149)   *blow-blew, grow-grew, know-knew, throw-threw*
        bind-bound, find-found, grind-ground, wind-wound

drink-drank, shrink-shrank, sink-sank, stink-stank
bear-bore, swear-swore, tear-tore, wear-wore
(Pinker 1999: 83; see also Pinker 1994: 138–145)

He claims that for irregular verbs speakers memorise two forms, the infinitive and the preterit, e.g. *drink drank*, as two linked roots. However, memory is not a list of unrelated slots, but is associative, he says. Speakers are aware of a link between *drink* and *drank*, based on the vowels and consonants in the two forms. He illustrates this principle for *string strung* with a diagram whose main points are reproduced in Figure 3, using terms from the structure of the syllable such as onset (the opening segment of a syllable), nucleus (the central segment of a syllable), and coda (the closing segment of a syllable) (Pinker 1999: 117–118). Pinker writes:

> The verbs undergoing a given irregular change are far more similar than they have to be. If you are a verb and want to undergo the *i-a-u* pattern, all you really need is an *i*. But the verbs that do follow the pattern (*drink, spring, shrink,* and so on) have much more in common; most begin with a consonant cluster like *st-, str-, dr-, sl-,* or *cl-,* and most end in *-ng* or *-nk*. ... Imagine a rule that said, 'If a verb has the sound *consonant-consonant -i-ng*, change *i* to *u*'.
>
> (Pinker 1999: 91)

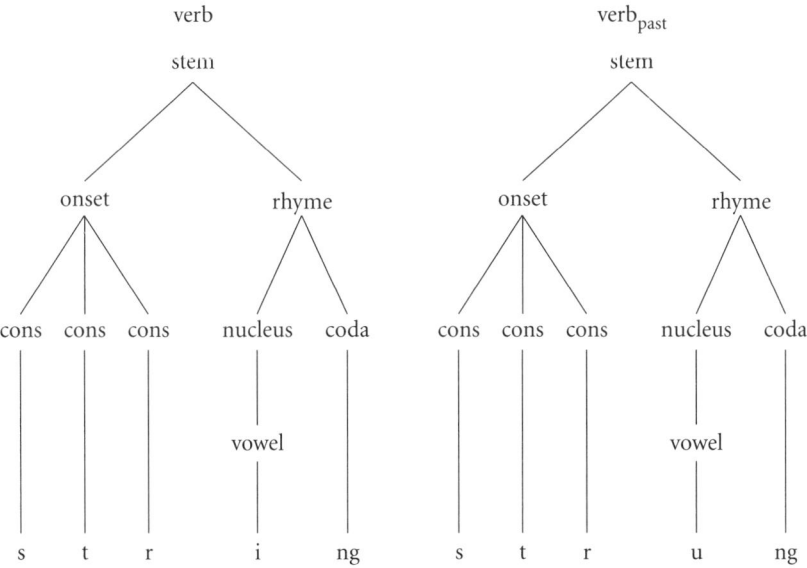

Figure 3. Pinker's dual root for *string strung* (based on Pinker 1999: 118)

Pinker (1999) presents a fascinating panoply of evidence – historical, dialectal, structural, psycholinguistic – in support of his view that the irregular verbs are alive and well in modern English, and exist in 'families' depending on the vowels and consonants which they contain. One particularly interesting piece of evidence comes from Bybee and Moder (1983). In a psycholinguistic experiment subjects were presented with made up verbs such as *to spling*, and asked to complete a sentence like (150):

(150)   Sam likes to spling. Yesterday he ——.

80% of people said *splang* or *splung*, because, Pinker claims, they link it up with the similar-sounding family *spring sprang sprung, ring rang rung* (Pinker 1999:84–85).[92]

Pinker also notes, as we did above, that some verbs which sound as though they ought to be strong, i.e. to link in with a particular family of irregular verbs, but which are weak, are weak because they are derived from nouns or adjectives, e.g. the verb *to ring* as in *Powell ringed the city with artillery*: "Verbs that are recognized as thinly disguised nouns or adjectives don't accept irregular forms, even when they sound like an irregular verb" (Pinker 1999:158). He also notes, as we also did above, that onomatopoeic verbs which sound as though they ought to be strong – i.e. belong to a particular irregular verb family – end up weak because of their onomatopoeia:

> Onomatopoeic verbs ... need past tense ... forms, but because they are not canonical roots, they cannot tap into the lexicon of roots and linked irregular forms that encourage irregular analogies. Onomatopoeic forms therefore are regular, even when their sound would otherwise tempt people to borrow an irregular pattern, *spling-splang-splung* style:
>
> > The engine *pinged* [not *pang* or *pung*].
> > ...
> > The canary *peeped* [not *pept*].   (Pinker 1999:155)

However, we still do not have rules and meanings for the strong verbs. There is still much work to be done. The next step was to see if the VCs and CVs of the strong verbs exist elsewhere in the vocabulary and grammar of English. Is it possible to link up the strong verbs via their VCs and CVs to a definable subset of vocabulary, e.g. a particular part of speech? In 1999 with the help of Wendy Anderson I conducted another experiment, to test this hypothesis. Since almost all the simplex strong verbs are monosyllabic we confined our search to monosyllabic words only, so that we were comparing like with like. All monosyllabic words except for verbs in the OALD were marked, and their VCs and CVs transcribed into IPA symbols. Since the OALD includes, of course, archaic forms we added archaic strong verbs to our list and expanded our list of VCs and CVs accordingly; and added modal verbs, for good measure. Appendix I on p.201 gives our complete list of the VCs of English strong and modal verbs. It was now simply a case of seeing which of the marked words from the OALD had a VC from that list, or a strong verb CV. As regards the CVs no pattern was found. For the VCs, however, a pattern was found, shown in Figure 4. Taken as a whole, i.e. without distinguishing between parts of speech, there is no pattern or correlation, viz. exactly 50% of the words examined contain a strong verb VC and 50% do not contain a strong verb VC. In order to see the pattern one has to distinguish between parts of speech, whereby we followed the categorisation given in the OALD. Moreover, one has to distinguish between lexical parts of speech such as noun and adjective on the one hand, and grammatical parts of speech (function words) such as preposition and conjunction on the other. Looking first at the lexical parts of speech, again no pattern is found, since 48% of the exemplars contain a strong verb VC, and 52% do not contain a strong verb VC, which can be considered a random distribution. However, when one looks at the exemplars of the grammatical parts of speech one sees that 72% contain a strong verb VC and only 28% do not contain a strong verb VC. In the case of personal pronouns the proportion is even higher at 87% (13 out of 15 word-forms). This percentage is too high to be chance. It strikes us as particularly high given that we have just seen an instance where the strong verb VCs *suppress* their appearance in another part of the lexicon, i.e. in weak verbs. Now suddenly the strong verb VCs are appearing in great numbers! There is obviously some link between the strong verbs and the grammatical parts of speech in English, manifest at the moment in the phonotactics of the words concerned. Strong verbs and (monosyllabic) function words share roughly the same VCs. The words behind the statistics in Figure 4 are given in Appendix II on pp. 203–206.

That is as far as I have got. I conducted the same two experiments for German and Russian and reached the same results, i.e. in German the VCs and CVs of its strong verbs, and in Russian just the VCs (not the CVs) of its nonproductive (= irregular) verbs, are also peculiar to the irregular verbs and tend not to appear on the (structurally comparable) regular verbs; and the irregular verb VCs in German and Russian have a surprisingly high rate of occurrence in (monosyllabic) function words and even in the inflectional endings of Russian (though not of German) – see below. So German and Russian confirm our results for English. But essentially that is where I am now.[93] The next step is to find out what lies behind the at the moment purely phonotactic link between

English monosyllabic words	with a strong verb VC	without a strong verb VC
lexical parts of speech		
nouns	614	747
adjectives	120	104
cardinal numbers	8	3
adverbs	80	57
interjections	15	9
abbreviations	5	4
Total lexical parts of speech	842 (= 48%)	924 (= 52%)
grammatical parts of speech		
prepositions	26	9
conjunctions	18	6
verb particles	9	5
personal pronouns	13	2
possessive pronouns	2	0
interrogative pronouns	2	1
indefinite pronouns	2	0
determiners	1	3
possessive determiners	6	2
indefinite determiners	4	4
interrogative determiners	1	1
negative determiners	1	0
definite article	1	0
indefinite articles	2	0
contractions	17	8
Total grammatical parts of speech	105 (= 72%)	41 (= 28%)
Grand total	947 (= 50%)	965 (= 50%)

Figure 4. Statistics of English monosyllabic words with a strong verb VC and without a strong verb VC, ordered by part of speech (based on the OALD)

irregular verbs and function words. Is the phonotactic link expression of a semantic common factor? Is the semantic common factor of an aspectual kind? What do the words in the left-hand column of Appendix II, i.e. the function words with an irregular verb VC, have in common? Do they have a semantic feature in common, perhaps of an aspectual kind? The answers to these questions will have to wait until my next research grant, and my next experiment (unless someone beats me to it!).

I am hopeful that the answers to these questions will deliver the looked for meaning which we know the strong verbs must have distinguishing them from the weak verbs, and rules for their formation. At the same time the answers should help resolve the contradictions discussed at the start of this chapter, i.e. the fact that the names of the tenses are complete misnomers, because the main meaning of the (simple) present tense is future time reference or else generic, the past tense can refer to present, future and imagined time as well as to past time, and the future tense can refer to present time as well as to future time. It is not by chance that Tobin called these tense-time mismatches 'exceptional', i.e. irregular uses (see p.108). By investigating the unexplained exceptions to tense formation, i.e. the irregular verbs, we hope to uncover a whole new analysis of the category tense, an analysis which will explain various problems associated with tense, especially the very exceptions which we hope will lead us to that analysis (more on exceptions later, in Chapter 7).

Irregular verbs in German

As one would expect, given that despite everything English is a Germanic language, German has a set of irregular or strong verbs, similar to English.[94] Most German verbs form their preterit by adding the infix -*t*- and a set of person endings to the stem of the verb, and their 2nd participle by adding the prefix *ge*- and the suffix -*t*, e.g. *sagen sagte gesagt* 'to say'. A small number of verbs, however, approx. 200 strong or irregular verbs, form their preterit with ablaut and a partially different set of person endings which includes ∅, and their 2nd participle with ablaut and the suffix -*en* (about a third of these also form their 2nd and 3rd pers. sing. pres. with ablaut), e.g. *gehen ging gegangen* 'to go'. Thus the forms which the strong verbs have and which the weak verbs do not have, and which we can expect to be bearers of a special meaning, are ablaut, the ending -*en*, and the ∅ person ending.

As in English, German is usually said to have three tenses, present, past, and future, which are reckoned to refer to present time, past time, and future time, respectively. Also as in English, German has plenty of examples which refute this analysis, i.e. each tense can refer to both the other times which are not in its canonical meaning, which are documented in Beedham (1995a: 123–126) and which we will not repeat here. For German, too, the question therefore arises: if not to time – or at least if not to those specific times – what do the German tenses refer to?

Mater (1966) lists 21,083 verbs, which means that if we took that as our yardstick the approx. 200 strong verbs would represent only 0.1% of all German verbs, a tiny number which one could perhaps dismiss as an aberration. However, it does not make sense structurally to compare the strong verbs with all verbs. Structurally, in German as in English, once a verb is strong it is strong in all its derivations, i.e. prefixed forms, so we confine our attention to *Grundverben* (non-prefixed verbs) only. Mater (1967:88) lists 3,205 *Grundverben*. Moreover, only verbs with the infinitive ending -*en* are strong, there are no strong verbs whose infinitive ends in -*eln*, -*ern*, -*igen*, -*lichen* or -*ieren* (Helbig & Buscha 1989:37). This means that in order to compare like with like structurally we must exclude such verbs from any comparison. Using Mater (1967) as a source, that leaves 1,467 weak *Grundverben* ending in -*en*. Thus the strong verbs represent approx. 10% of the structurally relevant *Grundverben* in German, a significant proportion which cannot be dismissed as an irregular aberration, but which must surely conceal regularities, if we can only find them.

In 1992 I conducted the same experiment for German as has been described already for English. The German irregular verb list, which contained strong, mixed and modal verbs, was pruned of archaic and regional forms,[95] which left 169 irregular *Grundverben*.[96] Thus we were comparing 169 irregular verbs with 1,467 regular verbs, i.e. there were 9 times as many regular verbs as irregular. Once again we compared the VCs and CVs of the (stems of the) irregular verbs with those of the regular verbs, and once again any VCs or CVs showing up in the irregular verb list had a remarkably low rate of occurrence in the regular verb list, and some did not show up there at all. Table 3a gives a

Table 3a. VCs and CVs which are unique to the German irregular verbs, i.e. which do not occur on a single structurally comparable regular verb (complete list from our data)

German VCs					
arf	aːx	ɛːf	ɪlt	ɔrb	ʊrd
arst	ɛrst	ɛːs	iːlt	ɔlt	uːb
alf	ɛlf	ɪrf	ɔʃ	ɔlf	uːd
aːp	ɛːp	ɪrst	ɔxt	øːg	uːks

German CVs					
pˏfa	biː	drɔ	vra	ʃviː	ʃlɔ
pˏfaː	braː	kaː	vrɪ	ʃvɔ	ʃluː
pˏfai	blai	kvɔ	vrʊ	ʃvʊ	rɛː
pˏfeː	bliː	krɔ	ʃɔ	ʃraː	møː
pˏfɪ	trai	gruː	ʃpra	ʃrai	neː
pˏfiː	treː	fliː	ʃpraː	ʃriː	lyː
pˏfoː	truː	floː	ʃpri	ʃmai	
tˏsoː	dai	viː	ʃprɔ	ʃlaː	
tˏsvʊ	dra	vɔ	ʃteː	ʃlɛ	
prai	driː	vuː	ʃtoː	ʃliː	

complete list from our data of the German VCs and CVs which are unique to the irregular verbs, i.e. which occur only on the irregular verbs, on not a single structurally comparable regular verb; and Table 3b gives a complete list of the irregular verb forms in which those VCs and CVs occur.

Most of the irregular verb VCs and CVs are represented amongst the regular verbs, but in very low numbers. However, when one looks more closely at those few regular verbs with irregular verb VCs and CVs one finds, as happened with English, that there are special circumstances which lead to them being there, viz. many of them are derived from nouns or adjectives (in contrast 95% of the German irregular verbs are base, i.e. non-derived, verbs), many are rare or specialized vocabulary, onomatopoeic and phonaesthetic, or colloquial, slang, and vulgar. For example, there are 6 strong verbs with the VC [ɪnd] – *binden* 'to tie', *empfinden* 'to feel', *finden* 'to find', *schwinden* 'to fade, die away', *verschwinden* 'to disappear', and *winden* 'to bind into a wreath or garland' – and only 2 weak verbs – *entrinden* 'to strip the bark off' and *erblinden* 'to go blind'. Since the regular verb list is 9 times longer than the irregular verb

Table 3b. German irregular verb forms containing VCs and CVs unique to the irregular verbs, i.e. containing VCs and CVs which do not occur on a single structurally comparable regular verb (complete list from our data)

Forms with both VC and CV unique			
infinitives	preterits	2nd participles	3rd pers. sing. pres.
mögen	brach	gedroschen	schläft
	drosch	gescholten	
	grub	geworben	
	sprach		
	wuchs		
Forms with a unique VC			
infinitives	preterits	2nd participles	3rd pers. sing. pres.
bersten	barst	erloschen	birst
helfen	erlosch	geflochten	bläst
	flocht	gefochten	darf
	focht	gegolten	gilt
	half	gehabt	gräbt
	hielt	geholfen	schilt
	lud	gestorben	wirft
	stach	verdorben	
	warf		
	wurde		

Table 3b. (*continued*)

| Forms with a unique CV | | | |
infinitives	preterits	2nd participles	3rd pers. sing. pres.
biegen	blieb	empfangen	empfiehlt
bieten	blies	empfohlen	gerät
bleiben	drang	geblieben	rät
braten	empfahl	gebraten	schlägt
empfangen	empfand	gedeihen	
empfehlen	empfing	geflogen	
empfinden	erschrak	geflohen	
fliegen	flog	gekrochen	
fliehen	floh	genesen	
fließen	kam	gepfiffen	
genesen	kroch	gequollen	
lügen	pfiff	geschlafen	
nehmen	quoll	geschlagen	
pfeifen	schlief	geschlossen	
preisen	schloss	geschossen	
schlafen	schlug	geschrieben	
schlagen	schoss	geschrien	
schließen	schrie	geschwiegen	
schmeißen	schrieb	geschwollen	
schreiben	schwieg	geschwommen	
schreien	schwoll	geschwunden	
schreiten	sprang	geschwungen	
sprießen	trug	gesprungen	
stehen	verdross	gestohlen	
stehlen	wies	gestoßen	
stoßen	wrang	getreten	
treiben	wusch	gewiesen	
treten	zog	gewonnen	
verbieten		geworden	
verbleichen		geworfen	
verdrießen		gewrungen	
verstehen		gezogen	
wiegen		gezwungen	
wringen		verdrossen	
		verschwunden	

list one would expect there to be 54 (i.e. 6 x 9) regular verbs with [ɪnd], or at least a lot of them, but there aren't, there are only two. Moreover, *entrinden* is derived from the noun *Rinde* 'bark', and *erblinden* is derived from the adjective *blind* 'blind'. Neither verb comes under pressure to undergo ablaut, because they have to retain the word from which they derive. Were it not for this special circumstance the number of regular verbs with the VC [ɪnd] would be zero.

To take another example, there are 14 irregular verb forms with the VC [an] (*begann* 'began', *brannte* 'burned', *gewann* 'won', *kannte* 'knew', *nannte* 'named', *rannte* 'ran, raced', *rann* 'ran, streamed', *sann* 'pondered', *spann* 'span', *gebrannt* 'burnt', *gekannt* 'known', *genannt* 'named', *gerannt* 'run, raced', *kann* 'can') and only 4 regular verbs, which are *bannen* 'to bewitch', *begrannen* 'to furnish with awns' (rare), *bemannen* 'to man', and *spannen* 'to tighten, tense'. *Begrannen* is derived from the noun *Granne* 'awn', and *bemannen* from the noun *Mann* 'man'; *bannen* probably avoids pressure from ablaut by virtue of its link with the noun *Bann* 'excommunication'; whilst *spannen* is a base verb and thus a counter-example, though even there one could point to special features which lead its participles to being full-blown adjectives, viz. *spannend* 'exciting' and *gespannt* 'taut; tense; eager'.[97] Thus again, were it not for special circumstances the already low figure of 4 regular verbs with [an] would be even lower.

Some examples of onomatopoeic/phonaesthetic regular verbs with an irregular verb VC or CV are *sirren* 'to buzz', *zischen* 'to hiss, sizzle', *schlürfen* 'to slurp, drink noisily', *traben* 'to trot', and *kläffen* 'to yap'. As was argued above for English, these verbs are excused the need to conjugate irregularly because of their overriding need to continue to imitate the sounds they denote, despite having VCs or CVs characteristic of irregular verbs.

Pinker (1999) has a chapter on German which, as for English, corroborates the findings and the analysis presented here for German, including the points about onomatopoeia and verbs derived from nouns and adjectives. Pinker writes:

> English speakers use *-ed* for onomatopoeia, as in *ping-pinged*, *ding-dinged*, and *peep-peeped*; German speakers use *-t* for onomatopoeia, as in *brummen-gebrummt* 'growl', *flüstern-geflüstert* 'whisper', and *klatschen-geklatscht* 'clap'. ... As with English ... German uses *-t* for verbs that are derived from other categories and thus cannot have special past-tense roots listed in memory. These include verbs derived from nouns, such as ... *hausen-gehaust* 'to house' from *Haus* 'house'. The same is true for verbs derived from adjectives, such as *kürzen-gekürzt* 'shorten' from *kurz* 'short'. (Pinker 1999: 218)

In 1999 I conducted the same experiment for German as has already been described for English, in terms of searching for the irregular verb VCs and CVs elsewhere in the monosyllabic[98] vocabulary and grammar of German, whereby the same pattern was found for German as was described above for English. The Duden-*Bedeutungswörterbuch* was used as a reference source. Again, no

pattern was found for CVs, but a pattern was found for VCs. If one distin-
guishes between lexical parts of speech and grammatical parts of speech, then
64% of the exemplars of grammatical parts of speech have an irregular verb
VC, and 36% do not. This proportion is particularly surprising, given that we
have just been looking at an area of German lexis, viz. regular verbs, where the
proportion of irregular verb VCs is very low. This distributional pattern es-
tablishes a phonotactic link between irregular verbs and grammatical parts of
speech in German, and invites us to go further and see if the phonotactic link
has a semantic basis to it, and if it can take us towards rules for the formation
of the irregular verbs.

Irregular verbs in Russian

In 2002, with the help of Albina Howard (née Ozieva), I conducted the same
two experiments for Russian (see Бидэм in press; also Beedham 1989). Russian
verbs fall into 6 groups, depending on the infinitive ending: *-at'*, *-ovat'*/*-evat'*,
-et', *-nut'*, *-it'*, and miscellaneous infinitive endings. Out of these groups verbs
in *-at'* and *-et'* have the largest number of irregular or 'non-productive' verbs,
as they are called, usually reckoned at approx. 200 and 65 respectively, and the
experiments were restricted to these two groups (Грамматика русского языка
1960:531–532, 551; *Die russische Sprache der Gegenwart* 1975:74, 84; Pulkina
& Zakhava-Nekrasova 1960:226–244). The irregularity of the Russian non-
productive verbs pertains to their present tense paradigm. Productive verbs in
-at' in their present tense retain the *-a-* in the stem, do not undergo consonant
interchange, and are 1st conjugation. For example, the present tense of *čitat'*
'to read' is: *čitaju' čitaješ' čitajet čitajem čitajete čitajut*. Non-productive verbs in
-at', on the other hand, in their present tense lose the *-a-* in the stem, undergo
consonant interchange in all persons,[99] and some (about 17%) are 2nd conjugation. For example, the present tense of *pisat'* 'to write' is: *pišu pišeš' pišet
pišem pišete pišut*, with the consonant interchange *s → š*. The irregularity of
verbs in *-et'* proceeds in an analogous way. Thus the forms which are special
to the non-productive verbs in *-at'* and *-et'*, which we can therefore – following the logic of structuralism – expect to carry meanings which the productive
verbs do not have, are: the vowel suffix[100] *-a-* or *-e-* is absent in the present
tense stem; (consequently) the present tense stem ends in a consonant; consonant interchange in all persons; 2nd conjugation (affects 17% of the relevant
verbs only).

As with English and German, a Russian verb, if it is non-productive, is non-productive in all its derived forms, prefixed and with suffixes. We therefore purged our non-productive verb list of all prefixed and suffixed verbs, leaving simplex verbs only. Because the experiments concerned the VCs and CVs of the stem of the verb, a small number of verbs whose stem consists of a consonant cluster only, e.g. *ždat'* 'to wait', with the stem *žd-*, were also deleted.[101] That left 132 simplex non-productive verbs in *-at'* and 51 in *-et'*. Using Daum and Schenk (1976) and the Обратный словарь русского языка a list of all productive verbs in *-at'* and *-et'* was drawn up, from which all prefixed and suffixed verbs were deleted, leaving 891 simplex productive verbs in *-at'* and 99 in *-et'*. Thus for verbs in *-at'* the productive verb list was 7 times as long as the non-productive verb list, and for verbs in *-et'* it was twice as long.[102]

It was now simply a case of, as before for English and German, comparing the VCs and the CVs of the stems of the verbs, to see where the distribution lay. As regards the CVs no pattern or tendency was found, in contrast to our findings for English and German. As regards the VCs, however, the same pattern was found as had been noted already on the English and German strong verbs, viz. the VCs of the Russian non-productive verbs had a remarkably low rate of occurrence on the productive verbs, and in some cases did not appear there at all. For the *-at'* verbs 24 out of the 87 VCs on the non-productive verbs do not occur on a single productive verb, and for the *-et'* verbs out of 57 VCs 40 VCs do not appear on a single productive verb – see Tables 4a and 4b. Some examples of non-productive verbs containing these unique VCs are *drebezžat'* 'to jingle', *deržat'* 'to hold', *šeptat'* 'to whisper', *burčat'* 'to mumble, mutter, grumble', *torčat'* 'to stick up, stick out', *letet'* 'to fly', *videt'* 'to see', *smotret'* 'to look'. Thus for the Russian irregular verbs, too, as for English and German, their VCs (though not their CVs) tend not to appear on the regular verbs and thus serve as phonotactic markers of irregular conjugation.

We then searched for the VCs of the non-productive verbs elsewhere in the vocabulary and grammar of Russian. In the light of our findings on English

Table 4a. VCs which are unique to Russian (simplex) non-productive verbs in *-at'*, i.e. which do not occur on a single (simplex) productive verb in *-at'* (complete list from our data). VCs which arise from present tense consonant alternation are given in brackets.

алк	ем	ест	олч	оск	урш
(ан)	епт	изж	опт	охт	ырч
езж	(ер)	(ов)	(опч)	узж	ыч
ей	ерж	(озъм)	орч	урч	юзж

Table 4b. VCs which are unique to Russian (simplex) non-productive verbs in -*et'*, i.e. which do not occur on a single (simplex) productive verb in -*et'* (complete list from our data). VCs which arise from present tense consonant alternation are given in brackets.

(аж)	(ахч)	(ерж)	ет	ип	(ищ)	орб	(оч)
алд	езр	ерп	(еч)	(ипл)	(ой)	(орбл)	(умл)
ап	(ей)	(ерпл)	(ещ)	ис	(опл)	орп	(ущ)
(апл)	(емл)	(ерч)	ид	ист	опт	(орпл)	ыхт
ахт	ерб	ест	(иж)	иш	(опч)	отр	(ыхч)

and German, to save time we went straight for the grammatical words, and added inflectional endings to the search. From the Словарь структурных слов русского языка (Морковкин 1997), a dictionary of grammatical/structural words in Russian, we selected those items which are not derived from other words, e.g. *on* 'he', *bez* 'without', *jesli* 'if', i.e. we excluded derived expressions like the preposition *v svjazi s* 'in connection with' (from *svjaz'* 'connection'), the conjunction *v sledstvie togo, čto* 'in consequence of the fact that; because' (from *sledstvie* 'consequence'). A small number of words which do not have a VC, e.g. *v* 'in', *kto* 'who', had perforce to be excluded from the counts. The results, using the part of speech categorisation of the Словарь структурных слов русского языка, were as follows. 79% of pronouns with a VC contain a VC from the non-productive verbs in -*at'* and -*et'*, 63% of prepositions, 59% of conjunctions, 81% of particles, 29% of exclamations. Thus four out the five grammatical parts of speech examined have an abnormally high density of non-productive verb VCs, i.e. for Russian, too, as for English and German, we have unearthed a phonotactic link between non-productive verbs and function words.

We then went on to check the situation with grammatical endings. Using the Грамматический словарь русского языка (1977:39–68, 77–135) (Зализняк 1977) and Русская грамматика (1980:760) as sources for an exhaustive list of endings we found that 63% of inflectional endings with a VC have a VC identical with those of the non-productive verbs in -*at'* and -*et'*. This proportion can also be regarded as abnormally high, thus it can be seen that a phonotactic link has been established between non-productive verbs and inflectional endings in Russian.[103] As for function words, this link needs to be investigated further, to see if it can lead us to special meanings for the non-productive verbs and rules for their formation.

Once again, the barriers between the Germanic and Slav languages are coming down. It used to be thought that the strong verbs of Germanic and the non-productive verbs of the Slav languages were very different animals. But we have found a common factor between them: in both English/German and Russian the VCs of (the stems of) the irregular verbs tend to occur only on the irregular verbs, not on the regular verbs. Moreover, those same VCs, now noted as characteristic of irregular verbs, have a surprisingly high rate of occurrence on monosyllabic function words. Structurally speaking, English and German from the Germanic language family and Russian from the Slav language family are not as dissimilar as we had thought.

[Handwritten annotations:]

simply

Maybe the VCs of strong verbs are Y PIE in nature?
and the new verbs which became strong ie not strong from
PIE, attracted on basis of analogy?
                              to vowel of infinitive and sometimes
                              also consonants = VCs

Ie when you look at a text, it is quite easy to identify language
simply based on how text looks, perhaps VCs of strong
verbs + function words are simply PIE, with new
strong verbs (ie. not strong in PIE) attracted by
analogy.

Just how irregular/ unproductive are the strong verbs?
paradigmatic   analogy | analogical   extension
      German-speaker's   Y hear to   have access
    to abstract vowel patterns

See Dutch also
diachronic developments of importance

CHAPTER 6

Text grammar

Parole versus *langue*

In Chapter 1 'Saussurean Structuralism' we pointed out that Saussure said in the *Cours* – or perhaps the editors of the *Cours* said it (see p.3) – that *langue*, not *parole*, is the proper *Untersuchungsobjekt* of linguistics. That is not to say, however, that *parole* can be ignored and has no role to play in the study of language, of course it does, and many linguists in the past half-century have conducted research on *parole* aspects of language, on texts.[104] A huge amount of fascinating and illuminating research has been conducted in areas such as styles and registers, functions of language, speech acts, discourse analysis, pragmatics, corpus studies, language and politics, and other such areas which are sometimes subsumed under the general heading of 'text grammar' (see e.g. Crystal & Davy 1969; Halliday & Hasan 1976; Halliday 1973; Searle 1969; Coulthard 1985; Levinson 1983; Kennedy 1998; Hodge and Kress 1993; Chilton et al. (Eds.) 1998).

In this chapter we will examine briefly four areas of text grammar: speech acts/communicative functions, theme-rheme analysis, styles and registers, and corpus studies. I hope to show that all these areas are of great interest and importance to linguistics. However, there are two points sometimes made by text grammarians which I do not accept. One of them is that by studying *parole* they are actually studying the structure of language and hence *langue* (see e.g. Searle 1969: 17); or they claim that Saussure never really said they are not allowed to study *parole* (see again p.3). That seems to me to be silly: if you study *parole* you study *parole* and you should be proud of it! The second point I disagree with, which is related to the first, is when some text grammarians assert that text grammar should replace sentence-grammar altogether. Such people claim that to remove a linguistic form from its context, from the text in which it was conceived, is to distort it and its meaning beyond recognition (see e.g. Stubbs 1996). I will show, however, that text grammar is simply different to sentence-grammar, and that the types of meaning displayed in texts is different to the types of meaning displayed in sentences, but that is all. They are different, but a full understanding of language requires the study of both, both (abstract) sentences and (concrete) texts. Moreover, I will show – using the passive as an example – that *langue* and *parole*, sentence-grammar and text grammar, are in a dialectical relationship with each other, such that they can help each other to solve each other's problems: text grammar can provide facts and observations which help us arrive at better sentence-grammatical analyses; and new sentence-grammatical analyses can solve certain problems of text grammar. Thus text grammar is justified both in its own right and as a means to assist research into sentence-grammar (cf. Frath 2007).

Let us start, then, with an area which emerged from EFL (English as a Foreign Language) under the guise of communicative functions (see e.g. Widdowson 1978), and from philosophy as speech acts (see Austin 1975; Searle 1969). Every utterance[105] in a text has a communicative function or performs a speech act, which is a crucial part of its meaning. For example, if you are walking through a wood and you hear somebody shout "Timber", and you respond by saying yes, there is a lot of timber around here, isn't there, you will be in danger of having a tree fall on your head. You would have missed the speech act *warning* in the utterance, misinterpreting it as the speech act *inform*. If you receive a letter from the Tax Office asking you to send them something, but because the letter is written in such gobbledegook you miss the point and file it away, saying I wonder why they sent me that letter, you would have missed the speech act *request* and again not grasped the full meaning of the text. Most people, both laymen and linguists alike, think that language has one function or speech act alone, and that is to inform. But there is no doubt that utterances in actual texts perform numerous speech acts, e.g. when somebody speaks to you they may be inviting you somewhere, they may be praising you or insulting you, thanking you, warning you, promising that they will do something, asking you to do something, ordering you to do something, conceding the point you just made or rejecting the point you just made, etc. If you fail to understand any of these functions you have obviously failed to understand the text in which they occurred, and you will suffer the consequences, dire or otherwise. Some speech acts are particularly important, e.g. declaring war, appointing government ministers, a judge passing sentence, baptisms, the vicar performing a wedding ceremony, to mention but a few. Some texts have no function other than that of establishing human contact, the famous 'phatic communion', which is the diametrical opposite of the function *inform*. If you meet someone on the street and they say to you 'How are you?', you do not give them a 10-minute medical report on your state of health, you say 'Fine, thanks', and move on to other things (Why did you thank them in response to their asking a question? You thanked them because they did not ask a question, i.e. requesting information, they showed concern for your state of health). It is a fundamental part of the meaning of any text that the reader/hearer understands the speech act(s) contained therein. And it is part of the human language faculty and human intelligence in general that we are able to understand the speech acts of texts.

Let us now examine a text, to see if we recognise and understand the communicative functions which it contains. Consider the text given in (151):

(151)

Betty Broadside, Kirkland Cottage, Main Street, St. Andrews

26 November 2002

Spanish Department
Lade Braes Comprehensive School
St. Andrews

Dear Colleagues

(1) As the outgoing president of the St. Andrews Friends of Logroño Association I would like to thank you all for supporting our exchange with Spain. (2) I am sure you will have noticed the improvements in your pupils' confidence in using Spanish and their interest in the language as a result of their exchange visit to Logroño. (3) Up till now, however, there has been no response from Lade Braes Comprehensive School about next year's exchange (4) although there are already seven pupils at Strathkinness Grammar School who want to go on the exchange next summer and the new parents' committee has been formed. (5) Could I perhaps suggest that you invite fourth year or sixth year students who have been on the exchange to talk to third year groups (and others) about the exchange so that they can make an informed decision on whether to join next year's group? (6) All pupils from third year upwards can take part whether they are learning Spanish or not.

(7) The next parents' meeting is on Tuesday 10 December at 7.30pm in Strathkinness Grammar School. (8) Any parents of pupils who wish to take part should attend this meeting as the exchange dates will be finalised and arrangements will be made to book the flights. (9) Further information can be obtained from Bruce Brain on 01631 957282 or by email: bb21@st-and.ac.uk.

(10) Many thanks for your help and cooperation.

Yours sincerely

Betty Broadside

The text in (151) is a reproduction of an actual letter which was sent by the outgoing president of the St Andrews Friends of Logroño Association to the Spanish Department of a local school. Only the names and addresses of people and schools have been changed, and the sentences have been numbered to facilitate analysis. If you had been a Spanish teacher at the local school who had received the letter would you have understood it fully? What does the letter say? Is it informative, congratulatory, or does it ask you to do something? Every sentence of the letter expresses a different communicative function or speech act. The first sentence *thanks* the Spanish teachers for their cooperation with the exchange with Spain, but the astute reader will notice in that an element of buttering up. The second sentence makes an *assertion* or *claim*, expressing a subjective opinion as if it were fact; the sentence expresses a hope and assumption more than a certainty, despite the phrase 'I am sure' at the beginning. If taken at face value sentence (3) does no more than *inform* the reader of a certain fact. But of course, it is not meant to be taken like that. Sentence (3) performs several speech acts at the same time: it *criticises* the teachers, *admonishes* them, and makes a *request* of them that they do something and make a response about next year's exchange, which is in danger of collapsing through lack of interest. Clause 4 makes a *comparison* with another school, *reinforcing* the criticism already made in sentence (3). Sentence (5), despite having the grammatical form of a question and ending with a question mark, and claiming explicitly to be a suggestion, is in fact a *request* for the recipients of the letter to take action to save next year's exchange. Sentence (6) has again superficially the speech act inform, but really is part of the request made in sentence (5). We come now to what is communicatively the crux of the letter. Superficially sentences (7)–(9) again merely inform the reader of certain facts. But if you understand the letter fully you will recognise that sentences (7)–(9) are again a request, *appealing* to the teachers' sense of commitment to the school and the subject: the teachers are asked to act, viz. they are asked to encourage their pupils to participate in the exchange and to tell them to tell their parents to attend the meeting on 10 December, which is coming up fast; and the teachers are asked to contact Bruce Brain themselves or else to tell their pupils to tell their parents to contact him. The letter ends in sentence (10) with what look likes a formulaic ending and thank you, but which again the astute reader will recognise as more a *request* for help and cooperation than a thank you for help and cooperation.

If you understood perfectly all the words in the text as vocabulary items, and if you understood perfectly the grammar of each sentence, such that you could parse them all, if you had not also understood the communicative function of each sentence and of the text as a whole you would not have understood the text fully, in any meaningful sense of the word 'understand'. Notice that the communicative functions arise on units bigger than the sentences of sentence-grammar, they arise at the level of the text.

So clearly, speech acts are a fundamental part of texts and our under-standing of texts. But where does that leave sentence-grammar and the gram-marian's abstract sentence? Should text grammar replace and take over from sentence-grammar, as some linguists believe should happen? Certainly not. Communicative meaning and (sentence-)grammatical meaning are different kinds of meaning, and speakers need and use both in the interpretation of texts. Communicative meaning arises as much from general intelligence and knowledge of the world as it does from purely linguistic knowledge. The notion that text grammar might obliterate sentence-grammar is, of course, ridicu-lous. The study of language will always require such basic notions as word, suffix, morpheme, clause, subject and object, nouns and verbs, tense, aspect, number, gender, agreement, etc., all of which exist quite independently of texts. And we will always need a notion of meaning which allows us to say, e.g. that the subject is usually agent, verbs usually express actions, etc., which again is inherent to sentences, not texts.[106] Such things may not be everyone's cup of tea, some strange and unfortunate people find them dry and boring, and find texts more interesting to study, but it does not alter the fact that they are the foundation and cornerstone of language, languages, and language study. We can build on them with text studies, but we cannot replace them with text studies. In fact, several generations of hapless British schoolchildren have been experimented on with the 'communicative method' of foreign lan-guage teaching, since the early 1970s, and the result has been a disaster. The great communicative experiment has produced generations of schoolchildren who learn short texts in French or Spanish off by heart and merrily recite them, but who cannot produce a single sentence – or utterance – in French or Spanish of their own, for the simple reason that they have not been taught the grammar to do so, and like it or not, grammar is a pre-requisite, via sentences, for the production of utterances. There is more to language than sentence-grammar, true, there are texts. But language does not consist of texts alone – there is still (sentence-)grammar. In British schools there was a reac-tion against the (sentence-)grammar method of foreign language teaching, but the pendulum has swung too far. It is time to recognise that pupils need both (sentence-)grammar and a communicative ability.

An interesting question which arises is, is it possible to find a set of forms, lexical and/or grammatical, which are typically associated with a given com-municative function (Coulthard 1977:8)? For example, if someone issues a warning, are there certain grammatical forms or constructions and certain lexical items which he or she would typically use? The answer is, for most communicative functions, no. There are three well-known exceptions to this 'No', and they are: the declarative mood used for the function 'giving information'; the interrogative mood used for the function 'asking questions'; and the imperative mood used for the function 'giving orders'. Admittedly, these three examples seem basic and frequent instances of a one-to-one correlation between form and communicative function, but they are actually severely limited and frequently broken. For example, when my wife asks me 'Isn't it time you did the hoovering?' – as she often does – if I interpreted it as a yes-no question and nothing more than that there would certainly have been a failure in communication between us. Almost all communicative functions can be realized by an infinite variety of grammatical forms and lexical items. Or, put the other way round, a given sentence with a given grammatical form can have an infinite number of communicative interpretations placed upon it, depending on the context. To give another example, the statement 'It's cold in here' is more likely to be a request to close the window than a meteorological observation. I did actually check this out once, with the help of my former colleague, Meriel Bloor, and spent a year trying to find a one-to-one correlation between the communicative functions in a particular register of English – it happened to be English for Computer Science – and the lexical and grammatical forms occurring there, but came to the conclusion, at the end of the research, that there really was no such correlation (Beedham & Bloor 1989). The question – and its answer – is important not least because there has been a trend, an unfortunate trend, in recent years for language course designers to base their courses on communicative functions, not grammar points.

Another interesting area of text grammar is theme-rheme analysis (also known as Functional Sentence Perspective, or Topic-Comment), which is concerned with the way in which a speaker/writer's desire to organise information in the sentence according to its importance or newness influences word order. The theme of a sentence is old information or less important information, rheme is new information or more important information. Linguists disagree on how theme-rheme is realized formally in language. Some linguists claim that word order realizes theme-rheme, whereby the theme usually occurs initially and the rheme second. Other linguists claim that theme-rheme is realized by stress and intonation, whereby the rheme of the sentence receives primary stress. Obviously, since primary stress can occur anywhere in a sentence the rheme can occur anywhere in the sentence, and hence also the theme, i.e. the two mooted realizations of theme-rheme contradict each other. Still another

group of linguists *define* the theme as the first item in the sentence, which is
yet a third way of looking at it. So there is a long way to go before we fully understand theme-rheme, but it is still a useful and necessary complement to a
purely syntactic (i.e. sentence-grammatical) approach to word order – i.e. the
first item in the stylistically neutral sentence is the subject, the second item is
the verb, the third item is the object, etc. (necessary because the first item in a
sentence/utterance is often precisely not the subject) – and a welcome refinement to what we used to say, which was simply and crudely that word order
could change because of emphasis.[107]

I have so far spoken of theme-rheme only insofar as it affects sentences,
but crucially, theme-rheme affects the organization of texts. Daneš (1974: 118–
121) analyses the following three texts according to their thematic progression
or communicative dynamism:

(152)   The first of the antibiotics was discovered by Sir Alexander Fleming in
        1928. He was busy at the time investigating a certain species of germ which
        is responsible for boils and other troubles.

(153)   The Rousseauist especially feels an inner kinship with Prometheus and
        other Titans. He is fascinated by any form of insurgency . . . He must show
        an elementary energy in his explosion against the established order and
        at the same time a boundless sympathy for the victims of it . . . Further
        the Rousseauist is ever ready to discover beauty of soul in any ne who is
        under the reprobation of society.

(154)   New Jersey is flat along the coast and southern portion; the north-western
        region is mountainous. The coastal climate is mild, but there is consid-
        erable cold in the mountain areas during the winter months. Summers
        are fairly hot. The leading industrial production includes chemicals, pro-
        cessed food, coal, petroleum, metals and electrical equipment.

Text (152) has a simple linear thematic progression, in which a theme is introduced followed by a rheme, the rheme becomes the theme of the next sentence
followed by another rheme, that rheme becomes the theme of the next sentence
or clause, and so on, as represented in the following diagram:

$$T_1 \rightarrow R_1$$
$$\quad \downarrow$$
$$T_2 (= R_1) \rightarrow R_2$$
$$\qquad \downarrow$$
$$T_3 (= R_2) \rightarrow R_3$$

In contrast, text (153) has a continuous or constant theme. In the first
sentence a theme is introduced, which leads on to a rheme. In the second sen-

tence the same theme is retained, but leading on to a different rheme. In the third sentence again the same theme is retained, but leading on to still another rheme, a third rheme. Diagrammatically:

$$T_1 \rightarrow R_1$$
$$\downarrow$$
$$T_1 \rightarrow R_2$$
$$\downarrow$$
$$T_1 \rightarrow R_3$$

Text (154), on the other hand, has a hypertheme – New Jersey – which leads first to a sub-theme T_1 and its rheme R_1, then to a sub-theme T_2 and its rheme R_2, then to a sub-theme T_3 and its rheme R_3, and so on, as shown in the following diagram:

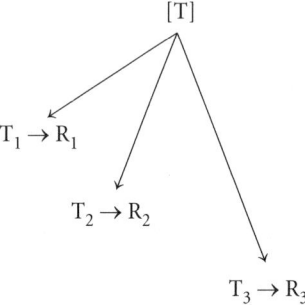

Thus we see that the text grammarians are right: a text is not a heap of sentences, but is organized in specific ways. I personally would hesitate to call it 'structure', since I prefer to reserve that term for the organization of sentences in *langue* or sentence-grammar, but I understand the temptation to extend the use of the term 'structure' to the organization of texts as well, using it, in fact, metaphorically.

Turning now to another area of *parole*-type linguistics, styles and registers, the days are long gone when language teachers taught their students the literary variety of language only, either unthinkingly or in the belief that literary style was the only kind of language worth learning. Every language learner now, both at school and at University, is presented with numerous non-literary varieties of language, such as the spoken language, journalese, officialese, scientific register, the language of advertisements, of politics, of sport, regional dialects, youth language, etc.[108] The styles and registers element of language study also requires, of necessity, a textual approach. Below are some samples of English journalese (text (155)), officialese/legalese (text (156)), and the language of science (text (157)):

(155)

Blair caught in Iraqi arms row

Sarah Hall, Patrick Wintour and Richard Norton-Taylor

Tony Blair's credibility over his use of intelligence before the Iraq invasion came under fresh assault yesterday when he said that at the time of the war he was personally unaware that Saddam Hussein did not have the ability to fire long-range chemical and biological weapons.

The prime minister's admission came in a day-long debate on the Hutton report yesterday and provoked heated exchanges.

Mr Blair made clear that at the start of the war he had had no knowledge of the fact that the government's infamous claim that Iraq could mobilise its banned weapons within 45 minutes of an order referred only to battlefield, as opposed to long-range, arms.

Yesterday's claim surprised MPs on both sides of the house and drew incredulous responses from opponents of the war. It is bound to be examined by the Butler inquiry into the collection and government use of intelligence on Iraq.

(The Guardian 5.2.2004, p. 1)

(156)

WILL

by

JOHN BROWN

2003

I, JOHN BROWN, residing at Castle House, Grannie Clark's Wynd, St Andrews, Fife, in order to settle the succession to my estate after my death provide as follows:

One   I revoke all prior wills and testamentary writings.

Two   I appoint my wife MRS MARY BROWN, residing with me and JAMES MCTAVISH, Solicitor of Thirty-five The Links, Pitscottie, Fife, to be my executors.

Three I direct my executors to give effect to any future writings subscribed by me however informal the same may be provided that in the opinion of my executors they clearly express my intentions.

Four   Unless otherwise specified any legacy granted by any writing shall be paid or made over as soon as my executors consider practicable after my death free of government duties in respect of my death and of delivery expenses but without interest.

Five   I direct my executors to make over the residue of my estate to my wife, the said Mrs Mary Brown, if she survives for thirty days after my death.

Six   If my said wife does not survive me for thirty days but in such event only, I direct my executors to make over the residue of my estate to such of my children Fiona Brown and Elspeth Brown as shall survive me equally between them if more than one, declaring that should either of my children predecease me leaving issue (including adopted issue) who shall survive me each member of a generation of issue of such predeceasing child shall share equally in the part of my estate, both original and accresced, which would have fallen to its parent if in life.

(reproduction of an actual will, in which the names and addresses have been changed)

(157)

Complex proximal deposition during the Plinian eruptions of 1912 at Novarupta, Alaska

Bruce F. Houghton, C.J.N. Wilson, J.Fierstein, W.Hildreth

Introduction

Explosive eruptions

Explosive eruptions occur across a wide range of volcano and magma types, yet the behavior of particulate-gas mixtures during explosive volcanism is inferred to be governed by a limited range of physical processes and parameters (e.g. Wilson et al. 1980). This behaviour is fundamentally controlled by conditions at the exit point, including the degree of overpressure (above local atmospheric conditions), temperature, mass fraction of exsolved volatiles, bulk grain size population, vent morphology, and the subsequent degrees of mixing with air and atmospheric moisture (see Sparks et al. 1997; Woods 1998, for reviews). These factors cause eruption mixtures to be partitioned, though with significant overlap, into one or more of four transport regimes (Figure 1): (1) jet/buoyant-plume behavior, (2) fountaining with co-current flow, (3) fountaining with countercurrent flow, and (4) direct lateral ejection. Theoretical models and field examples are widely documented for the end-member conditions represented by these four regimes.

(Bulletin of Volcanology 2004/66:95–133:95)

I will now present a brief analysis of these three passages, in order to illustrate the usefulness and indeed necessity of analysing language in terms of styles and register (on journalese in English see Fowler 1991; Bell 1991; on legalese see Crystal & Davy 1969: 193–217; Di Pietro (Ed.) 1982: 99–154; Bhatia et al. (Eds.) 2003; on the language of science see Halliday & Martin 1993; Swales 1990; Gledhill 2000). There is not the space here to go into any great detail, but the case for a styles and register approach to language is so obvious that even a brief examination of the texts will serve to achieve our aims. We will restrict our analysis to the following dimensions (see Brinker 2001):

> communicative function of the text
> situation of the text
> content of the text
> typical vocabulary
> typical grammatical forms
> compounds
> hyphenated compounds
> sentence length

It is immediately obvious that the three texts differ hugely in their language, both from literature and from each other. Let us begin with communicative function. When ascertaining the communicative function of the texts one is really going back to the communicative functions commonly found in the registers which the texts have been chosen to illustrate. The communicative function of text (155), the newspaper article, is a mixture of informing and opinion-influencing, like all media reports, despite the claim by newspapers of every political persuasion to be objective and merely reporting what happened. The communicative function of text (156), on the other hand, is completely different, it is to issue instructions: the signatory of the text instructs his solicitor as to who gets what after his death, and even makes the instructions explicit with the performative verbs "I provide …", "I revoke …", "I appoint …", "I direct …". The communicative function of the scientific text, (157), on the other hand, is different again, it is to present new scientific research, which involves such functions as describing, explaining, and criticising previous research.

'Situation of the text' refers to such factors as the social roles of addresser and addressee, and whether addresser and addressee are together or separate spatially or temporally, as in e.g. a book, a face-to-face conversation, an e-mail exchange, a dialogue on the telephone, etc. It so happens that addresser and addressee in all three of our chosen texts are spatially and temporally separated. But in other respects of their situation our three texts are very different. The situation of text (155) is that it is an article in a daily newspaper, whereby the addresser is 'the newspaper' – this is not the place to go into the social and economic implications of that phrase – and the addressee is anyone willing to buy and read that particular newspaper. The situation of text (156) is that it is a document having legal force, a will, drafted by one person (a lawyer) but signed by somebody else (the person making the will). The addresser is someone making a will, the addressees are the person's family, the law-courts, and anyone who might claim to have an interest in that person's estate after his death. The situation of text (157) is that it is a research paper in a scientific journal: the addressers are four scientists, and the addressees are fellow-scientists in the same area of specialism as the addressers, i.e. volcanoes. This is not the book in which to enter upon a discussion of the role of the media, of legal systems, and of science in society, in order to gain a fuller understanding of our texts. But we note that the situations of the three texts are completely different from each other, each situation influencing massively the language of the text which it conceives.

Turning to our next dimension, the three texts have vastly different contents. The content of (155) is war, weapons, and what a British Prime Minister knew or did not know about certain weapons. The content of (156) is the future death of a particular individual, his property, and his family members. The content of (157) is volcanoes and different types of volcanic eruptions. Once again, very different contents, each determining a very different (style of) language.

Typical vocabulary, i.e. vocabulary typical and representative not just of the given text but of the register which the text exemplifies, from the newspaper text are *arms, weapons, war, battlefield, intelligence, debate, inquiry*. Typical vocabulary from the legal text are *to reside, estate, testamentary, executor, legacy, duties, to predecease, issue, accresced, to give effect to, the same* (as anaphoric pronoun), *in respect of*. Typical vocabulary items from the scientific text are *deposition, magma, volcanism, exsolved, volatiles, lateral, behaviour, parameters, to infer, to cause, model*. Once again, we are confronted by very different vocabularies for very different registers.

Grammatical constructions and forms in the newspaper text which are typical of journalese are the use of reported speech ("he said that ... he was unaware", "Mr Blair made clear that ... he had had no knowledge"), modal verbs ("Iraq could mobilise"), and a wide range of tenses: preterit ("came under assault"), present ("is bound"), and future ("bound to be examined"). Grammatical constructions typical of legalese in (156) are the performative verbs ("I revoke all prior wills"), a pronoun in the agentive *by*-phrase of a passive ("subscribed by me"), *shall* instead of *will* for the 3rd pers. future, unusual attributive 2nd participles (e.g. *my said wife*), and concessive clauses with *if* and *should* ("should either of my children ..."). Typical grammatical constructions and forms in the scientific text (157) are the passive ("the behavior ... is inferred to be governed"), and the present tense for general truths ("eruptions occur across a wide range of volcano ... types").

Turning to compounds, our newspaper text has a classic compound noun in headlines, *Iraqi arms row*. The legal text has no noteworthy compounds, whereas the scientific text abounds with them: *bulk grain size population, transport regimes*. Hyphenated compounds – whereby the hyphen indicates a greater degree of lexicalisation – are also to be found in the newspaper text (*long-range, day-long*) and the science text (*particulate-gas, buoyant-plume*).

The three texts also differ in respect of sentence length. The newspaper article – which is from a broadsheet newspaper, as opposed to the tabloid press – tests the reader's stamina initially with a first sentence 46 words long, but immediately rests him or her with a second sentence only 18 words long, before launching again into another 46-word third sentence. That, however, is again followed by a shorter, less demanding sentence. The legal text is true to form in having the longest sentence out of the three passages, though at a mere 101 words it is a modest example by the standards of legal language. The science text gives no quarter on readability and has a succession of three fairly long sentences – 40, 52 and 40 words – before ending the paragraph with a short 17-word sentence.

The analysis of our three texts and registers is summarised in Figure 5. We have seen that in all eight parameters the three texts differ from each other hugely. It is obvious that the notion of 'the standard language' is an abstraction which dissolves rapidly as soon as one looks at a particular text, and that the language of literature – the 'literary language' – is just one style or register amongst many, it is no more representative of a language than many other text types that one could take. We see once again that *langue* and sentence-grammar has its place, but that we ignore *parole* and text grammar at our peril.

The analysis of language varieties has been much enhanced by the advent of the computer, and Stubbs (1996) claims that the computer has done for linguistics what the telescope did for astronomy (mentioned by Gledhill 1999: 227). A computer can analyse in certain ways large corpora consisting of hundreds of texts and millions of words, producing, for example, word frequencies and concordances. A concordance program searches a corpus for all the occurrences of a given word or form, and lists them in the centre of the page, one per line, with a context of up to 10 words either side (Stubbs 1996: xviii–xix). This provides a convenient format in which the linguist can study the words or forms he is interested in. If he wishes, the researcher can easily see a bigger context for the word or form he is investigating. An example of a concordance for the passive in English, taken from Stubbs (1996: 141–142),

	function	situation	content	vocabulary	grammar	compounds	hyphenated compounds	sentence length
Text (155): journalese	inform, and influence opinion	article in newspaper; addresser: 'the newspaper'; addressee: (potential) purchasers	war, weapons, and what a British Prime Minister knew about certain weapons	*arms, weapons, war, battlefield, intelligence, debate, inquiry*	reported speech, modal verbs, wide range of tenses	*Iraqi arms row*	*long-range, day-long*	quite long (46 words) followed by quite short (18 words)
Text (156): legalese	(legally-binding) instructions	legal document, a will; addresser: someone making a will; addressee: family and law-courts	future death of someone, their property, and family members	*to reside, estate, testamentary, executor, legacy, duties, to predecease, issue, accresced*	performative verbs, pronoun in by-phrase of passive, *shall* instead of *will*, attributive 2nd part.	(none)	(none)	contains one very long sentence (101 words)
Text (157): language of science	present new scientific research	research paper in scientific journal; addresser: scientists; addressee: fellow scientists	volcanoes and different types of volcanic eruptions	*magma, volcanism, exsolved, volatiles, lateral, behavior, parameters, to cause*	passive, present tense for general truths	*bulk grain size population, transport regimes*	*particulate-gas, buoyant-plume*	mostly quite long sentences (40–52 words)

Figure 5. Analysis of English texts (155), (156) and (157): journalese, legalese, and the language of science

is given in Figure 6. By using a computer instead of speculating on the types of passive that might occur in a given language the researcher can very quickly have hundreds of authentic examples at his disposal for study and analysis.

We have now seen four areas of text grammar or *parole*-style linguistics which are interesting in their own right: speech acts, theme-rheme analysis, styles and registers, and corpus studies. However, the study of *parole* and texts also has a bearing on *langue* or sentence-grammar. In our discussion of the passive in Chapter 3 we encountered three instances where observations on texts fed into our *langue* analysis of the passive. And there was movement in the opposite direction as well, viz. our new sentence-grammatical analysis of the passive – the passive as an aspect of the verb, not a voice of the verb – helped explain some problems and mysteries of a textual nature. Thus *langue* studies and *parole* studies – sentence-grammar and text grammar – stand in a dialectical relationship with each other, mutually reinforcing one another.

The first piece of textual evidence we encountered in our discussion of the passive was the fact that corpus linguists have discovered that four fifths of actually occurring passive sentences in texts appear without the agentive *by*-phrase. This was an unexpected finding, we said, because under the voice analysis passives are derived from an underlying active, where the subject (i.e. expressing the agent) is obligatory. Thus there is a contradiction between the fact that in the active the subject (= agent) is obligatory, whilst in the passive the agent (= the subject in the active) is rare. The contradiction is there not just for sentence-grammar but for text grammar as well. At least it is unless you think that corpus studies produces statistical data and observations which serve no purpose. A corpus studies that did that would be very dry and un-interesting indeed. But no, the findings of corpus studies can be put to use in sentence-grammar, and that is what we did. The fact that four fifths of passives in texts appear without the *by*-phrase is evidence against the voice-analysis, and in favour of the aspect analysis. What we said was that if you posit an 'active' 'voice' 'underlying' a passive voice, then you have made for yourself various problems, including explaining why four fifths of passives have no agentive *by*-phrase realized. But if you recognise that the passive is an aspect of the verb (like the perfect and the progressive in English), meaning 'action + state', from which meaning it so happens that the subject is patient, then the agentive *by*-phrase becomes an ordinary prepositional phrase in which *by* is an ordinary preposition, meaning 'through the agency, means, or instrumentality of', and optional like most prepositions. Thus the fact that many passives appear with-out a *by*-phrase is to be expected, and not a problem. Corpus studies has helped holera and typhoid killed thousands of Britons. These diseases were caused by infected water. Now all the water supplied to homes ca

Wells: Permeable rocks such as chalk, limestone and sandstone are called aquifers because they bear water. The water usually remain

can be artificially pumped out through wells. When the aquifer is sandwiched between two impermeable rocks, pressure can build up at

pplied to the water system. Water in the storage reservoirs is purified naturally and is readily available in times of shortage.

rally and is readily available in times of shortage. The water is passed through filter beds before it can be used. Figure E shows t

ary Reservoir which is over twice the size of Hyde Park. Water is pumped into the Thames from the ground water stored within the lim

system linking rivers by pipelines and tunnels (Fig. E). Water is transferred from the wetter areas to the drier areas of the countr

ewers and eventually to the local sewage works. Sewage works are located beside rivers in or near towns. The water discharged into

the water you drink comes from C 500 million litres of water are used in Greater London every day. Discuss the problems associated

, England's largest natural lake. One and a half million trees were felled to make way for it, and a hamlet, several buildings and t

r it, and a hamlet, several buildings and the main valley road were drowned by the rising water. Why was this remote Northumberland

opment Fund and the British government. A further £43 million was loaned by the EEC at reduced rates of interest. Kielder Water wi

ng permits are sold direct to the public. Worm and fly fishing are permitted and motorboats are available for hire. Water sports:

ion of the water takes place further downstream. The reservoir is used by small boats of all kinds, and water skiers. Boat trips:

a farmer in the Kielder Valley when the Kielder Water Scheme is announced. You learn that half your land is to be flooded. What ar

mand for consumer goods increased. The new industrial growth was concentrated in the Midlands and south. In the older industrial a

e distribution of old people. (c) How do you think old people are distributed in your area? (d) Are some areas especially attracti

because there was little money available. 1930s More success was achieved through the creation of trading estates such as Trefores

three-tier system shown on Fig D. 1982 The three-tier system was retained but the size of the assisted areas was greatly reduced.

ze of the assisted areas was greatly reduced. Enterprise zones were established. Figure F lists the incentives provided by the gove

of investment costs for industry in the assisted areas, which is used to top up national regional development grants. Between 1975

as crops are continuously grown. Nutrients and minerals which were replaced by roots and fallow years are now replaced by soil cond

uch 'free range' chickens are rare. Most eggs and chicken meat are produced on factory farms like that illustrated. There are thousa

completely sterile so that no disease can enter. The chickens are fed on concentrated feed pellets and may be injected with drugs t

y per cent of the EEC's budget is spent on the CAP. The farmer is guaranteed a price which is fixed each year. An intervention price

et is spent on the CAP. The farmer is guaranteed a price which is fixed each year. An intervention price is set up for each product,

often surplus production with the EEC. The surplus products are stored (butter 'mountains' and wine 'lakes') or sold cheaply with

Figure 6. Concordance: Passives in a school textbook (from Stubbs 1996:141)

sentence-grammar reach a new analysis, and sentence-grammar has helped to explain a curious finding of corpus studies (see pp.35, 37, 43).

The second instance of the dialectic between sentence-grammar and text grammar which we came across in our discussion of the passive was to do with odd passives. We noted that, although according to the voice analysis of sentence-grammar all transitive verbs form a passive, when you take a text and try to convert the transitive actives occurring there into the passive you end up for the most part with grotesque curiosities. Why? And why can most odd passives be made grammatical by tinkering around, changing certain bits of them? Many linguists have noticed this problem, and tried to explain it with theme-rheme analysis, from text grammar. But we proposed a different explanation, within sentence-grammar, viz. that because the passive is an aspect of the type Auxiliary + Participle it has to obey the constraints of compositional aspect: because it means 'action + state' it requires a telic sentence, i.e. one with an inherent end-point in it (which becomes the state bit of 'action + state'). The tinkering that one does to odd passives achieves the effect of altering the compositional aspect of the sentence, and hence passivizability. Once again, a new sentence-grammatical analysis explains a textual problem: most active transitive sentences in texts will not convert into the passive because they do not have the right compositional aspect (see pp.35–36, 45–46).

The third textual mystery which we encountered in our discussion of the passive was the fact that Quirk et al. 1985's typical passive sentence, based on corpus studies, was *This difficulty can be avoided in several ways*, which looks nothing like the favourite example of the voice analysis from sentence-grammar, *John was hit by Bill*. Once again, the problem is one which affects both sentence-grammarians and text grammarians. The solution to the mystery came with our new, sentence-grammatical analysis of the passive: the *hit* example supports the voice analysis of the passive, because it emphasises the idea that the subject 'receives the action of the verb'. But both things are wrong, both the sentence-grammatical voice analysis and the textual notion that *John was hit by Bill* is a typical passive sentence. On the other hand, the new aspect analysis ties in with the typical passive which emerges from corpus studies, because the sentence *This difficulty can be avoided in several ways* has numerous typical aspectual features on it, in particular indefiniteness and plurality. Thus in the case of the aspect analysis both things are right, both the sentence-grammatical analysis of the passive as an aspect and the observation from corpus studies that *This difficulty can be avoided in several ways* is a typical passive sentence. Once again *langue* and *parole*, sentence-grammar and text grammar, have worked dialectically to help each other out in the solving of a mystery (see pp.39, 46).

We have seen in this chapter examples of text grammar which show that text grammar is both valid in its own right, quite independently of sentence-grammar, and helpful to sentence-grammarians in their analyses. Let us now return to the point made by some text grammarians that only text grammar is valid, sentence-grammar is misguided, because words and forms only have meaning in texts, to take a word or form out of its co-text is to distort it beyond recognition. The sentence-grammarian's answer to this criticism is as follows. The sentence-grammarian analyses words and forms by deliberately abstracting away from their specific contexts in order to arrive at generalizations. This is the essence of science. If one did not abstract away from specific instances generalizations would be impossible. Such ancient, familiar, and incontrovertible concepts of sentence-grammar as word, clause, noun, and subject are generalizations of this kind, they exist on the sentence, not on the text. The staple diet of our work is invented sentences, true, some of which sound a bit odd, e.g. *la plume de ma tante* 'my Aunt's pen', *mensa* (Voc.) 'O, table', or *The student wrote the essay*. But they serve their purpose. We rely on grammaticality judgements of native speakers, also true, but as long as we genuinely consult native speakers and do not rely solely on our own judgement, and as long we get several different opinions on a sentence, not just one, the method works. Moreover, sentence-grammar has one fundamental advantage over text grammar and corpus studies, and that is that the sentence-grammarian can say that such-and-such a form or sentence will never occur in a language, whereas the most that a text grammarian and corpus linguist can say is that it is not in my corpus: which is not to say that it does not exist or is ungrammatical, merely that it does not happen to occur in your corpus. That is what makes sentence-grammar grammar, and why the term 'grammar' in the phrase 'text grammar' is actually a metaphor.

CHAPTER 7

The method of lexical exceptions

After our *excursus* into the realms of *parole* let us now return to matters of *langue*. According to Saussure a language is a structure or system. System implies regularity implies rules, and any learner of a foreign language knows that learning a foreign language entails learning rules. But what about the (unexplained) exceptions to rules? In grammar there always are exceptions to rules. Where do they fit in?[109]

A commonly held view is that in grammar (unexplained) exceptions to rules are inevitable and unavoidable, and we just have to put up with them. But that seems to me a misguided view. If a language really is systematic it should not allow any exceptions at all, i.e. items which stand outside the system, not a part of it. Yet exceptions do exist, so how do they arise? It seems to me that they arise to the extent that we, the grammarians, have got it wrong. We introduce them from outside with rules that are not quite right. If a rule is 100% correct it will have no (unexplained) exceptions whatsoever, if it is almost exactly right it will have a small number of exceptions, and if it is badly wrong it will have lots of exceptions.

Can exceptions be eliminated? Yes, they can. In fact, unexplained exceptions to rules are an open invitation to the grammarian to come and investigate. If there is an area of grammar which has a large number of unexplained exceptions we should home in on them and investigate them, trying to find out what causes them, and by eliminating the cause – a faulty analysis – eliminate the exceptions. We have seen two sets of exceptions in this book: non-passivizable transitive verbs, and strong or irregular verbs. In fact, we used both sets of exceptions in a parallel way, to gain deeper insights into the faulty rules which produced them, in what may be termed a 'method of lexical exceptions'. Let us now review what we did with those two sets of exceptions, to see what the method of lexical exceptions involves and how it works.

The method of lexical exceptions is a dialectical method of research in grammar, which can be thought of in terms of the Hegelian triad of thesis, antithesis, and synthesis. The thesis are the currently accepted views on a given area; the antithesis are the problems, contradictions, flaws, exceptions, etc. thrown up by the thesis; and the synthesis is the new analysis which arises from the dialectical interaction between thesis and antithesis, explaining and thus removing the contradictions. Philosophers say that the antithesis negates the thesis, and the synthesis arises by a negation of that negation (see under *dialectic* and *dialectical materialism* in Edwards (Ed.) 1967; Sowell 1985:6–65; Marx 1976; Engels 1987; Mueller 1958).

Earlier in this book we tackled the passive construction and the tense system in the same way, by attacking their respective unexplained exceptions: in the case of the passive transitive verbs which do not form a passive, in the case of tense formation the strong/non-productive/irregular verbs. The thesis or currently accepted theory of the passive was that passives are derived from an underlying active. The antithesis or contradictions of this theory were the five formal differences between active and passive leading to no semantic difference, the agentive *by*-phrase, non-passivizable transitive verbs, etc. We used the problems and contradictions of the antithesis – particularly the (unexplained) lexical exceptions non-passivizable transitive verbs – to arrive at a new analysis of the passive, viz. the passive as an aspect. A crucial part of the new analysis is that the exceptions disappear, i.e. are explained, and that is what happened in Chapter 3 – the explanation under the aspect analysis was that some transitive verbs do not form a passive because transitivity is not the criterion for passivizability, lexical/compositional aspect is.

The thesis or currently accepted theory of tense was that tenses refer to times, and that in English, for example, verbs form their preterit and 2nd participle by adding -*ed* to the verb. The antithesis or contradictions of this theory were the fact that all the tenses can refer to virtually all the times (i.e. the present tense can refer to future and past time, and indeed by itself (i.e. without the help of the progressive) cannot refer to present time at all, etc.), and the approx. 200 English strong verbs which do not form their preterit and 2nd participle with -*ed*. Our work on tense and irregular verbs is not complete, such that we could offer a finished solution and synthesis, as was the case with the passive. However, we have made significant progress in the direction of finding one. We have found that the VCs and the CVs of the strong verbs are phonotactic markers of strong conjugation; and that the strong verbs share their VCs (though not their CVs) to a surprisingly high degree with (monosyllabic) function words (and in Russian even with grammatical endings). There is still some way to go, but we have unearthed hitherto unnoticed patterns and regularities on the strong verbs which point to the possibility of a solution and synthesis eventually being found.

category	thesis	antithesis	synthesis
passive	voice analysis	5 formal differences to no semantic effect; agentive *by*-phrase; non-pass. trans. verbs; etc.	aspect analysis: various problems explained, particularly non-pass. trans. verbs (passivizability dependent on lexical/compositional aspect, not transitivity)
tense	tenses refer to times; verbs form preterit and 2nd part. with *-ed*	all tenses refer to (virtually) all times; strong verbs	(thus far:) VCs are phonotactic markers of strong conjugation; strong verb VCs shared with function words

Figure 7. The method of lexical exceptions viewed in terms of thesis, antithesis, and synthesis

Thus if we view an area of grammar in terms of the Hegelian triad of thesis, antithesis, and synthesis, unexplained lexical exceptions are part of the antithesis, and if used dialectically can lead to the discovery of a synthesis. This is summarised in Figure 7.

We use lexical exceptions because they offer a practical way of overcoming the fact that the number of sentences in a language is infinite. If the number of sentences in a language were finite, then in order to investigate a given construction one would naturally begin by examining all the sentences in which that construction occurred. But the number of sentences in a language is not finite, it is infinite. Thus it is impossible to examine all the sentences in which a given construction occurs. However, by examining all the sentences in which a given construction can *not* occur and yet ought to occur (going by our current state of knowledge), it is as if one had examined all the sentences in which the construction could occur.

We also use lexical exceptions because they render theoretical linguistics an empirical science. I am not *claiming* or *proposing* that the passive is an aspect, I have *discovered* that the passive is an aspect. Linguistics is finally truly an empirical science.

In both instances, the passive and tense, we identified the object of study by virtue of their grammatical form realized by a given phonological shape,[110] and approached them in terms of their category-meaning-syntax (syntax in the sense of combinatorial possibilities); this is a Saussurean element which is crucial to the method of lexical exceptions. For the passive the grammatical form we were investigating was auxiliary + passive participle, realized in English in the phonological shape of *be* + V-*ed*; its category under the old analysis was voice of the verb, under the new analysis aspect of the verb; its meaning under the old analysis was synonymous with underlying active, under the new analysis 'action + state'; and its syntax under the old analysis was that only transitive verbs form a passive, under the new analysis that only telic verbs form a passive. For tense the grammatical form that we were looking at was verbs which deviate from the regular pattern in their tenses, realized in English in the phonological shape of ablaut and -*en*. The category of such verbs under the old analysis is that they are called 'strong' verbs, which is merely a label for a set of verbs which we don't know what to do with synchronically;[111] under the new analysis thus far it is the phonotactics of the irregular verbs which places them within the system of English, German, and Russian, respectively. The meaning of the strong verbs under the old analysis is that they don't have one, i.e. it is not the case that the strong verbs have an identifiably different meaning to the weak verbs (also, present tense means present time, etc.); we do not yet have a *langue*-based new meaning for the strong verbs, though Tobin suggests on the basis of textual evidence that they are resultative. Once we have a meaning for the strong verbs grounded in *langue* we will revisit the meanings of the tenses, and the new analysis should explain the semantic anomalies of the old analysis, such that we revise the meaning of the present tense to something other than present time, and so on, for all the tenses. On the syntax[112] of the strong verbs, or, to put it more appositely, the combinatorial possibilities of the strong verbs, or, to put it more appositely still, how can one tell with which verbs ablaut and -*en* combine, under the old analysis one can't tell, one can only list them, whilst under the new analysis thus far ablaut and -*en* combine with monosyllabic verbs containing a specified set of VCs and CVs. Thus we see the same approach to the passive and tense, to non-passivizable transitive verbs and strong verbs, based on their grammatical-form-as-realized-by-a-phonological-shape, category, meaning, and syntax/syntagmatics. This is summarised in Figure 8.

It is important to emphasise that one starts with form and goes from there to meaning, not the other way round, and here we are back with the main theme of this book, that language creates the reality that we perceive (Beedham 2007). The linguist who starts with meaning is doomed to be trapped in the analysis which produced that meaning. The method of lexical exceptions is a practical way of circumventing the Sapir-Whorfian fact that we are trapped in the meanings and categories imposed on us by language – it is a way out of the trap.

The method of lexical exceptions is helped enormously by working with more than one language, e.g. three languages, as I do. The reason for this is that, if one identifies the same grammatical form in more than one language,

area of study	grammatical form	phonological shape		category	meaning	syntax/syntagmatics
passive	auxiliary + passive participle	(English) be + V-ed	old analysis	voice of the verb	synonymous with underlying active	only transitive verbs form a passive
			new analysis	aspect of the verb	action followed by resulting state	only telic verbs form a passive
tense (irreg. verbs)	verbs which deviate from the regular pattern in their tense formation	(English) verbs with ablaut and -en	old analysis	strong verbs (just a label, no category given, verbs have to be listed)	no meaning given	no criteria given, verbs have to be listed
			new analysis	(thus far:) strong verbs have a special phonotactics	no langue-based meaning yet, though textual evidence that they are resultative	ablaut and -en combine with verbs containing a specified set of VCs and CVs

Figure 8. The grammatical form/phonological shape/category /meaning/syntagmatics of the passive and tense

grammatical form		phonological shape	
	English	German	Russian
auxiliary + passive participle	*be* + V-*ed*	*werden/sein* + *ge*-V-*t*	*byt'* + V-*n*-/-*en*-

Figure 9. The passive formally identified in English, German, and Russian

because each language has a different lexico-morpho-syntactic structure you get three different perspectives on the same form. You can use the insights that one language gives you as clues about where to look in the other two languages. Having then made advances in the other two languages, you can use those new insights as clues about where to look in the first language. And so on, ad infinitum. Each language gives you a step up in the other two languages in a mutually reinforcing and supportive way, in a virtuous circle and upward spiral of scientific discovery. The crucial thing is at the start to identify *formally*, not semantically, in all three languages the area you wish to investigate, and that area must have a substantial set of (unexplained) exceptions in all three languages. For the passive the grammatical form to be identified was auxiliary + passive participle. In English the phonological sequence which realized this grammatical form was *be* + V-*ed*, in German it was *werden/sein* + *ge*-V-*t*, in Russian it was *byt'* + V-*n*-/-*en*-[113] (see Figure 9). The voice-based rule that all and only transitive verbs form a passive was valid in all three languages, and all three languages had their exceptions to this rule, e.g. in English *have, resemble, marry*; in German *haben* 'to have', *bekommen* 'to receive', *mögen* 'to like'; in Russian *poblagodarit'* 'to thank', *uvidet'* 'to see', *požalet'* 'to feel sorry for'.[114]

To give an example of one language giving clues of where to look in another language, it is possible or perhaps even likely that the Russian constraint whereby usually only perfective verbs, not imperfective, form a participial passive led me to test the English and German non-passivizable transitive verbs for their compatibility with the resultative perfect. I was not aware of it happening, if it happened it happened subconsciously, but looking back on it it seems likely. I should emphasise at this point that I am not talking here comparative linguistics in the sense that one says because a form is one thing in one language it must be the same thing in another language. On the contrary, in order to argue for a particular analysis in a language one must have evidence which is internal to that language.

It is also advantageous if at least one of the languages you are investigating is a foreign language to you. This is because it is easier to appreciate in a foreign language than in one's native tongue that the meanings encoded by that language are specific to that language and arise from the lexico-morpho-syntactic structure of that language (in other words, form determines meaning). It is all too easy when examining one's native language to fall into the trap of believing that the meanings which you see in it are natural and logical. If you do that, however, you will obviously never find new meanings. But a foreign language gives you the necessary psychic distance from your *Untersuchungsobjekt*. You must speak the foreign language fluently, however, i.e. have near-native speaker fluency, because you will need to use the intuitive part of your brain to help you decide where to look for a solution, and you will also need to arbitrate and make the final decision when your native speaker informants disagree on the grammaticality of the test sentences which you present them with. Having said that, however, one of the languages you investigate can be your native language – the extra fluency and intuitions you have in your native language are helpful – as long as at least one of the languages you investigate is foreign to you.[115]

In either case, native language or foreign language, you have to have a feel for the language, like a poet.[116] That is the beauty of the method of lexical exceptions: it uses the rational part of your brain, when you work like a scientist; it uses the intuitive part of your brain, when you act like a poet; and it exploits serendipity as well, since, in the course of testing the verbs for their various properties you may stumble across a correlation and a solution by chance.

We come now to the core of the method. Having identified the form you want to investigate and its lexical exceptions, what do you do with those exceptions? What you do is you try to find a consequence of their exceptional status elsewhere in the grammar and/or vocabulary of the language concerned. You try to find a link between your exceptions and some other point in the lexico-grammar of the language concerned.[117] It is almost inevitable that that 'some other point' will also be mysterious and unexplained. You are tracing a path of disruption through the ordered system. It is like tracing a path of untidiness through a tidy room. Initially the link will be of a formal kind – morphological, syntactic, or phonotactic – and you may at first not see the semantic link. But as sure as the sign is indivisible the penny will drop and you will eventually see the semantic link. When that happens a new analysis will become apparent and the pieces of the jig-saw will fall into place.

Let me describe how it happened in the case of non-passivizable transitive verbs. First of all the verbs themselves had to be identified. This was done by going through a dictionary – for English it was the OALD – and marking all transitive verbs listed. Another crucial element in the method of lexical exceptions is that the investigation be exhaustive, i.e. it was crucial to get *all* the non-passivizable transitive verbs of each language, not just a sample. The verbs so marked were then put into a passive sentence – the OALD was used to find good example sentences of English to put into the passive – and the passive sentences thus constructed presented to three native speakers for their grammaticality judgements: they were asked if the sentences were A grammatical, B borderline, C ungrammatical, D don't know.[118] It is important not to rely on one's own grammaticality judgements but to seek the judgements of other (native) speakers. It is also important not to rely on one person's judgement, even if that person is not you, but to get at least three judgements. Since I was in Leipzig when I was working on the passive in the 1970s there was a convenient supply of native speaker informants for all three of my languages, German, Russian, and English. In the cases of disagreement between informants – and it is inherent to what one is doing here, i.e. working at the outer edge of grammaticality, that there will be disagreements – it was my job to decide whether a verb was non-passivizable or not. This part of the research took up the most time. I ended up with 108 transitive verbs in English for which I had at least one ungrammatical passive sentence. The waters were muddied by the fact that many verbs were non-passivizable in one meaning but not in another, and even with a consistent meaning many verbs were non-passivizable in one sentence but not in another – it was only later that I realised that this was because the compositional aspect of the sentence was affecting passivizability – but one way or another, after much head-scratching and soul-searching, I ended up with 108 transitive verbs in English which could be called more or less non-passivizable. The same was done for German and Russian.

The verbs were then examined in detail to try to find out what made them special or peculiar such that they did not form a passive, despite being transitive. Were their non-passives affected by question or negation or the presence of an adverb or a modal verb, i.e. did an ungrammatical passive sentence suddenly become more acceptable in a question or negated or with an adverb added or a modal verb added (once again the grammaticality judgements of native speaker informants were crucial)? In some cases yes, though not in sufficient numbers to appear significantly so. The results of the tests were drawn up in the format of a table to help me focus on them – see Table 5 on p.162 – and I spent many happy hours staring at rows and columns of pluses and minuses stuck on the wall of my flat – this was before the age of the computer! – trying to see a pattern. Then I started to test the verbs for their possibilities of co-occurrence in other constructions, other than the passive.[119] This was also a time-consuming part of the exercise, but it was also the most interesting and most rewarding. It was here that the real science was done; it was here that one made new observations, uncovered new facts, which lead to new insights and new analyses (Augst 1975a: 283–284). It is here that you can follow up hunches empirically and experimentally, test out an idea. If you are right you will discover a correlation, if you are wrong you won't, but no matter, you simply try out another avenue. For some reason, I don't know why, I tested my verbs to see if they formed a resultative perfect. I had no great expectations from this experiment, no more than all the others performed over many months which had drawn a blank. To my surprise about two-thirds of the verbs did not form a resultative perfect. Why was that? Was that normal, that most of a random group of 108 verbs should not form a resultative perfect (I knew nothing about aspect – after all, I was working on voice)? Surely all or most verbs form a resultative perfect? The rest is history – see Chapter 3!

The method of lexical exceptions allows the sentence-grammarian to carry out experiments in the manner of the natural sciences. This is highly unusual. Usually sentence-grammar is considered to be and is practised as a pure arts and humanities subject, conducted entirely rationally, not empirically. But the method of lexical exceptions allows the grammarian to conduct empirical enquiries, to investigate systematically, to experiment. It turns the study of *langue* into an empirical science. It is the methodological corollary of the notion that linguistics is a search for meanings, whereby the meanings that we are looking for are determined by the form of language.

Having used the method of lexical exceptions successfully once I wanted to use it again, and so cast around for another set of exceptions to investigate. The strong verbs of English and German, and non-productive verbs of Russian, presented themselves immediately as obvious candidates, and they became my next research project. I tackled them in the same way as non-passivizable transitive verbs, with two differences. Firstly, whereas for the passive most of my time was spent identifying its exceptions, for tense that bit was already done for me – every grammar and dictionary lists the irregular verbs, indeed the irregular verbs are famous amongst linguists and non-linguists alike, as Pinker (1994 and 1999) so entertainingly points out. Secondly, the stage in which one makes explicit the syntactic properties of the verbs by testing them for their compatibility with other constructions – I tested the English verbs for their ability to form an actional passive, statal passive, attributive 2nd participle, expanded attributive 2nd participle, progressive, and imperative (see Beedham (1994a) for an account of the German part of this research) – did not produce a result, so I did something which I had not done with the non-passivizable transitive verbs, and that is I looked at the internal phonotactic structure of the verbs, i.e. their VCs and CVs, as described in Chapter 5. It is possible that the syntactic properties will still come into play, viz. whatever meaning is eventually found for the irregular verbs will have a syntactic manifestation in that they will be precluded

Table 5. The syntactic properties of some English non-passivizable transitive verbs (Beedham 1982:139)

	passive	agent oblig. present	agent oblig. absent	agent optional	passive in questions	passive in negative	passive with modal	action nomin. + gen.	action nomin. with *by*	passive with adverb	resultative ... perfect
comprise	–	+	–	–	–	–	–	–	–	–	–
contain	+	+	–	–	+	+	+	–	–	–	–
cost	–	+	–	–	–	–	–	–	–	–	±
deserve	±	–	–	+	+	+	–	–	–	+	–
detest	+	+	–	–	+	+	–	–	–	+	±
dignify	–	–	–	+	–	–	+	+	+	–	+
dream	–	+	–	–	–	–	+	–	–	–	–

from a particular construction which exhibits that meaning; in other words, the irregular verbs will have their version of the perfect-passive correlation. But for the moment the syntactic stage of research is on ice, and I am concentrating on phonotactics. Of course, every set of exceptions has its idiosyncrasies, and it may well turn out that, whilst syntax was the thing of non-passivizable transitive verbs, phonotactics is the irregular verbs' thing. But we don't know yet, we will have to wait and see, when we have a result. Anyway, the point is that the method of lexical exceptions did again produce a correlation, only this time it is phonotactic instead of syntactic.

My work on the irregular verbs has the further difference that I put the syntactic properties onto computer and got a colleague to write a program which helps you look for patterns, and have used research assistants, none of which I had for my passive research. However, these are incidental factors.

Although I have not yet solved the irregular verbs, the progress made is every bit as spectacular as that achieved on the passive. To have discovered that the VCs and CVs of the strong verbs of English and German are effectively unique to the strong verbs and hence serve as phonotactic markers of strong conjugation, that those self-same strong verb VCs have an unexpectedly high rate of occurrence in (monosyllabic) function words (and grammatical endings in Russian), and that this generalization holds in a non-Germanic, a Slav language, Russian, is equally as important as the discovery that the passive is an aspect. The length of time taken on each project so far is broadly similar, though the irregular verbs are taking longer than the passive. Whilst I worked for 3 years full-time on the passive, I have been working for 18 years part-time on the irregular verbs, spending approx. a sixth of my time on them, which works out as equivalent to 3 years full-time (plus approx. one year's worth of research assistance, a mixture of full-time and part-time). There is still a long way to go on the irregular verbs, and I don't know how much longer it will take to crack them, but as a return on the investment of time and energy the results are already impressive.

To say out loud what is implicit in this chapter, I hope that other linguists will try out the method of lexical exceptions on other areas of grammar in other languages. The stages of research that one goes through may be summarised as follows:

Phase 1
Choose a formal construction which is present in at least two languages which you speak fluently and which has a substantial set of unexplained

lexical exceptions in each language. It will almost certainly be a construction which foreign learners find particularly difficult to master.

Phase 2

Identify the problems, anomalies, contradictions, etc. associated with your chosen construction, making special note of the semantic ones. In particular:

Phase 3

Identify and list the unexplained lexical exceptions to your construction – all of them – if necessary using dictionaries and native speaker informants.

Phase 4

Identify the properties of your exceptions, especially their formal properties (though their semantic characteristics may also be helpful), e.g. morphological, syntactic, phonotactic. This phase may well involve the use of native speaker informants.

Phase 5

Try to find out what is special about your lexical exceptions, which might lead them to be exceptions. Do they and they alone (or most of them, anyway, say at least 60%) exhibit a particular formal characteristic which emerges from your work in Phase 4? If so, you have found a formal correlation between your exceptions and that characteristic. This is the key to the solution you are looking for.

Phase 6

This is the semantic phase. Can the meaning associated with the formal characteristic discovered in Phase 5 be found in your chosen construction and its exceptions? Is it a meaning which no one has ever noticed before? Is it a meaning which would explain the semantic anomalies of your chosen construction noted in Phase 2? If so you are home and dry, you have found a new analysis for your chosen construction and an explanation for its lexical exceptions. The new analysis will have different and better rules for the formation of your chosen construction, which do not produce the exceptions of the old analysis, and a new meaning for your chosen construction which both sounds intuitively right and explains the semantic anomalies noted in Phase 2.

All things being equal, in addition to being recognised and accepted by other theoretical linguists the new analysis will enter pedagogical grammars, both for foreign learners and native speakers. Though it may not be in your lifetime.

Conclusion

This book has been about language and meaning, whereby our main thesis has been that the reality which we perceive is not merely *influenced* by language and other facets of the human perceptual apparatus – mind, biochemical make-up, physical attributes, the five senses – it is *created* by them. That is to say, the world without an observer is not there. This is an idea usually found in philosophy, where it goes by the name of subjective idealism, but we have approached it from linguistics. The accepted wisdom on this matter is the very opposite, viz. that the world pre-exists language. Most people – scientists, scholars, and laymen alike – think that the objects of the universe such as tables and chairs, dogs and cats, houses and trees, exist already in the world, and language comes along later and labels them. But Saussure 1983 showed that words and morphemes only have meaning within the terms of the linguistic system which they constitute; it is linguistic structure which endows a word or a morpheme with meaning, not its reference to reality. Saussure expressed this view by saying that words and morphemes are signs consisting of *signifiant* (form) and *signifié* (meaning), whereby the sign is indivisible, i.e. you don't get *signifiants* without a *signifié* and you don't get *signifiés* without a *signifiant*. He also expressed it by saying that language consists of *langue* – the self-contained system (= (sentence)-grammar) – and *parole* – the realization of the system in actual speech (or texts) – but it is *langue* which is or should be the main object of study in linguistics.

The methodological point to be inferred from this is that linguists must have a formal, not semantic approach to language. Linguists who start from meaning and attempt to go from there to form are trapped in the old meanings of old analyses. It is only if we start from form, as realized by a given phonological shape, that we can make progress in linguistics and uncover new meanings on the basis of new formal analyses.

We noted in passing two common misinterpretations of Saussure: firstly, that some linguists who consider themselves to be structuralists believe that meanings exist independently of language, such that one can or indeed must start with meanings and go from there to forms; and secondly, some linguists believe that language can only be properly investigated by looking at it in context, in actual speech or texts, i.e. they believe that *parole* is the proper *Untersuchungsobjekt* of linguistics.

So far so good. But so far we have only used other people's arguments, fairly familiar ones, in support of the idea that language creates reality. What do I have to offer that is new? What I offer is the aspectual analysis of the passive, which claims to replace the voice analysis of the passive, i.e. the practice of deriving passives from an underlying active. But give us a break, you say, how does the aspectual analysis of the passive support the view that language creates reality? It works like this. One has to appreciate that many of the things which we talk about and think about are abstract, not concrete, things such as love and hate, socialism and the market system, innocence and guilt, etc. Moreover, one has to appreciate that when we perceive reality we do so largely in terms of words and their meanings. Now, the aspect analysis of the passive brings with it a new meaning for *be* + V-*ed* in English: it claims that *be* + V-*ed* means 'action + state', i.e. the expression of a new state which arises on the subject as the result of a preceding action. The point is, where does this meaning come from? If you believe the old view then you presumably must believe that the meaning 'action + state' was there all along, we just hadn't seen it (assuming you accept the aspect analysis as being correct). Now that we have seen it we can revise our view of the meaning of *be* + V-*ed*, and say OK, we got it wrong before, but now you mention it I can see quite clearly that *be* + V-*ed* means 'action + state', it does not mean the same as a purported underlying active after all. I can definitely see a piece of the universe, action + state, labelled by the form *be* + V-*ed*. But it wasn't like that, that is not how I came across the meaning 'action + state'. The way I saw the meaning 'action + state' was through the spectacles of the perfect-passive correlation. It was only when I noticed that the same verbs were unexpectedly excluded from both the passive and the resultative perfect that I began to see a meaning 'action + state'. Without that syntactic correlation I would never have seen that meaning, that slice of reality, because it is the syntactic correlation which *creates* the meaning and hence the slice of reality. The recognition that the passive is an aspect of the verb, not a voice of the verb, is proof positive that form determines meaning and hence language creates the reality that we perceive.

But what about concrete objects, I hear you say. Much of the world we perceive may well be abstract, but in the final analysis we stand on hard ground and we ourselves are hard. Ultimately the universe comes down to solid objects, what do you have to say about that? My answer is that at this point, when it comes to solid objects, language is not enough to explain the creation of reality, other facets of the human perceptual apparatus come into play, e.g. our physical size. It is only because we are the size we are that other parts of the universe are solid to us. If we were smaller than the smallest sub-atomic particle in the solid objects around us we would pass right through them without even knowing that they were there. So once again, even in the case of solid objects, the perceiving being creates for itself the reality which it perceives.

In addition to showing how language creates reality three other things arose from our exploration of language and meaning. Firstly, we showed that the analyses of traditional grammar are not self-evident facts, but are theories or hypotheses open to refutation, the passive being a case in point: in traditional grammar passives are derived from an underlying active (the voice analysis), but we showed that that analysis is wrong, the passive is an aspect of the verb, like the perfect and the progressive in English, not a voice of the verb. From this it follows that the model-building approach, particularly as represented by generative grammar, is misguided. We looked at several models of language, e.g. Minimalism and Lexical-Functional Grammar, and their way of handling the passive, and noted that despite numerous superficial differences they are all based on the view from traditional grammar that passives are derived from actives. Thus what they do in effect is to formalize a particular descriptive analysis, but one which has been shown to be false. If you strip away the notations and the model-specific assumptions you are left with a common or garden analysis which every schoolchild knows anyway. The features of the models – their notations and their special assumptions and postulations – add nothing to the sum of human understanding whatsoever, they simply act as a mysterious, albeit extremely scientific-looking code, which has to be cracked before you can get at the descriptive truths lying hidden beneath them.

We also noted that generative grammar confuses notation with form. Generative grammarians borrow symbols from mathematics, logic, and computer science, as well as using their own abbreviations and mnemonics, but notational is not the same as formal. A formal approach in the descriptive sense can lead to explanations, but if formal means nothing more than notational, which it does in generative grammar, the outcome is trivial, not explanatory.

The second thing to arise from our exploration of language and meaning, in addition to our main thesis, was that we applied the lessons of the passive to irregular verbs. We said that if there is no difference in form without a difference in meaning the irregular verbs must have a meaning different to the regular verbs, carried in English by ablaut and -*en*. Moreover, if a language is a system in which everything hangs together, the irregular verbs must hang together with something, if we can only find with what, i.e. there must be rules by which the irregular verb-forms are formed, if we could only find them. In the same way that the irregularity of non-passivizable transitive verbs dissolved away in the aspect analysis of the passive, so the irregularity of the irregular verbs will disappear if we can find rules for them. If we find the meaning and the rules at all we will find them together, at the same time, because the linguistic sign is indivisible, i.e. form and meaning are indivisible. Although, unlike for the passive, we could not give a completed analysis for the irregular verbs, we pointed to some considerable progress made en route to a solution. It is highly likely that the irregular verbs will be shown to have a resultative meaning, in contrast to the process-oriented meaning of the regular verbs. At the moment we only have textual evidence, from Tobin and Quirk, pointing in that direction, but further *langue*-style research will hopefully bring out formal – e.g. syntactic, morphological, or phonotactic – evidence of a meaning for the irregular verbs. We have made a start on that track, and showed that the irregular verbs differ phonotactically from the regular verbs: the English irregular verbs contain VCs and CVs which the regular verbs tend not to contain (the German irregular verbs also, for Russian just the VCs). Moreover, the English irregular verb VCs show up to a surprisingly high degree in monosyllabic function words, e.g. pronouns (the German and Russian irregular verbs show the same phenomenon, and Russian even has it, incredibly, vis-à-vis grammatical endings). This is the latest stage of my research. It remains to be seen where this line of investigation will take us in the future, conducted either by me or by others.

Finally, I introduced you to the method of lexical exceptions. The aspectual analysis of the passive arose from a detailed examination of non-passivizable transitive verbs. Non-passivizable transitive verbs are exceptions to the rule that all transitive verbs form a passive. At the time they were the biggest mystery of the passive, and hence the most inviting area for research. They also offered an extremely empirical line of research, since they could be examined in detail from every possible angle. It was from that experience that I chose irregular verbs as my next area for research, since irregular verbs are also unexplained exceptions to a grammatical rule, viz. in English to preterit and 2nd participle formation. Indeed, in general I offer to you the method of lexical exceptions as an empirical method by which to investigate the grammar of natural language. The method of lexical exceptions is a way around the language trap, a way around the fact that form determines meaning, a way around the fact that linguists have to think about the very thing that allows them to think. It turns the study of *langue* into a natural science, in which you can conduct experiments. And it sidesteps the fact that the number of sentences in which the construction you wish to analyse can occur is infinite: by investigating the sentences in which your construction ought to occur, going by our current state of knowledge, but doesn't, it is as if you were investigating all the sentences in which it could occur. Choose an area of grammar which has a suspiciously large number of unexplained lexical exceptions, and use the exceptions as a way in to the problem and its solution. Choose an area of grammar which is present in two or three languages, to give you several perspectives on the same problem; all the better if one of the languages is not your native tongue, so as to give a psychic distance between you and the language you are analysing – you are unlikely then to fall into the trap of thinking that the categories of that language are natural and semantically/pragmatically logical. The method of lexical exceptions has been used once already to produce the aspectual analysis of the passive, and again to expose the role of VCs and to a certain extent CVs in irregular verbs. It is a method which draws on the poet, scientist and engineer in us all, and which I hope will lead to further interesting discoveries within grammar and linguistics. If reality does not exist except in terms of the perceptual apparatus which creates it, there is no more important element of that perceptual apparatus than language. Sorry, Stephen Hawking, but Wittgenstein was right: "The sole remaining task for philosophy *is* the analysis of language" (my italics).[120] Study language and study the reality which language creates, study languages and study the realities which they create, and study varieties of language and study the realities which they create.

Notes

1. Morphemes are meaningful bits of words, e.g. the suffix -er in English as in *singer* means 'doer, agent', the prefix *re-* as in *to re-enact* means 'again', the ending -s on nouns as in *cats* means 'plural'.

2. '... the fundamental idea of this course: *the only true object of linguistics is* <u>*la langue*</u>*, taken in itself and for itself* ' (translation by CB).

3. Saussure speaks of a unit of language having a 'value' in a system: "A language is a system in which all the elements fit together, and in which the value of any one element depends on the simultaneous coexistence of all the others" (Saussure 1983:113). See also Gamkrelidze 2006.

4. St. John's Gospel, Chapter 1, verse 1. For an exegesis of this famous phrase from the Bible see the *Encyclopedia of Early Christianity* (1997:687–691); Bultmann (1971:19–36); Newman and Nida (1980:6–9).

5. "What takes place, is a somewhat mysterious process by which 'thought-sound' evolves divisions, and a language takes shape with its linguistic units in between those two amorphous masses" (Saussure 1983:111).

6. In generative grammar this debate is known as the relationship between 'syntax and semantics'.

7. For example, Leech and Svartvik (1975) is a semantically based version of the more formally oriented Quirk et al. (1972).

8. In the words of Benveniste (1971:132): "Notions like process or object do not reproduce objective characteristics of reality but result from an expression of reality which is itself linguistic ... . These notions are not intrinsic properties of nature recorded in language; they are categories that have been formed in certain languages and projected onto nature."

9. I suspect that a clue to what is going on here is given in pedagogical grammars of the modern language written by historical linguists. A pedagogical grammar, written for the foreign learner of a modern language, does not normally attempt to introduce new analyses of familiar areas of grammar, it takes the generally accepted analyses. On the other hand, if you are a theoretical linguist it is your job to produce new and better analyses of familiar points of grammar. I suspect that the historical linguist writing pedagogical grammars thinks that he is doing synchronic, theoretical linguistics. Of course, he is not – there is a difference between pedagogical grammar and theoretical grammar. A pedagogical grammar draws on theoretical work but it is not itself a theoretical work. That a historical linguist does not produce a new synchronic analysis in a pedagogical grammar is not a problem, it is normal, but if that linguist is also not taking a synchronic approach to earlier stages

of the languages whose history he researches into, but works atomistically instead, that is a problem, and is worrying.

10. The data for historical linguistics is what was written down, mostly literary texts, on the basis of which the historical linguist has to reconstruct the spoken language. Because of this necessary link between language and literature it seems to me that the term 'philology' is more accurate than the term 'historical linguistics', which is misleading, omitting as it does the literature part of historical linguistics.

11. It always amazes me to hear generativists described as structuralists, and even more so to hear myself described as a 'syntactician', implying generative grammarian. Both these descriptions are based on a misconception of the generative method and of *langue*/competence. The fact of the matter is that descriptive *langue*-oriented linguists like myself are far closer to *parole*-oriented linguists (because the latter tend not to be generative) than to generative grammarians.

12. On the first use and turbulent history of the famous phrase *un système où tout se tient* see Koerner (1999).

13. It is not surprising that people think this way, given that the brain undergoes physical and chemical changes during first language acquisition (Lenneberg 1967).

14. A reader of an earlier version of this book wondered if I accepted that the earth is round, and if so, does my acceptance of that fact not destroy the very case I brought the flat earth debate in to support, in other words, is it not a fact independent of the observer that the earth is round? The answer is, I do accept that the earth is round, but only because of the perspective I have, i.e. a perspective from outer space which photographs from outer space have given me. But a few thousand years ago I would doubtless have been, like everybody else, a keen member of the flat earth society, again simply because of my (earth-bound) perspective. So once again, "c'est le point de vue qui crée l'objet". Yes, but is the earth not really round, you ask, irrespective of your beliefs, well-informed or ill-informed as they might be by science? The answer is the same as given above, particularly in the conversation with the jellyfish. To human beings the earth appears round, but only because of the biochemical and physical attributes which we possess and the perceptual apparatus which they provide us with. The roundness of the earth is a projection of those attributes and that perceptual apparatus. To a sentient being which were smaller than the smallest sub-atomic particle in the universe (except for the particles of which the being itself were made) the earth would not even be there to be perceived, let alone be round.

15. The notion that language determines thought, and that we are trapped in the conceptual categories of our native language, is known in linguistics as the Sapir-Whorf hypothesis (also: the theory of linguistic relativity), named after the American linguists and anthropologists Edward Sapir (1884–1939) and Benjamin Lee Whorf (1897–1941). See Whorf (1956); Sapir (1949); Niemeier and Dirven (Eds.) (2000); Pütz and Verspoor (Eds.) (2000).

16. Pullum (1991) points out that since the Eskimo-Aleut languages are polysynthetic, i.e. use inflectional and derivational morphology to form words of almost infinite length which express what in English would be expressed by a phrase or clause, words in Eskimo are not comparable with words in Indo-European languages. The question therefore becomes not how many words do the Eskimo-Aleut languages have for snow but how many morphemes.

17. Names are usually considered to be meaningless (apart from etymological vestiges of meaning), but we see here that they are capable of carrying very significant meanings. On names and naming see Anderson (2003).

18. The United States of America had a Department of War from 1789 to 1949, when it was renamed the Department of Defense. The British War Office was renamed the Department of Defence in 1964. 1949, with the formation of West and East Germany, was the start of the Cold War proper and the start of the language of the Cold War. For a discussion of the language of nuclear 'defence' matters see Chilton (Ed.) (1985), *Multilingua* (1988), Beedham (1983).

19. The perfect also has some characteristics of a tense. Furthermore, when the perfect is combined with a tense the resulting form, e.g. pluperfect, future perfect, is usually considered to be a tense. Here we will concentrate on the aspectual properties more than the tense properties of the perfect.

20. I hesitate to use the phrase 'common sense', since as is well-known by now – indeed it is one of the inferences to be drawn from structuralism and from this book – every age, every society, and every scientific analysis creates its own common sense. But notwithstanding all of that, the phrase is still useful.

21. The practice has survived for the English present and past participles, which are sometimes called the 1st and 2nd participles. After a discussion of the meaning of the participles in which he was unable to reach a definitive conclusion Jespersen (1924: 284) wrote: "I see no other way out of the terminological difficulty than the not very satisfactory method of numbering the forms, calling the *-ing-* participle the first and the other the second participle".

22. In doing so we are using orthographic letters to allude to the phonolog shape of the morphological form in question. Put like that it sounds convoluted, but fortunately the phrase 'the *-ed* form in English' is not convoluted and is very simple to use.

23. In traditional grammar the perfect is glossed as 'completed action'. Once again we have the problem of overcoming a meaning which previous linguists have attempted to set in stone by naming the form after the Latin word *perfectus*, meaning 'performed'. I.e. if one were to take the term 'perfect' etymologically literally the statement 'The perfect does not mean completed action' would be a self-contradiction. But the form *have* + V-*ed* in English, commonly known as the 'perfect', does not mean completed action, as can be readily seen from the fact that this meaning does not distinguish the perfect from the preterit. In most preterit sentences the action is just as complete as in the perfect, e.g. for most imaginable contexts in both *He closed the door* and *He has closed the door* he completed the action of closing the door. The difference between the two sentences is that in the latter perfect sentence the fact that he closed the door is still relevant for some reason to the speaker at the time of speaking, whereas in the former preterit sentence it is not.

24. I use the term syntax to mean combinatorial possibilities, not word order, the latter being the more usual understanding of the term 'syntax', especially in generative grammar (see Beedham 1995a: 19–23).

25. McCoard (1978: 23) speaks of lexical aspect in English being 'covert' in a kind of 'crypto-aspect'.

26. Hornby (1949) called them non-conclusive verbs, implying a slightly different meaning. Once again, we are confronted with a terminological problem, caused by linguists naming aspects after what they think is their meaning. It is somewhat harder to name syntactically determined aspects as opposed to morphologically realized aspects, since one does not have the option of calling them, for example, 'the -*ed* form'. In this case one might speak of -[Progressive] verbs, or something similar. However, there is also a political dimension to grammatical baptisms, and in this case since the majority of linguists seem happy with the idea that verbs in English which resist -*ing* are stative I am prepared to go along with them.

27. McCoard (1978: 142–144) is quite right to point out that the sub-meaning of the perfect you end up with depends on other elements in the sentence as well, not just the verb. For example, if in (1) we delete the time phrase *for 20 years* we are left with an experiential perfect – another recognised sub-meaning of the perfect – in which the living in Scotland is understood to have come to an end, and the verb *to live* appears to behave like a telic verb. This is because aspect is compositional, which we examine next.

28. I hope the reader will not quibble, and say that in order to judge the grammaticality of a sentence you have to interpret it semantically. That is true up to a point, but for most sentences it is still easier to give grammaticality judgements than semantic interpretations, and the former provide scientific formal evidence whereas the latter only provide intuitive semantic evidence.

29. Other terms for telic/atelic are bounded/unbounded, terminative/aterminative, and conclusive/non-conclusive (McCoard 1978: 161). Once again, I prefer the opaque term with the classical root, telic/atelic (from Greek *telos* 'end'), which hints at a particular meaning but at the same time allows us to argue over whether the meaning of these verbs is bounded, or terminative, or conclusive, etc. The main thing is that we agree on the formal indications of telic aspect, and a name for it. That part of the exercise need contain no doubt or grey areas. Then we can go on to debate the meaning, and if there is disagreement between scholars and grey areas on the semantics – and there always are on the semantics – then at least the debate can be conducted sensibly and rationally.

30. There is also a similarity with syntax as combinatorial possibilities, i.e. structuralism, aspect, and syntax all boil down to the same thing, viz. combinability.

31. It is surely a mistake for Quirk et al. (1985) to use the term 'perfective', with all its connotations of the Russian aspect system, for the English perfect.

32. Even within the same language two words can have what looks to be the same meaning, yet differ syntactically, thus indicating a difference in meaning. For example, *to vanish* and *to disappear* look like synonyms, yet you can say *the vanished treasure*, as stated above, but you cannot say **the disappeared treasure*. So *to vanish* and *to disappear* are not exact synonyms after all, and do not have exactly the same lexical aspect.

33. At this point I would emphasise again that these are meanings which are special to the Russian verbal and lexical system. Although there are similarities for example between Russian imperfective on the one hand and English progressive, French *imparfait*, etc., on the other, the differences are more important than the similarities, and it is a mistake to try to carry over Russian meanings to English, or French, or any other language. English no more has a Russian-style perfective aspect than Russian has an English-style perfect aspect.

34. Zifonun et al. (1997) use the term 'transformative' where Helbig and Buscha use 'perfective'. Abraham (1990) speaks of 'terminative'. Once again, the way out of this terminological conundrum is to call the lexical aspect after the formal indication of it, so in this case we should speak of '*sein*-verbs', i.e. verbs which form their perfect with *sein*. If we could at least agree on that it would make a debate about the meaning of such verbs – perfective, transformative, terminative, or whatever – much more sensible.

35. Actually an action followed by the resulting state, which we will see in the next chapter.

36. The asterisk in (11b) applies to a statal passive interpretation only. One could interpret the sentence as *Der Student ist gelobt worden*, with elision of *worden*, in which case it would be a pluperfect of an actional passive and grammatical.

37. Once again there is a terminological dilemma, since the V-*ed* form is commonly called the past participle, but I will follow Jespersen (1924: 283–284) in calling it the 2nd participle in order not to prejudice the issue of its meaning.

38. 'Patient' is the semantic role associated with the object of the sentence, and is defined as the participant in the sentence affected by the action of the verb (Quirk et al. 1985: 741; Fillmore 1968: 25) or created by the action of the verb (*Kleines Wörterbuch sprachwissenschaftlicher Termini* 1975: 193).

39. 'Cognitive' is another term for referential or denotational (Lyons 1977: 175). Thus the phrase 'cognitively synonymous' means referentially or denotationally synonymous. Quirk et al. (1985: 159) define 'active' as follows: "A passive verb phrase (i.e. one containing a construction of type D [passive aux (BE) + -*ed* participle]) contrasts with an active verb phrase, which is simply defined as one which does not contain that construction". They define a transitive verb as follows: "Verbs used in monotransitive function require a direct object . . . . Direct objects are typically noun phrases which may become the subject of a corresponding passive clause". Transitive verbs which do not form a passive they call 'middle' verbs (Quirk et al. 1985: 1176, 735–736). In languages with cases on the noun transitive verbs are usually restricted to those governing the accusative case, cf. Helbig and Buscha (1989: 53): "*Transitive Verben* sind solche Verben, bei denen ein Akkusativobjekt stehen kann, das bei der Passivtransformation zum Subjektsnominativ wird" *transitive verbs* are verbs with which an accusative object can stand, which under the passive transformation becomes the subject in the nominative. The reader will note the circularity of all of this, but we will not dwell on that here, but will rather press on to the aspect analysis, where the circularity of these definitions disappear along with a whole host of other problems raised by the voice analysis.

40. The theme of a sentence is old or less important information, usually placed at the beginning of a sentence, whilst rheme is new or more important information, usually placed after the theme. In the active the agent is theme, whilst in the passive the patient (underlying object) is theme. On theme/rheme see pp. 140–142.

41. We will soon see that the 'actional' passive actually means 'action + state', but we will nevertheless stick with the voice-based practice of calling it the actional passive.

42. Schoenthal (1976: 183) makes a similar finding for German, viz. 83% of the actional passives in her German corpus appear without an agentive *von*-phrase.

43. In generative grammar numerous devices have been postulated to explain them, but a postulation – even a formalized one – does not constitute an explanation: see Chapter 4.

44. It is often said that the passive exists to make the patient theme, i.e. to put a patient NP in the more prominent initial or subject position (Keenan 1976:310; Bolinger 1975:155). Halliday (1967b:213, 216) refines this explanation by adding that the passive makes the patient unmarked theme, thus distinguishing *The book John bought* (with marked theme) from *The book was bought by John* (with unmarked theme). There are two objections to this explanation. Firstly, it does not work for inflecting languages such as Russian, in which an object NP in the accusative case in initial position is commonly unmarked. Secondly, theme-rheme analysis is fine at the level of texts, in *parole*, but it cannot substitute for or replace grammatical explanations at the level of the sentence within *langue* (see Chapter 6). In other words, no matter to what good theme-rheme effect *be* + *V-ed* is put in texts one still wants to know what it means *qua* grammatical form.

45. The aspectual analysis of the passive presented here is based on Beedham (1979, 1981, 1982, 1987a, 1987b, 1990, 1998a), Бидэм (1988); Schoorlemmer (1995); Пупынин (1980), Poupynin (1996, 1999). For reactions (positive and negative), discussion and development regarding English see Tobin (1993:77, 278, 280–313, 1994:117, 264–265, 289, 372); Verkuyl (1993:29, 275–276); Siewierska (1984:139, 143, 160, 191); Andersen (1990:196); Levin (1993:85, 86); Winford (1988:277); Dagut (1985:10); Terasawa (1984:302–303); Van Langendonck (1982:135); Salkie (1987:92, 99). Regarding Russian see Schoorlemmer (1995:256–257, 263–265); Poupynin (1996:132); Chvany (1985:22, 1987, 1990). Regarding German see Abraham (2000); Zifonun et al. (1997:1876); H. Gross (1998:63–64, 232); Helbig (1987:225–226); Leiss (1985:264, 1992:2, 71); Darski (1999:196); Kotin (1995:62, 1997:482, 497, 1998:19, 37); Leys (1989:110). Regarding Spanish see Gregory (2006).

46. Thus transitivity is still relevant to passivizability, but in the sense that it contributes to telic aspect. Intransitive telic verbs such as *to die*, *to arrive* do not on the whole form an 'action + state' passive with *be* + *V-ed*, they form rather an 'action + result' perfect with *have* + *V-ed*. But notice the similarity in meaning between the passive of a telic transitive verb and the perfect of a telic intransitive verb: *They were rescued* (the end-state of which is they are safe) – *They have arrived* (the result of which is they are here). The similarity is so close that a few intransitive verbs which allow a telic interpretation can form their perfect with the auxiliary *be* instead of *have*, and hence look formally like a passive, e.g. *They are gone* instead of *They have gone*. The similarity – both formal and semantic – between the passive of transitive verbs and the perfect of telic intransitive verbs is particularly striking in German, where telic intransitive verbs form their perfect with *sein* 'to be' not *haben* 'to have', so that you have such parallels and resemblances as *Die Frucht ist gereift* 'the fruit has ripened' (perfect) and *Das Fenster ist geöffnet* 'the window is opened' (passive); see pp. 49–50.

47. Some atelic verbs can form a passive, but only after aspectual-compositional tinkering such as deletion of a *by*-phrase. For example, *She was missed/loved/hated* are all grammatical, but only because they do not have a *by*-phrase. If you add a *by*-phrase with a singular definite NP, e.g. *by John*, they all sound less good. On the other hand, an indefinite NP in the *by*-phrase such as *everyone* sounds fine. These examples show that compositional aspect plays a role in passivizability, confirming that the passive is an aspect of the type Auxiliary + Participle, reacting to compositional aspect, as Auxiliary + Participle aspects do. See the discussion of odd passives on pp. 35–36. Further research will hopefully bring out the details of exactly what compositional changes affect the passivizability of which verbs, but for the moment we can note that the phenomenon of compositional aspect affecting passivizability really does exist and further research on the passive needs to go down those lines.

48. We can see now why it is that the 2nd participle appears both in the passive and the perfect, such that it used to be called in traditional grammar 'the perfect passive participle'. It is not fortuitous homonymy but grammatically motivated homonymy.

49. I am grateful to Warwick Danks and Cobi Gray for this point.

50. Formal in the descriptive, not generative sense.

51. Syntax in the sense of combinatorial possibilities.

52. The perfect-passive correlation as described here is 100% valid, because it just so happens that all six verbs chosen by Quirk et al. (1985) to exemplify transitive non-passivizability fit the correlation, i.e. do not form a resultative perfect. If one enquires a little deeper into the problem, however, one finds that the correlation is not 100%: some transitive verbs do not form a passive but do form a resultative perfect, and conversely others do form a passive but do not form a resultative perfect. After testing an exhaustive list of non-passivizable transitive verbs in English and German it turned out that the correlation holds about two-thirds of the time – see Beedham (1982: 59–74, 92–113). The reason that the correlation is not 100% is that the passive and the resultative perfect are not exactly synonymous, since one means 'action + state' whilst the other means 'action + result'. They are, nevertheless, sufficiently close in meaning to deliver the syntactic proof that the passive behaves like the perfect, i.e. is an aspect.

53. PF: perfective; IMPF: imperfective; INSTR: instrumental case. Whereas in English the agent is contained in the *by*-phrase, in Russian the agent appears in the instrumental case.

54. Abraham (2000: 154) says:

> Allein diese syntaktische, nahezu ausnahmslose syntaktische Verteilung spricht dafür, daß das Passiv im Russischen aspektuell begründet ist 'this syntactic, almost exceptionless syntactic distribution alone speaks in favour of the fact that the passive in Russian is to be accounted for aspectually'. [my translation]

55. Following Halliday (1976: 161–162) I use the term 'receptive' to mean any sentence in which the subject is patient, for whatever reason, covering *My house was burgled*, *The cakes are selling well*, *The shop closes at 10.00*, *The hat blew into the river*, the Russian reflexive passive, the Latin passive *amor* 'I am loved', etc.

56. Numerous linguists describe the perfective, unlike the imperfective, as being the aspect in Russian which is capable of expressing a result, in the manner of a perfect in those languages like English which have a perfect: see for example Бондарко (1971); Виноградов (1972: 439–440); Isačenko (1972: 717); Wade (1992: 285); Comrie (1976: 63–64, 84–86). (That is not to say, of course, that the Russian perfective formally realizes (or 'encodes') the perfect, merely that it is capable of expressing what in some languages would be expressed with a perfect – see next footnote).

57. Chvany (1985: 22, 1990) is mistaken in her belief that I said in Beedham (1982) that the perfective aspect encodes a perfect of result. I agree with her most emphatically that it does not. To have said that would have been to commit the very error which I am cautioning against in this book, viz. that of transferring meanings encoded (i.e. formally realized) in one language – for example the resultative perfect in English – across to another language, for example Russian and its perfective aspect. The perfective aspect in Russian (viewing an action in its entirety, from beginning to end) is not the same as the perfect in English (past action with current relevance). What I am saying is that the perfective aspect in Russian, because it encompasses the end of an action, provides the pre-requisite necessary for the participial *byt'* passive. In other words the perfective is telic, as Schoorlemmer (1995) puts it, i.e. it contains a *potential* end-point. But it is the participial *byt'* passive not the perfective aspect which means 'action + state' (I did not actually say that either the *byt'* passive or the perfective means 'perfect of result' at all, as Chvany implies, what I said was that the *byt'* passive means 'action + state' and in so doing is the nearest that Russian has to an English perfect of result).

58. The grounds that Helbig (1987:225–226) gives for rejecting this meaning of the *werden*-passive are clearly not sustainable. He writes: "[Es] ist einzuwenden, daß das Passiv nicht gleichzeitig Handlung und Zustand ausdrücken kann, weil beide Begriffe sich ausschließen" (The objection to it is that the passive cannot express action and state simultaneously, because the two concepts are mutually exclusive – my translation). It is true that actions and states are mutually exclusive, i.e. a thing cannot be both an action and a state at the same time, but I am not saying that. What I am saying is that *first* an action occurs, *then* a state arises as a result of it, i.e. the action and state do not happen simultaneously, one follows the other. It is, of course, entirely normal for a single form to express two or even more components of meaning, a pertinent example of which would be the resultative perfect in German, which Helbig himself recognises as expressing an action and the result which ensues from that action (Helbig & Buscha 1989:151–152). Just as there is no contradiction in saying that the German resultative perfect means 'action + result', so there is no contradiction in saying that the *werden*-passive means 'action + state'.

59. Further research will have to look into the details of what lexical/compositional aspect a German intransitive verb must have to form a passive – *tanzen* in *Es wurde getanzt* is atelic, not the expected telic. Although it is a familiar and much used construction very few intransitive verbs can enter into it, and the construction has a nuance of intensity: *Es wurde die ganze Nacht getanzt* 'they danced the whole night long', *Es wurde laut gesungen* 'there was loud singing'. Intensity is a semantic feature which crops us frequently in discussions of aspect, and no doubt it is significant here, in the passive of intransitives.

60. In fact, that the perfect-passive correlation in German is presented here as being as high as 91% valid arises from my confining my examples to those given in grammars of German. As was explained above for English, however, if one enquires a little further into the problem one finds that for German also the correlation holds in about two-thirds of cases – see Beedham (1982:59–74, 92–113). The reasons for the one-third discrepancy have to do with the fact that the *werden*-passive and the resultative perfect are not exactly synonymous, and with the specific lexical semantics of the verbs concerned, as here with *bekommen* and *ergeben*.

61. (71c) is interpretable as a resultative perfect if one imagines a situation in which you are observing someone walking along who suddenly grimaces with pain, from which you as an observer deduce that the leg is now suddenly hurting him. But the result in question is on you as an observer, not on the subject of the sentence. Moreover, without that special context, i.e. in most contexts, *schmerzen* is not open to a resultative interpretation. The same argument applies to *wundern*, *freuen*, and *ärgern* in (72)–(74).

62. Granted that the formal nature of the correlation is diluted by the fact that it requires a semantic interpretation, viz. one has to imagine the c sentences in the perfect as resultative.

63. It is not, however, what generative grammarians mean by a formal generalization. By 'formal' they mean the linguist's assumptions formalized in a notation, i.e. they obtain generalizations by constructing a formal model – see Chapter 4.

64. Syntax in the sense of combinatorial possibilities, not word order.

65. At this point an anonymous reader of an earlier version of this book said (s)he thought that by saying one analysis was wrong and another analysis was right I was undermining my thesis that it all depends on your point of view. If it all depends on your point of view then surely everybody is right? No, that is not how it works, and that is not what I have been saying. Even under structuralism there is still right and wrong, true and false; there is even still 'common sense' (see fn. 20). Within the terms of the passive construction I am saying that if you believe the passive is a voice of the verb (its form) you will believe that actives and passives are synonymous (its meaning), whereas if you believe the passive is an aspect of the verb (its form) you will believe it means 'action + state' (its meaning). There are two different assessments of the form of the passive leading to two different versions of its meaning. In both cases form determines meaning, and that is an important message of this book. But one of the assessments is wrong and one of them is right. The assessment that the passive is a voice of the verb and that actives and passives are synonymous is wrong, whilst the assessment that the passive is an aspect of the verb and that the passive means 'action + state' is right. And that is another important message of this book. In broader terms it is not correct to infer from structuralism that everybody is right, it just depends on your point of view. That would make science, logic and reason impossible – that is the very opposite of what structuralism is about. The structuralist thesis is that the beliefs which individuals hold dearly and often consider to be God-given, objective and irrefutable are actually subjective and based on a particular point of view. The same situation considered from a different perspective leads to very different beliefs. The argument then shifts from beliefs to perspectives. Of course there is still an argument to be had – which perspective is the one we should have or want to have – but at least the argument can now take place on a more rational basis.

66. I have to admit, though, that Schoorlemmer (1995) does just that for Russian (see Beedham 1998a).

67. A reader of an earlier version of this book made the following objection:

> [B's] personal discovery path does not constitute any sort of proof that 'form deter-
> mines meaning and hence language creates the reality that we perceive'. Between,
> on the one hand, the establishment of the validity of a personal discovery path
> from form to meaning in the passive, and, on the other, generalizations about
> the form-meaning relationship and further about language and reality, there is
> an enormous logical gap. . . . whatever path each of us takes in each particular case,
> we [linguists] *discover* and not *create* those meanings.

My answer to this objection is as follows. I have not said that *we* create those meanings, it is form and our attempts to describe those forms which create the meanings. What I discovered was not a meaning but an analysis, the aspectual analysis. It was then that I noticed, and the semantic intuition developed inside me, that the passive means something different to what I used to think it meant, when I believed the voice analysis. The analysis created the meaning (in other words, the grammatical analysis which I ascribed to the phonological form in question), not me.

68. What needs to happen now is that someone else should repeat that experiment, i.e. the experiment of seeing whether the same set of transitive verbs form neither a passive nor a resultative perfect, either for one of the languages already tested, i.e. English and German (it could not be done for Russian because Russian does not have a formal perfect with *have* + 2nd participle), or else for another language which has both a formal passive with *be* + passive participle and a formal perfect with *have* + perfect participle. Such an experiment would confirm or refute the aspectual analysis of the passive.

69. Since, as was said earlier (p. 25 and fn. 30), syntax in the sense of combinatorial possibilities amounts to the structuralist tenet that a language is a system whose units are determined by their place in the system, it follows that to say that syntax is primary is merely another way of saying that a language is a Saussurean system.

70. Works on generative grammar are best divided into *pro* and *contra*. The best and most readable *pro* introduction to generative grammar is undoubtedly Radford (1997); the best *contra* work is undoubtedly Gross (1979). Other works *pro* generative grammar are Chomsky (1995, 1986), Martin et al. (Eds.) (2000), Bresnan (2001), Gazdar et al. (1985), Smith (1999), Cook and Newson (1996), Lyons (1991), Horrocks (1987), Newmeyer (1986). Other works *contra* generative grammar are Lamb (1967), Hall (1987), Putnam (1967), Harman (Ed.) (1982), Koerner (Ed.) (1975), Robinson (1975), Uhlenbeck (1975), Derwing (1973), Lamendella (1969), Bolinger (1960), Hockett (1968), Jakobson (1971), Twaddell (1973), Chafe (1968), Winter (1965), Moore and Carling (1982), Ney (1983), Hervey (1976), Davies (Ed.) (1995). For earlier attempts of mine to debunk the generative myth see Beedham (2001, 1995b, 1986a, 1982: 133–134).

71. Whilst it is true that for many years now generativists have not generated the passive using a single transformation or device but have split it up into several operations, that does not alter the fact that behind the several operations lies the active-passive relation.

72. The resultative perfect means 'action + result', a meaning very similar to the passive meaning 'action + state', therefore it is to be expected that roughly the same verbs will be incompatible with both the resultative perfect and the passive.

73. On the one hand it is comforting that there is at least something right about generative grammar, on the other hand, because the descriptive element lends plausibility to an otherwise nonsensical method it is annoying that the generativists trade on the very approach which they have destroyed.

74. Langacker (1982, 1991: 200–225) puts the passive in relation to the perfect and the progressive, under the heading of aspect. But Langacker the cognitive grammarian will not talk to Bresnan the lexical functionalist or to Schoorlemmer the minimalist about it, and the first two at least are oblivious to my work on the perfect-like qualities of the passive because it is

not framed in a model at all. So we all go on re-inventing the wheel, duplicating analyses, proliferating terminology and missing out on the possibility of potentially fruitful debate and cooperation. We don't even get to disagree with each other, we just ignore each other! This situation, which is endemic to the model-building approach, is deplorable and risible. Generative grammar and the model-building approach have made linguistics a laughing stock of the academic world. They have also led to a decrease in the popularity of linguistics courses in universities, after the initial upsurge of interest in the 1960s and 1970s, so much so that in Britain we are even seeing now the closure of linguistics departments. Generative grammar is unpopular with students because it is unteachable, and it is unteachable because it is untenable. You cannot fool students into believing that a notation is formal and explanatory, or that you can do science by inventing devices which are explanations by fiat.

75. It is from computer programming languages that the generativist phrase 'syntax and semantics' comes. To speak of 'syntax and semantics' is doubtless appropriate to programming languages, but it is not appropriate to natural language, where we speak more properly of 'form and meaning'. Computer languages differ from natural language in not having a morphology – they really do only have a syntax – and in being constructed for communication between man and machine, not between people. That is for starters, even before we consider how on earth anyone can possibly believe that by rendering the grammar of a natural language in computer programming formalisms one has thereby achieved a theory and explanation of natural language.

76. Forbes (1994), Read (1995), and Lemmon (1965) are excellent introductions to formal logic.

77. I.e. generative grammar.

78. A well-known introduction to the methods of science is Chalmers (1999).

79. In this subsection I will use mainly quotations in order to communicate these ideas on physics to the reader straight from the horse's mouth and not via a paraphrase by me.

80. The historical approach is so all-pervasive in modern languages that in academia the phrase 'modern languages' means the literature and language of a modern language studied from a historical perspective. We cannot therefore say 'the descriptive linguistics of a modern language' (with *a*) because that would still imply primarily historical linguistics. To unambiguously exclude the historical we have to say 'the descriptive linguistics of the modern language' (with *the*). An alternative formulation would be 'the descriptive linguistics (non-historical) of a modern language'.

81. Examples (124), (126)–(129), (131)–(137), and (141)–(147) are taken from Quirk et al. (1985: 179–188, 213–214, 228–229).

82. Even the present progressive, associated as it is with a present meaning of the present tense, is more often used with future reference – e.g. *They are leaving tonight* – than with present reference.

83. The analysis of English irregular verbs presented here is based on Beedham (1989, 1994c, 1995–1996, 2006); see also Beedham (2002a). Although the irregular verbs are actually irregular with respect to tense and aspect, we follow the usual practice in abbreviating this fact to saying that they are irregular with respect to tense. For a reaction and some discussion see Tobin (1993: 324–327, 350, 353).

84. The ending which we write as -ed is realized phonetically as [t], [d], or [ɪd], depending on the nature of the preceding sound.

85. On *snuck* see Hogg (1988).

86. Of course, language never stops changing, and some of these forms are reverting to weak conjugation again, others are marked as archaic.

87. There are irregular verbs for which this happens, viz. verbs in the process of switching from strong to weak, and verbs with their own dialect forms in addition to the standard irregular forms. But the point is that there remains a solid residue of less common verbs (in addition to all the common irregular verbs) for which it does not happen, for which speakers do not hesitate. Incidentally, modern Russian has about 400 irregular verbs, and Russian native speakers never 'make mistakes' or have doubts about their irregular forms, except in the case of literally one or two verbs (Бидэм in press). This may be connected with the fact that Russian has very few dialects, despite having a large number of speakers covering a huge territory.

88. He claims the same semantic distinction applies in the Romance languages and in Hebrew.

89. Pinker momentarily considers the question of whether the irregular verbs might have their own, separate meaning, but regrettably and in my view prematurely rejects the notion: "Could we reduce the difference between regular and irregular verbs to a difference in meaning between the two kinds of verbs ...?" (Pinker 1999:42).

90. At this point we see that the overwhelming monosyllabicity of the irregular verbs is more important than we had realised earlier. Monosyllabicity is a phonetic pre-requisite to the salience of the VCs and CVs of the irregular verbs.

91. Historically it is well known that weak verbs in Germanic were derived or secondary (Lockwood 1968:99). However, we are concerned here with the structure of English today, not with its structure at an earlier stage of its development, i.e. we are conducting a synchronic analysis of modern English, in which, following Saussure, we do not allow diachronic considerations to distort our synchronic analysis. This is not so much a profound insight of Saussurean structuralism as plain common sense. Pinker puts it nicely when he says, in the context of a discussion about speakers being aware of the difference between foreign words and native words: "Modern English speakers, of course, do not have a collective memory of the cadences of an ancient Saxon fatherland. There must be a source in a speaker's own experience for the inkling that a word is not of native stock" (Pinker 1999:156).

92. A similar experiment but from a diachronic perspective was carried out for German by Augst (1975a:269–274) with similar results.

93. What needs to happen now is that someone else should repeat my two experiments, i.e. examine the VCs and CVs of the irregular verbs to see if they have a low rate of occurrence on the regular verbs and a high rate of occurrence on monosyllabic function words and grammatical endings, either for one of the languages already investigated, i.e. English, German, and Russian, or else on some other language which has irregular verbs. Such repeated experiments would confirm or refute the findings and analysis presented here.

94. The analysis of German irregular verbs presented here is based on Beedham (1989, 1994a, 1994b, 1994c, 1995–1996, 2005a, Ms); see also Beedham (1995a: 121–143); and Köpcke (1998). For reactions, positive and negative, and discussion see Darski (1999: 25); Durrell (2001).

95. Verbs with both strong and weak forms, e.g. *melken molk/melkte gemolken/gemelkt* 'to milk', were excluded, but verbs with both strong and weak forms according to known criteria were retained, e.g. *erschrecken* (intrans.) 'to be frightened' strong but *erschrecken* (trans.) 'to frighten' weak.

96. Prefixed verbs with a different meaning from the simplex verb were retained, e.g. *verstehen* 'to understand' alongside *stehen* 'to stand'.

97. *Spannen* in West Germanic was strong (see Grimms' *Deutsches Wörterbuch*), but that does not help us here, since we are conducting a synchronic analysis of modern German, not a diachronic study.

98. Most of the stems of the German non-prefixed irregular verbs are monosyllabic, between 84% and 91%, depending on how you count them.

99. All productive verbs in *-it'* undergo consonant interchange, but only in the 1st pers. sing.

100. They are actually infixes, not suffixes, but it is customary in Russian grammar to refer to all morphemes after the stem as suffixes (Russian суффикс).

101. In the case of such verbs for which a vowel is introduced in the present tense, e.g. *vrat' veru* 'to lie', thus giving a VC and CV, the VCs and CVs were retained in brackets. All VCs and CVs arising from consonant alternation were placed in brackets. The brackets indicate that at this stage of the investigation we are not certain whether those VCs and CVs should be included in the counts or not. We will decide later, when we have more information.

102. To return to our discussion which we had with English and German about whether the irregular verbs could be learned exceptions, we see that 13% of Russian simplex verbs in *-at'* and 34% of simplex verbs in *-et'* are irregular. These are even bigger proportions than in English and German, and Russian native speakers never make mistakes or hesitate with them (except for one or two verbs), despite Russian being an inflecting language and the Russian verb having dozens of different forms. Russian shows more clearly than ever that the irregular verb forms are not learned off by heart like new lexical items, rather, there are rules and meanings underlying their formation, if we can only uncover them.

103. At this point I checked on the German endings and found that the same correlation does not apply there, i.e. the inflectional endings of German do not contain a preponderance of strong verb VCs.

104. As already mentioned, a text may be spoken or written.

105. I follow the useful terminological convention under which *langue* has 'sentences', whilst texts have 'utterances'.

106. The counterpart to sentence-grammars is dictionaries. Dictionaries depend on there being a notion of word and word meaning which is independent of specific texts. Do text grammarians want to abolish dictionaries, as well as sentence-grammar? They may well produce different kinds of reference works, e.g. usage dictionaries based on texts, and I welcome that, but the central position of the traditional dictionary based on words and word meanings, abstracting away from specific texts and specific genres, will never alter.

107. Some theme-rheme analysts call what they do 'syntax'. However, this is a metaphorical and very misleading use of the term syntax. Theme-rheme considerations operate at a different level to syntax.

108. Sadly, once again the pendulum has swung too far, and literature in British schools is now severely neglected, to the detriment of language learning.

109. This chapter is based on Beedham (1982:135–146, 1986b, 1989, 1994a, 1994b, 1995a:135–143, 1998b, 2002a); see also Beedham, Danks & Soselia (Eds.) (in prep.); and Danks (in prep.). On exceptions in general see Simon & Wiese (Eds.) (in press).

110. It is confusing when linguists speak of 'form' and it is not clear whether they mean a grammatical form (e.g. Auxiliary + Participle) or a phonological form (e.g. *be* + V-*ed*). The confusion can be avoided by speaking about phonological 'shape' instead of 'form'. It is important to make the distinction because grammatical form is rather abstract and theoretical, whilst phonological forms/shapes are more concrete and more like data, and we want to be clear about what is data and what is theory. Data is the phonological form/shape *be* + V-*ed*. If you say that your data is the grammatical form Auxiliary + Participle you have already introduced, perhaps unwittingly, some theory – perhaps *be* is not an auxiliary, perhaps V-*ed* is not a participle.

111. Jacob Grimm called them 'strong' because they are the original verbs of Proto-Indo-European, and must be very strong, i.e. resilient, to have survived so long. So the term 'strong' is a metaphorical-historical term which says nothing about the synchronic status of these verbs in the modern language.

112. At this point the term 'syntagmatics' is perhaps more appropriate, indicating the combinability not just of words but of morphemes and VCs/CVs.

113. Notice that the requirement that we identify our object of study formally cuts out the reflexive passive with -*sja* 'self ' in Russian, since clearly -*sja* is not an auxiliary + passive participle.

114. It turned out that a perfect-passive correlation for Russian was not possible in the way that it was for English and German, for the simple reason that Russian does not have a perfect (i.e. a construction with *have* + participle); but it was obviously not possible to know this in advance, i.e. to know what the crucial correlation would be. However, this gap was more than compensated for by Russian having an aspectual constraint vis-à-vis the passive which English and German do not have, viz. the fact that the participial passive in Russian is confined on the whole to perfective verbs only.

115. Abraham (2000) ends with the statement:

> Man lernt erst durch das Beispiel und durch die feinfasrige Analyse etwa des Englischen und Russischen (vgl. Beedham 1981!) die Besonderheiten des Deutschen zu erkennen. Erst der über die Einzelsprache hinausgreifende typologische Vergleich vermag die nötigen Einsichten zu erbringen. 'It is only through the example of and through the fine-grained analysis of, for example, English and Russian (cf. Beedham 1981!) that one learns to recognise the special features of German. Only

a typological comparison which reaches out beyond the individual language can deliver the necessary insights.'   (Abraham (2000:163), my translation)

116. A poet is particularly sensitive to the meanings of the words and forms he uses, even if he cannot explicitly state what those meanings are. The linguist, as a scientist, wants to state explicitly what they are. I don't know where the physicist or the chemist gets his hunches from, but I would guess that the linguist gets his hunches from a poet's intuition about the meaning of the words and forms he is investigating, not forgetting that there is something of the poet in all of us.

117. Tobin (1993) emphasises the interlocking of vocabulary and grammar, in contrast to our usual practice of keeping grammars and dictionaries apart. The method of lexical exceptions involves the researcher behaving very much like both a grammarian and a lexicographer.

118. On using informants for grammaticality judgements see Quirk and Svartvik (1966), Cowart (1997).

119. Gross (1975, 1979, 1994)'s method is similar, but he tests every verb of a language for its syntactic behaviour, whereas the method I am advocating homes in on a subset of verbs, defined by their status as exceptions. Cf. also Levin (1993).

120. On the final page of his *A Brief History of Time* the theoretical physicist Stephen Hawking says: "Philosophers reduced the scope of their enquiries so much that Wittgenstein, the most famous philosopher of this century, said, 'The sole remaining task for philosophy is the analysis of language.' What a comedown from the great tradition of philosophy from Aristotle to Kant!" (Hawking 1988:193). (No source is given for the words in single quotation marks, but the Wittgenstein experts I have consulted tell me that it does not ring true as a direct quotation, and is more likely a paraphrase by Hawking of Wittgenstein's views – cf. Wittgenstein (1971:§4.0031), where it is asserted: "All philosophy is a 'critique of language'").

References

Dates of first editions or when first published are given in square brackets.

Abraham, W. (1984). "Transitivity – a variable in concept formation." In J. J. van Baak (Ed.), *Signs of Friendship: To Honour A. G. F. van Holk, Slavist, Linguist, Semiotician* (pp. 1–28). Amsterdam: Rodopi.

———. (1990). "How much of the German tense system is 'aspect' and 'Aktionsart'?" In C. Vetters & W. V. Vandeweghe (Eds.), *Perspectives on aspect and Aktionsart, Belgian Journal of Linguistics* 1991 (6) (pp. 133–150). Bruxelles: Université de Bruxelles.

———. (2000). "Das Perfektpartizip: seine angebliche Passivbedeutung im Deutschen." *Zeitschrift für germanistische Linguistik, 28* (2), 141–166.

Allen, R. L. (1966). *The Verb System of Present-Day American English*. The Hague: Mouton.

Allen, W. S. (1974). *Living English Structure*. London: Longman.

Andersen, P. (1989). "Gibt es Passivmorphologie?" *Linguistische Berichte, 121*, 185–204.

———. (1990). "Typological approaches to the passive." Review of Shibatani (Ed.). (1988). *Journal of Linguistics, 26* (1), 189–202.

———. (1991). *A new look at the passive*. Frankfurt am Main: Peter Lang.

Anderson, J. (2003). "On the structure of names." *Folia Linguistica, XXXVII* (3–4), 357–398.

Augst, G. (1975a). *Untersuchungen zum Morpheminventar der deutschen Gegenwartssprache*. Tübingen: Narr.

———. (1975b). "Wie stark sind die starken Verben? Überlegungen zur Subklassifizierung der nhd. Verben." In G. Augst (Ed.), *Untersuchungen zum Morpheminventar der deutschen Gegenwartssprache* (pp. 231–281). Tübingen: Narr.

Austin, J. L. (1975 [1962]). *How To Do Things With Words*. London: Oxford University Press.

Bartsch, W. (1969). "Über ein System der Verbformen." In *Der Begriff Tempus – eine Ansichtssache?*, Beihefte zur Zeitschrift *Wirkendes Wort, 20* (pp. 90–110). Düsseldorf: Pädagogischer Verlag Schwann.

Baugh, A. C. & Cable, T. (2002 [1951]). *A History of the English Language*. Fifth Edition. London: Routledge.

Beedham, C. (1979). "The perfect passive participle in English." *Zeitschrift für Anglistik und Amerikanistik, 27*, 75–81.

———. (1981). "The passive in English, German and Russian." *Journal of Linguistics, 17*, 319–327.

———. (1982). *The Passive Aspect in English, German and Russian*. Tübingen: Narr.

———. (1983). "Language, indoctrination and nuclear arms." *UEA Papers in Linguistics* [University of East Anglia] *19*, 15–31.

———. (1986a). "Descriptive Versus Generative Grammar: The Passive." *Language Sciences, 8*, 103–128.

———. (1986b). "Form, Meaning and Syntax as Interdependent Hypotheses." *Journal of Literary Semantics, XV*, 3–11.

———. (1987a). "The English passive as an aspect." *Word, 38*, 1–12.

———. (1987b). "Das deutsche Passiv: Aspekt, nicht Genus verbi." *Deutsch als Fremdsprache, 24*, 160–165.

———. (1989). "Investigating Grammar through Lexical Exceptions: tense and irregular verbs in English, German and Russian." *Journal of Literary Semantics, XVIII*, 187–202.

———. (1990). "Das deutsche Passiv: Aspekt, nicht Genus verbi." In W. Bahner, J. Schildt, & D. Viehweger (Eds.), *Proceedings of the Fourteenth International Congress of Linguists, Berlin/GDR, August 10 – August 15, 1987* (pp. 722–725). Berlin: Akademie-Verlag.

———. (1994a). *Die Methode der lexikalischen Ausnahmen: die Untersuchung von syntaktischen Eigenschaften unregelmäßiger Verben*. Duisburg: *L.A.U.D.*, Series A: General & Theoretical Papers, Paper No. 348.

———. (1994b). "Die starken Verben als Analogon zu transitiven, nicht passivfähigen Verben: eine methodologische Skizze." *Deutsch als Fremdsprache, 31*, 163–167.

———. (1994c). "The Role of Consonants in Marking Strong Verb Conjugation in German and English." *Folia Linguistica, XXVIII*, 279–296.

———. (1995a). *German linguistics: An introduction*. München: Iudicium.

———. (1995b). "Critique of Generative Grammar." [Based on English data]. In C. Beedham (Ed.), *German linguistics: An introduction* (pp. 177–223). München: Iudicium.

———. (1995–1996). "Vowel + consonant and consonant + vowel sequences in the strong verbs of German and English." *Cahiers Ferdinand de Saussure, 49*, 139–163.

———. (1998a). "The perfect passive participle in Russian." A review of *Participial passive and aspect in Russian*, by Maaike Schoorlemmer. *Lingua, 105*, 79–94.

———. (1998b). "Structuralism and lexical exceptions in three languages." In B. Caron (Ed.), *Proceedings of the Sixteenth International Congress of Linguists* (*Paris 1997*) Paper No. 0195. Oxford: Elsevier/Pergamon. [CD-ROM].

——— (Ed.). (1999a). *Langue and Parole in Synchronic and Diachronic Perspective: Selected Proceedings of the XXXIst Annual Meeting of the Societas Linguistica Europaea, St. Andrews, 1998*. Oxford: Elsevier/Pergamon.

———. (1999b). "Introduction." In C. Beedham (Ed.), *Langue and Parole in Synchronic and Diachronic Perspective: Selected Proceedings of the XXXIst Annual Meeting of the Societas Linguistica Europaea, St. Andrews, 1998* (pp. 1–15). Oxford: Elsevier/Pergamon.

———. (2001). "A critique of the model-building approach." Review of Schoorlemmer 1995. *Word, 52*, 79–94.

———. (2002a). "Irregularity in language: Saussure versus Chomsky versus Pinker." A review of Words and Rules, by S. Pinker. *Word, 53*, 341–367.

———. (2002b). "Über die Anwendbarkeit der theoretischen Grammatik in pädagogischen Grammatiken: Saussure, das Passiv und starke Verben." In P. Wiesinger (Ed.), *Akten des X. Internationalen Germanistenkongresses Wien 2000: "Zeitenwende – Die Germanistik auf dem Weg vom 20. ins 21. Jahrhundert"* Band 4 (pp. 37–42). Bern: Peter Lang.

. (2005a). "Eine phonotaktische Verbindung zwischen starken Verben und grammatischen Wörtern der deutschen Gegenwartssprache." *Deutsch als Fremdsprache, 42*, 167–172.

——. (2005b). *Language and Meaning: The structural creation of reality.* Amsterdam/ Philadelphia: Benjamins.

——. (2006). "A phonotactic link between strong verbs and function words in English." *Word, 57*.

——. (2007). "La méthode des exceptions lexicales et la relation entre la langue et la réalité." *Res per nomen 2007. Actes du 1er colloque Res per nomen, Reims, du 24 au 26 mai 2007.* Coordinateurs: P. Frath, J. Pauchard, C. Gledhill. Reims: Université de Reims. To be reprinted in P. Frath et al. (Eds.), *Le point sur la référence en langue*, 2008. Reims: Presses Universitaires de Reims.

——. Ms. Eine phonotaktische Verbindung zwischen starken Verben und grammatischen Wörtern der deutschen Gegenwartssprache: Die Daten.

Beedham, C. & Bloor, M. (1989). "English for Computer Science and the Formal Realization of Communicative Functions." *Fachsprache, 11*, 13–24.

Beedham, C., Danks, W. & Soselia, E. (Eds.). (In preparation). *Proceedings of the Conference on the Method of Lexical Exceptions, St Andrews, 2007.*

Bell, A. (1991). *The language of news media.* Oxford: Blackwell.

Benveniste, É. (1971 [1966, in French]). *Problems in General Linguistics.* Translated from the French by M. E. Meek. Coral Gables, Florida: University of Miami Press.

Bergen, B. K. (2004). "The psychological reality of phonaesthemes." *Language, 80*, 290–311.

Berger, P. & Luckmann, T. (1966). *The Social Construction of Reality: A Treatise in the Sociology of Knowledge.* London: Penguin.

Berkeley, G. (1998 [1734]). *A Treatise Concerning the Principles of Human Knowledge.* Ed. by Jonathan Dancy. Oxford: Oxford University Press.

Berlin, B. & Kay, P. (1999 [1969]). *Basic Color Terms; Their Universality and Evolution.* Leland Stanford Junior University, USA: CSLI [Centre for the Study of Language and Information] Publications.

Bhatia, V., Candlin, C. N., & Gotti, M. (Eds.). (2003). *Legal Discourse in Multilingual and Multicultural Contexts.* Bern: Peter Lang.

Bittner, A. (1996). *Starke 'schwache' Verben – schwache 'starke' Verben: deutsche Verbflexion und Natürlichkeit.* Tübingen: Stauffenburg.

Bloor, T. & Bloor, M. (2003 [1995]). *The functional analysis of English: A Hallidayan approach.* 2nd ed. London: Arnold.

Blust, R. A. (1988). *Austronesian Root Theory: An Essay on the Limits of Morphology.* Amsterdam/Philadelphia: Benjamins.

Bolinger, D. (1960). "Linguistic science and linguistic engineering." *Word, 16*, 374–391.

——. (1974). "Meaning and Form." In L. Motz (Ed.), *Transactions of the New York Academy of Sciences*, Series 11, Vol. 36, No. 2 (pp. 218–233).

——. (1975). *Aspects of Language.* Second Edition. New York: Harcourt Brace Jovanovich.

Bresnan, J. (2001). *Lexical-Functional Syntax.* Oxford: Blackwell.

Brinker, K. (2001 [1985]). *Linguistische Textanalyse: Eine Einführung in Grundbegriffe und Methoden.* 5. Aufl. Berlin: Erich Schmidt.

Brinton, L. J. (1988). *The Development of English Aspectual Systems: Aspectualizers and Post-Verbal Particles*. Cambridge: Cambridge University Press.

Bühler, K. (1990 [1934, in German]). *Theory of Language: The Representational Function of Language*. Translated from the German by D. F. Goodwin. Amsterdam/Philadelphia: Benjamins.

Bultmann, R. (1971 [1964, in German]). *The Gospel of John: A Commentary*. Translated from the German by G. R. Beasley-Murray, R. W. N. Hoare & J. K. Riches. Philadelphia: The Westminster Press.

Bybee, J. L. & Moder, C. L. (1983). "Morphological classes as natural categories." *Language, 59*, 251–270.

Bybee, J. L. & Slobin, D. I. (1982). "Rules and schemas in the development and use of the English past tense." *Language, 58*, 265–289.

Carpenter, B. (1992). *The Logic of Typed Feature Structures*. Cambridge Tracts in Theoretical Computer Science no. 32. New York: Cambridge University Press.

Chafe, W. L. (1968). "Idiomaticity as an anomaly in the Chomskyan paradigm." *Foundations of Language, 4*, 109–127.

Chalmers, A. F. (1999 [1976]). *What is this thing called Science?* Third edition. Buckingham: Open University Press.

Chilton, P. (Ed.). (1985). *Language and the Nuclear Arms Debate: Nukespeak Today*. London: Frances Pinter.

Chilton, P. A., Ilyin, M. V., & Mey, J. L. (Eds.). (1998). *Political discourse in transition in Europe 1989–1991*. Amsterdam/Philadelphia: Benjamins.

Chomsky, N. (1957). *Syntactic Structures*. The Hague: Mouton.

——. (1959). Review of Skinner 1957. *Language, 35*, 26–58.

——. (1962). "Explanatory models in linguistics." In E. Nagel, P. Suppes, & A. Tarski (Eds.), *Logic, Methodology and Philosophy of Science: Proceedings of the 1960 International Congress* (pp. 528–550). Stanford, CA: Stanford University Press.

——. (1964). "The logical basis of linguistic theory." In H. G. Lunt (Ed.), *Proceedings of the Ninth International Congress of Linguists, Cambridge, MA, August 27–31, 1962* (pp. 914–1008). Mouton: The Hague.

——. (1965). *Aspects of the Theory of Syntax*. Cambridge, MA: MIT Press.

——. (1982). *Some Concepts and Consequences of the Theory of Government and Binding*. Cambridge, MA: MIT Press.

——. (1986). *Knowledge of Language: Its Nature, Origin, and Use*. New York: Praeger.

——. (1995). *The Minimalist Program*. Cambridge, MA: MIT Press.

Chvany, C. V. (1985). "Foregrounding, 'Transitivity', Saliency (in Sequential and Non-Sequential Prose)." *Essays in Poetics, 10* (2), 1–27.

——. (1987). Review of Beedham 1982. *Folia Slavica, 8* (2 & 3), 352–360.

——. (1990). "Verbal aspect, discourse saliency, and the so-called 'Perfect of result' in modern Russian." In N. B. Thelin (Ed.), *Verbal aspect in discourse* (pp. 213–235). Amsterdam/Philadelphia: Benjamins (reprinted in O. T. Yokoyama & E. Klenin (Eds.). (1996), *Selected Essays of Catherine V. Chvany* (pp. 286–299). Columbus, Ohio: Slavica).

Comrie, B. (1976). *Aspect: An introduction to the study of verbal aspect and related problems*. Cambridge: Cambridge University Press.

——. (1985). *Tense*. Cambridge: Cambridge University Press.

Cook, V. J. (1988). *Chomsky's Universal Grammar: An Introduction*. Oxford: Blackwell.

Cook, V. & Newson, M. (1996 [1988]). *Chomsky's Universal Grammar: An Introduction*. 2nd ed. Oxford: Blackwell.

Coulthard, M. (1985 [1977]). *An Introduction to Discourse Analysis*. New ed. London: Longman.

Cowart, W. (1997). *Experimental Syntax: Applying Objective Methods to Sentence Judgments*. Thousand Oaks, CA: Sage.

Crystal, D. & Davy, D. (1969). *Investigating English style*. London: Longman.

Dagut, M. B. (1985). "A 'teaching grammar' of the passive voice in English." *IRAL* (International Review of Applied Linguistics in Language Teaching) *XXXIII*, 1–12.

Dahl, Ö. (1985). *Tense and aspect systems*. Oxford: Blackwell.

———. (1987). "Comrie's Tense: Review Article." Review of Comrie 1985. *Folia Linguistica*, *XXI*, 489–502.

Daneš, F. (1974). "Functional Sentence Perspective and the Organization of the Text." In F. Daneš (Ed.), *Papers on Functional Sentence Perspective* (pp. 106–128). The Hague: Mouton.

Danks, W. (In preparation). "Modern Standard Arabic: In search of irregularity." In Beedham, Danks & Soselia (Eds.), *Proceedings of the Conference on the Method of Lexical Exceptions, St Andrews, 2007*.

Darski, J. (1999). *Bildung der Verbformen im Standarddeutschen*. Tübingen: Stauffenburg.

Daum, E. & Schenk, W. (1976 [1954]). *Die russischen Verben*. Mit einem Aufsatz zur Syntax und Semantik der Verben des modernen Russisch von Prof. Dr. Rudolf Růžička. Leipzig: Enzyklopädie.

Davies, P. W. (Ed.). (1995). *Alternative Linguistics: Descriptive and Theoretical Modes*. Amsterdam/Philadelphia: Benjamins.

Derwing, B. L. (1973). *Transformational Grammar as a Theory of Language Acquisition: A Study in the Empirical, Conceptual and Methodological Foundations of Contemporary Linguistics*. Cambridge: Cambridge University Press.

Die russische Sprache der Gegenwart. Band 2: Morphologie (1975). Verfaßt von einem Autorenkollektiv unter Leitung von Herbert Mulisch. Leipzig: Enzyklopädie.

Dillon, G. L. (1973). "Perfect and other aspects in a case grammar of English." *Journal of Linguistics*, *9*, 271–279.

Dingle, H. (1931). *Science and Human Experience*. London: Williams & Norgate.

———. (1972). *Science at the Crossroads*. London: Martin Brian & O'Keeffe.

Di Pietro, R. J. (Ed.). (1982). *Linguistics and the Professions: Proceedings of the Second Annual Delaware Symposium on Language Studies*. Norwood, NJ: ABLEX.

Dowty, D. R. (1991 [1979]). *Word Meaning and Montague Grammar: The Semantics of Verbs and Times in Generative Semantics and in Montague's PTQ*. Dordrecht: Kluwer.

Duden: Das Bedeutungswörterbuch. (1985). Duden Bd. 10, 2. Auflage. Mannheim: Dudenverlag.

Duden: Grammatik der deutschen Gegenwartssprache. (1998). Duden Bd. 4, 6. Auflage. Mannheim: Dudenverlag.

Durrell, M. (2001). "Strong verb Ablaut in the West Germanic languages." In S. Watts, J. West, & H.-J. Solms (Eds.), *Zur Verbmorphologie germanischer Sprachen* (pp. 5–18). Tübingen: Niemeyer.

——. (2002 [1971]). *Hammer's German Grammar and Usage*. Fourth Edition. London: Arnold.

Edwards, P. (Ed. in chief). (1967). *The Encyclopedia of Philosophy*. Vols. 1–8. New York: The Macmillan Company & The Free Press.

Encyclopedia of Early Christianity. (1997). E. Ferguson (Ed.). 2 vols. Second Edition. New York: Garland Publishing.

Engels, F. (1987 [1878, in German]). "Anti-Dühring. Herr Eugen Dühring's Revolution in Science." In K. Marx & F. Engels (Eds.), *Collected Works* Vols. 1–49, 1975–2001, Vol. 25 (pp. 1–309). London: Lawrence & Wishart.

Essen, L. (1971). *The Special Theory of Relativity: A Critical Analysis*. Oxford: Clarendon Press.

Fillmore, C. J. (1968). "The Case for Case." In E. Bach & R. T. Harms (Eds.), *Universals in Linguistic Theory* (pp. xii, 1–88). New York: Holt, Rinehart and Winston.

Forbes, G. (1994). *Modern Logic: A Text in Elementary Symbolic Logic*. Oxford: Oxford University Press.

Forsyth, J. (1970). *A grammar of aspect: Usage and meaning in the Russian verb*. Cambridge: Cambridge University Press.

Fowler, R. (1991). *Language in the news: Discourse and ideology in the press*. London: Routledge.

Frath, P. (2007). *Signe, référence et usage*. Paris: Manuscrit-Université.

Freed, A. F. (1979). *The semantics of English aspectual complementation*. Dordrecht: Reidel.

Friedrich, P. (1974). *On Aspect Theory and Homeric Aspect*. International Journal of American Linguistics 40, Memoire 28.

Fries, C. C. (1952). *The Structure of English*. London: Longmans, Green and Company.

——. (1961). "The Bloomfield 'School.'" In C. Mohrmann, A. Sommerfelt, & J. Whatmough (Eds.), *Trends in European and American Linguistics 1930–1960* (pp. 196–224). Utrecht: Spectrum.

Gamkrelidze, T. V. (2006). "The problem of 'L'arbitraire du signe.'" In T. V. Gamkrelidze, *Selected Writings: Linguistic Sign, Typology and Language Reconstruction*, ed. by I. Hajnal (pp. 56–64). Innsbruck: Institut für Sprachen und Literaturen der Universität Innsbruck.

Gamkrelidze, T. V. & Ivanov, V. V. (1995 [1984, in Russian]). *Indo-European and the Indo-Europeans: A Reconstruction and Historical Analysis of a Proto-Language and a Proto-Culture*. Vols. I and II. Translated from the Russian by J. Nichols. Berlin: Mouton de Gruyter.

Gazdar, G., Klein, E., Pullum, G., & Sag, I. (1985). *Generalized Phrase Structure Grammar*. Cambridge, MA: Harvard University Press.

Gelhaus, H. & Latzel, S. (1974). *Studien zum Tempusgebrauch im Deutschen*. Tübingen: Narr.

Gledhill, C. (1999). "Towards a Description of English and French Phraseology." In C. Beedham (Ed.), *Langue and Parole in Synchronic and Diachronic Perspective: Selected Proceedings of the XXXIst Annual Meeting of the Societas Linguistica Europaea, St. Andrews, 1998* (pp. 221–237). Oxford: Elsevier/Pergamon.

——. (2000). *Collocations in Science Writing*. Tübingen: Narr.

Gregory, A. (2006). Review of Beedham 2005b. LINGUIST List 17.3168.

Grimm, J. & W. (1984 [1854]). *Deutsches Wörterbuch Bd. 1–33*. Munich: dtv.

Gross, H. (1998). *Einführung in die germanistische Linguistik.* 3. Aufl. Munich: Iudicium.

Gross, M. (1975). *Méthodes en syntaxe.* Paris: Hermann.

——. (1979). "On the Failure of Generative Grammar." *Language, 55*, 859–885.

——. (1994). "Constructing Lexicon-Grammars." In B. T. S. Atkins & A. Zampolli (Eds.), *Computational Approaches to the Lexicon* (pp. 213–263). Oxford: Oxford University Press.

Grundzüge einer deutschen Grammatik (1980). Von einem Autorenkollektiv unter der Leitung von K. E. Heidolph, W. Flämig und W. Motsch. Berlin: Akademie-Verlag.

Hall, R. A. Jr. (1987). *Linguistics and Pseudo-Linguistics: Selected Essays 1965–1985.* Amsterdam/Philadelphia: Benjamins.

Halliday, M. A. K. (1967a). "Notes on transitivity and theme in English. Part 1." *Journal of Linguistics, 3*, 37–81.

——. (1967b). "Notes on transitivity and theme in English. Part 2." *Journal of Linguistics, 3*, 199–244.

——. (1973). *Explorations in the Functions of Language.* London: Edward Arnold.

——. (1976). *System and function in language.* Selected papers. Ed. by G. R. Kress. London: Oxford University Press.

Halliday, M. A. K. & Hasan, R. (1976). *Cohesion in English.* London: Longman.

Halliday, M. A. K. & Martin, J. R. (1993). *Writing Science: Literacy and Discursive Power.* London: Falmer Press.

Halliday, M. A. K. & Matthiessen, C. (2004 [1985]). *An Introduction to Functional Grammar.* 3rd ed. London: Arnold.

Hardin, C. L. & Maffi, L. (Eds.). (1997). *Color categories in thought and language.* Cambridge: Cambridge University Press.

Harman, G. (Ed.). (1982 [1974]). *On Noam Chomsky: Critical Essays.* Sec   l Edition. Amherst: University of Massachusetts Press.

Hartmann, R. A. (1999). "Gegen eine herkömmliche Interpretation von Saussures *Langage, Langue* und *Parole* – ein Merkzettel." In C. Beedham (Ed.), *Langue and Parole in Synchronic and Diachronic Perspective: Selected Proceedings of the XXXIst Annual Meeting of the Societas Linguistica Europaea, St. Andrews, 1998* (pp. 35–45). Oxford: Elsevier/Pergamon.

Hawking, S. (1988). *A Brief History of Time: From the Big Bang to Black Holes.* Introduction by Carl Sagan. Toronto: Bantam Books.

Helbig, G. (1983). *Geschichte der neueren Sprachwissenschaft.* Opladen: Westdeutscher Verlag.

——. (1987). "Zur Klassifizierung der Konstruktionen mit *sein* + Partizip II (Was ist ein Zustandspassiv?)." In Centre de Recherche en Linguistique Germanique (Nice) (Ed.), *Das Passiv im Deutschen: Akten des Kolloquiums über das Passiv im Deutschen, Nizza 1986* (pp. 215–233). Tübingen: Niemeyer.

Helbig, G. & Buscha, J. (1989 [1970]). *Deutsche Grammatik: Ein Handbuch für den Ausländerunterricht.* Berlin: Langenscheidt/Enzyklopädie.

Hempen, U. (1988). *Die starken Verben im Deutschen und Niederländischen: Diachrone Morphologie.* Tübingen: Niemeyer.

Hervey, S. G. J. (1976). "Is deep structure really necessary?" *Lingua, 39*, 227–239.

Hinton, L., Nichols, J., & Ohala, J. J. (Eds.). (1994). *Sound symbolism.* Cambridge: Cambridge University Press.

Hockett, C. F. (1968). *The State of the Art.* The Hague: Mouton.

Hodge, R. & Kress, G. (1993 [1979]). *Language as Ideology.* 2nd edition. London: Routledge & Kegan Paul.

Hogg, R. M. (1988). "Snuck: The Development of Irregular Preterite Forms." In G. Nixon & J. Honey (Eds.), *An Historic Tongue: Studies in English Linguistics in Memory of Barbara Strang* (pp. 31–40). London: Routledge.

Hopper, P. J. & Thompson, S. A. (1980). "Transitivity in grammar and discourse." *Language,* 56, 251–299.

Hornby, A. S. (1949). "Non-Conclusive Verbs: Some Notes on the Progressive Tenses." *English Language Teaching,* 3, 172–177.

Horrocks, G. (1987). *Generative Grammar.* London: Longman.

Huddleston, R. (1971). *The sentence in written English: A syntactic study based on an analysis of scientific texts.* Cambridge: Cambridge University Press.

Isačenko, A. V. (1962). *Die russische Sprache der Gegenwart. Teil I: Formenlehre.* Halle (Saale): Niemeyer.

———. (1972). Review of A grammar of aspect: Usage and meaning in the Russian verb, by J. Forsyth. *Language,* 48, 715–719.

Jakobson, R. (1971). "Boas' view of grammatical meaning." In R. Jakobson (Ed.), *Selected Writings,* Vol. II (pp. 489–496). The Hague: Mouton.

Janssen, T. & Redeker, G. (Eds.). (1999). *Cognitive Linguistics: Foundations, Scope and Methodology.* Berlin: Mouton.

Jespersen, O. (1924). *The Philosophy of Grammar.* London: George Allen & Unwin.

———. (1933). *Essentials of English Grammar.* London: George Allen & Unwin.

Kabakčiev, K. (2000). *Aspect in English: A "Common-Sense" View of the Interplay between Verbal and Nominal Referents.* Dordrecht: Kluwer.

Kant, I. (1933 [1781, in German]). *Critique of Pure Reason.* Transl. from the German by N. K. Smith. 2nd ed. London: Macmillan.

Keenan, E. L. (1976). "Towards a Universal Definition of 'Subject.'" In C. N. Li (Ed.), *Subject and Topic* (pp. 303–333). New York: Academic Press.

Keller, R. E. (1978). *The German Language.* London: Faber and Faber.

Kennedy, G. D. (1998). *An introduction to corpus linguistics.* London: Longman.

Klein, W. (2000). "An analysis of the German perfekt." *Language,* 76, 358–382.

Kleines Wörterbuch sprachwissenschaftlicher Termini (1975). Autoren: B. Bartschat, R. Conrad, W. Heinemann, G. Richter, A. Steube. Leipzig: Bibliographisches Institut.

Koerner, E. F. K. (Ed.). (1975). *The Transformational-Generative Paradigm and Modern Linguistic Theory.* Amsterdam/Philadelphia: Benjamins.

———. (1999). "Three Saussures – One 'Structuralist' *Avant la Lettre.*" In C. Beedham (Ed.), *Langue and Parole in Synchronic and Diachronic Perspective: Selected Proceedings of the XXXIst Annual Meeting of the Societas Linguistica Europaea,* St. Andrews, 1998 (pp. 19–34). Oxford: Elsevier/Pergamon.

Köpcke, K.-M. (1998). "Prototypisch starke und schwache Verben der deutschen Gegenwartssprache." In M. Butt & N. Fuhrhop (Hg.), *Variation und Stabilität in der Wortstruktur,* Sonderheft Germanistische Linguistik 141–142 (pp. 45–60).

Kotin, M. (1995). "Probleme der Beschreibung der deutschen Verbalmorphologie: Zur Herausbildung der grammatischen Kategorie des Genus verbi." *Deutsche Sprache, 23*, 61–72.

——. (1997). "Die analytischen Formen und Fügungen im deutschen Verbalsystem: Herausbildung und Status (unter Berücksichtigung des Gotischen)." *Sprachwissenschaft, 22* (4), 479–500.

——. (1998). *Die Herausbildung der grammatischen Kategorie des Genus verbi im Deutschen. Eine historische Studie zu den Vorstufen und zur Entstehung des deutschen Passiv-Paradigmas.* Hamburg: Buske.

Lakoff, G. (1970). *Irregularity in Syntax*. New York: Holt, Rinehart and Winston.

Lakoff, R. (1970). "Tense and its Relation to Participants." *Language, 46*, 838–849.

Lamb, S. M. (1966). *Outline of stratificational grammar*. Washington: Georgetown University Press.

——. (1967). Review of Chomsky 1964 and 1965. *American Anthropologist, 69*, 411–415.

Lamendella, J. (1969). "On the Irrelevance of Transformational Grammar to Second Language Pedagogy." *Language Learning, 19*, 255–270.

Langacker, R. W. (1982). "Space grammar, analysability, and the English passive." *Language, 58*, 22–80.

——. (1987). *Foundations of Cognitive Grammar. Vol. I: Theoretical Prerequisites.* Stanford, California: Stanford University Press.

——. (1991). *Foundations of Cognitive Grammar. Vol. II: Descriptive Application.* Stanford, California: Stanford University Press.

Leech, G. N. (1971). *Meaning and the English Verb*. London: Longman.

Leech, G. & Svartvik, J. (1975). *A Communicative Grammar of English*. London: Longman.

Leiss, E. (1985). "Zur Entstehung des neuhochdeutschen analytischen Futurs." *Sprachwissenschaft, 10*, 250–273.

——. (1992). *Die Verbalkategorien des Deutschen: Ein Beitrag zur Theorie der sprachlichen Kategorisierung.* Berlin: de Gruyter.

Lemmon, E. J. (1965). *Beginning Logic*. Wokingham: Van Nostrand Reinhold.

Lenneberg, E. H. (1967). *Biological Foundations of Language*. New York: John Wiley & Sons.

Levin, B. (1993). *English Verb Classes and Alternations: A Preliminary Investigation*. Chicago: University of Chicago Press.

Levin, B. & Rappaport, M. (1989). "An approach to unaccusative mismatches." *Proceedings of NELS, 19*, 314–328. Amherst, MA: GLSA.

Levinson, S. C. (1983). *Pragmatics*. Cambridge: Cambridge University Press.

Leys, O. (1989). "Aspekt und Rektion räumlicher Präpositionen." *Deutsche Sprache, 17* (2), 97–113.

Lockwood, W. B. (1968). *Historical German Syntax*. Oxford: Clarendon.

Lyons, J. (1968). *Introduction to Theoretical Linguistics*. Cambridge: Cambridge University Press.

——. (1977). *Semantics*. Vols. 1 and 2. Cambridge: Cambridge University Press.

——. (1991 [1970]). *Chomsky*. Third Edition. Fontana Modern Masters. Hammersmith: Fontana.

Marchand, H. (1969). *The Categories and Types of Present-Day English Word-Formation: A Synchronic-Diachronic Approach*. Second edition. Munich: C. H. Beck'sche Verlagsbuchhandlung.

Martin, R., Michaels, D., & Uriagereka, J. (Eds.). (2000). *Step by Step: Essays on Minimalist Syntax in Honour of Howard Lasnik*. Cambridge, MA: MIT Press.

Marx, K. (1976 [1847, in French]). "The Poverty of Philosophy. Answer to the Philosophy of Poverty by M. Proudhon." In K. Marx & F. Engels, *Collected Works* Vols. 1–49, 1975–2001, Vol. 6 (pp. 105–212). London: Lawrence & Wishart.

Mater, E. (1966). *Deutsche Verben. Bd. 1: Alphabetisches Gesamtverzeichnis*. Leipzig: Bibliographisches Institut.

——. (1967). *Deutsche Verben. Bd. 2: Grundwörter und deren Zusammensetzungen*. Leipzig: Bibliographisches Institut.

McCawley, J. D. (1968). "Lexical Insertion in a Transformational Grammar without Deep Structure." *Papers from the Fourth Regional Meeting of the Chicago Linguistic Society*, 71–80. Reprinted in J. D. McCawley (Ed.), *Grammar and Meaning: Papers on Syntactic and Semantic Topics* (pp. 155–166). New York: Academic Press.

——. (1971). "Tense and Time Reference in English." In C. J. Fillmore & D. T. Langendoen (Eds.), *Studies in Linguistic Semantics* (pp. 97–113). New York: Holt, Rinehart & Winston.

——. (1974). "English as a VSO language." In P. A. M. Seuren (Ed.), *Semantic Syntax* (pp. 75–95). London: Oxford University Press.

——. (1982). *Thirty Million Theories of Grammar*. Chicago: University of Chicago Press.

McClelland, J. L. & Rumelhart, D. E. (Eds.). (1986). *Parallel Distributed Processing: Explorations in the Microstructure of Cognition. Volume 2: Psychological and Biological Models*. Cambridge, MA: MIT Press.

McClelland, J. L., Rumelhart, D. E., & Hinton, G. E. (1986). "The Appeal of Parallel Distributed Processing." In D. E. Rumelhart & J. L. McClelland (Eds.), *Parallel Distributed Processing: Explorations in the Microstructure of Cognition. Volume 1: Foundations* (pp. 3–44). Cambridge, MA: MIT Press.

McCoard, R. W. (1978). *The English perfect: Tense-choice and pragmatic inferences*. The Netherlands: North Holland.

Miyahara, F. Ms. What time does tense denote? The status of tense in the English verb system. Paper given at the *XVIth International Congress of Linguists*, Paris 1997.

Moore, T. & Carling, C. (1982). *Understanding Language: Towards a Post-Chomskyan Linguistics*. London: Macmillan.

Mueller, G. E. (1958). "The Hegel legend of 'thesis-antithesis-synthesis'." *Journal of the History of Ideas, XIX*, 411–414.

Multilingua: Journal of Cross-Cultural and Interlanguage Communication. Vol. 7, Nos. 1/2. 1988. Special Issue: Discourse of the nuclear arms debate.

Newman, B. M. & Nida, E. A. (1980). *A Translator's Handbook on The Gospel of John*. London: United Bible Societies.

Newmeyer, F. J. (1986 [1980]). *Linguistic Theory in America*. Second Edition. San Diego: Academic Press.

Ney, J. W. (1983). Review of Chomsky 1982. *Language Sciences, 5*, 219–232.

Niemeier, S. & Dirven, R. (Eds.). (2000). *Evidence for Linguistic Relativity*. Amsterdam/ Philadelphia: Benjamins.

Nordenson, H. (1969). *Relativity: Time and Reality*. London: George Allen and Unwin.

OALD. See *Oxford Advanced Learner's Dictionary of Current English*.

Orwell, G. (1989 [1949]). *Nineteen Eighty-Four*. London: Penguin.

Oxford Advanced Learner's Dictionary of Current English (1989). Ed. by A. S. Hornby. Fourth Edition. Chief Editor: A. P. Cowie. Oxford: Oxford University Press [cited in the text as OALD].

Palmer, F. R. (1974). *The English Verb*. 2nd ed. London: Longman.

Parsons, T. (1990). *Events in the Semantics of English: A Study in Subatomic Semantics*. Cambridge, MA: MIT Press.

Pereira, F. & Shieber, S. (1987). *PROLOG and Natural Language Analysis*. CSLI Lecture Notes no. 10. Stanford: Center for the Study of Language and Information (distributed by the University of Chicago Press).

Pinker, S. (1984). *Language Learnability and Language Development*. Cambridge, MA: Harvard University Press.

——. (1994). *The Language Instinct: The New Science of Language and Mind*. London: Penguin.

——. (1999). *Words and Rules: The Ingredients of Language*. London: Weidenfeld & Nicolson.

Pollard, C. & Sag, I. A. (1987). *Information-Based Syntax and Semantics*. Stanford: CSLI [Centre for the Study of Language and Information].

——. (1994). *Head-Driven Phrase Structure Grammar*. Chicago: University of Chicago Press.

Poupynin, Y. A. (1996). "Central and Peripheral Connections between Aspect and Voice in Russian." *Folia Linguistica, XXX*, 129–140.

——. (1999). *Interaction between Aspect and Voice in Russian*. München: Lincom Europa. [Translation of Пупынин 1980].

Pulkina, I. & Zakhava-Nekrasova, E. [No date given; c. 1960]. *Russian (A Practical Grammar with Exercises)*. Moscow: Progress.

Pullum, G. K. (1991). "The great Eskimo vocabulary hoax." In G. K. Pullum (Ed.), *The Great Eskimo Vocabulary Hoax and Other Irreverent Essays on the Study of Language* (pp. 159–171). Chicago: University of Chicago Press.

Putnam, H. (1967). "The 'Innateness Hypothesis' and Explanatory Models in Linguistics." *Synthese, 17*, 12–22.

Pütz, M. & Verspoor, M. H. (Eds.). (2000). *Explorations in Linguistic Relativity*. Amsterdam/Philadelphia: Benjamins.

Quirk, R. (1970). "Aspect and Variant Inflection in English Verbs." *Language, 46*, 300–311.

Quirk, R., Greenbaum, S., Leech, G., & Svartvik, J. (1972). *A Grammar of Contemporary English*. London: Longman.

Quirk, R., Greenbaum, S., Leech, G., & Svartvik, J. (1985). *A Comprehensive Grammar of the English Language*. London: Longman.

Quirk, R. & Svartvik, J. (1966). *Investigating Linguistic Acceptability*. The Hague: Mouton de Gruyter.

Radford, A. (1997). *Syntactic theory and the structure of English: A minimalist approach*. Cambridge: Cambridge University Press.

Read, S. (1995). *Thinking About Logic: An Introduction to the Philosophy of Logic.* Oxford: Oxford University Press.

Robins, R. H. (1967). *A Short History of Linguistics.* London: Longman.

——. (1980). *General Linguistics. An Introductory Survey.* Third Edition. London: Longman.

——. (1999). "Key Dates in Twentieth Century Linguistics." In C. Beedham (Ed.), *Langue and Parole in Synchronic and Diachronic Perspective: Selected Proceedings of the XXXIst Annual Meeting of the Societas Linguistica Europaea, St. Andrews, 1998* (pp. 63–72). Oxford: Elsevier/Pergamon.

Robinson, I. (1975). *The New Grammarians' Funeral: A critique of Noam Chomsky's linguistics.* Cambridge: Cambridge University Press.

Rumelhart, D. E. & McClelland, J. L. (Eds.). (1986a). *Parallel Distributed Processing: Explorations in the Microstructure of Cognition. Volume 1: Foundations.* Cambridge, MA: MIT Press.

Rumelhart, D. E. & McClelland, J. L. (1986b). "On Learning the Past Tenses of English Verbs." In J. L. McClelland & D. E. Rumelhart (Eds.), *Parallel Distributed Processing: Explorations in the Microstructure of Cognition. Volume 2: Psychological and Biological Models* (pp. 216–271). Cambridge, MA: MIT Press.

Růžička, R. (1967). "Korrelation und Transformation." In *To Honor Roman Jakobson* (pp. 1709–1733). The Hague: Mouton.

Salkie, R. (1987). Review of Dahl 1985. *Lingua, 72* (1), 79–99.

Sampson, G. (1987). Review of Rumelhart and McClelland (Eds.) 1986a/McClelland and Rumelhart (Eds.) 1986. *Language, 63,* 871–886.

Sapir, E. (1949). *Selected Writings of Edward Sapir in Language, Culture, and Personality.* D. G. Mandelbaum (Ed.). London: Cambridge University Press.

Saussure, F. de (1972 [1916]). *Cours de linguistique générale.* Édition critique préparée par Tullio de Mauro. Paris: Payot.

——. (1983 [1916, in French]). *Course in General Linguistics.* Ed. by Charles Bally & A. Sechehaye. Translated from the French and annotated by R. Harris. London: Duckworth.

Schoenthal, G. (1976). *Das Passiv in der deutschen Standardsprache: Darstellung in der neueren Grammatiktheorie und Verwendung in Texten gesprochener Sprache.* München: Hueber.

Schoorlemmer, M. (1995). *Participial Passive and Aspect in Russian.* OTS Dissertation Series. Utrecht: OTS [Onderzoeksinstituut voor Taal en Spraak/Research Institute for Language and Speech].

Searle, J. R. (1969). *Speech Acts: An Essay in the Philosophy of Language.* Cambridge: Cambridge University Press.

Shibatani, M. (Ed.). (1988). *Passive and voice.* Amsterdam/Philadelphia: Benjamins.

Siewierska, A. (1984). *The Passive: A Comparative Linguistic Analysis.* London: Croom Helm.

Simon, H. & Wiese, H. (Eds.). (In press). *Expecting the Unexpected – Exceptions in Grammar.* Berlin/New York: Mouton de Gruyter.

Skinner, B.F. (1957). *Verbal Behavior.* New York: Appleton-Century-Crofts.

Smith, N. (1999). *Chomsky: Ideas and Ideals.* Cambridge: Cambridge University Press.

Sowell, T. (1985). *Marxism: Philosophy and Economics.* London: Allen & Unwin.

Stein, G. (1979). *Studies in the Function of the Passive.* Tübingen: Narr.

Stevenson, L. (1981). "Three Kinds of Transcendental Idealism." In G. Funke (Ed.), *Akten des 5. Internationalen Kant-Kongresses, Mainz 4–8 April 1981*, I. 2 (pp. 1050–1059). Bonn: Bouvier Verlag Herbert Grundmann.

——. (1982). "Wittgenstein's Transcendental Deduction and Kant's Private Language Argument." *Kant-Studien, 73*, 321–337.

Stubbs, M. (1996). *Text and Corpus Analysis: Computer-assisted Studies of Language and Culture*. Oxford: Blackwell.

Svartvik, J. (1966). *On voice in the English verb*. The Hague: Mouton.

Swales, J. (1990). *Genre Analysis: English in Academic and Research Settings*. Cambridge: Cambridge University Press.

Terasawa, J. (1984). "The function of the passive in Old English and present-day English." *Studies in English Literature* (Tokyo) *61* (2), 287–304.

Theocharis, T. & Psimopoulos, M. (1987). "Where science has gone wrong." *Nature, 329*, 595–598.

Tobin, Y. (1989). "Space, time and point-of-view in the Modern Hebrew verb." In Y. Tobin (Ed.), *From Sign to Text: A Semiotic View of Communication* (pp. 61–92). Amsterdam/Philadelphia: Benjamins.

——. (1990). *Semiotics and Linguistics*. London: Longman.

——. (1993). *Aspect in the English Verb: Process and Result in Language*. London: Longman.

——. (1994). *Invariance, Markedness and Distinctive Feature Analysis: A Contrastive Study of Sign Systems in English and Hebrew*. Amsterdam/Philadelphia: Benjamins.

Townsend, C. E. (1975). *Russian Word-Formation*. Cambridge, MA: Slavica.

Twaddell, W. F. (1973). "Straw Men and Pied Pipers." *Foreign Language Annals, 6*, 317–329.

Uhlenbeck, E. M. (1975). *Critical comments on transformational-generative grammar 1962–1972*. The Hague: Smits.

Van Langendonck, W. (1982). "Passive in a semantic-syntactic dependency network." *Communication & Cognition, 15* (3/4), 407–428.

Verkuyl, H. J. (1972). *On the compositional nature of the aspects*. Foundations of Language, Supplementary Series, Volume 15.

——. (1993). *A Theory of Aspectuality: The Interaction between Temporal and Atemporal Structure*. Cambridge: Cambridge University Press.

Wade, T. (1992). *A Comprehensive Russian Grammar*. Oxford: Blackwell.

Waterman, J. T. (1966). *A History of the German Language*. Seattle: University of Washington Press.

Watkins, C. (1962). "The origin of the *t*-preterite." *Eriu, 19*, 25–46.

Whorf, B. L. (1956). *Language, Thought, and Reality: Selected Writings of Benjamin Lee Whorf*. J. B. Carroll (Ed.). Cambridge, MA: MIT Press.

Wickelgren, W. A. (1969). "Context-sensitive coding, associative memory, and serial order in (speech) behavior." *Psychological Review, 76*, 1–15.

Widdowson, H. C. (1978). *Teaching Language as Communication*. London: Oxford University Press.

Wilding, J. M. (1978). "Indefinacy as Hyper-Case for the Agentive By-phrase in English Full Passives." In W. Dressler & W. Meid (Eds.), *Proceedings of the Twelfth International Congress of Linguists, Vienna, August 28 – September 2, 1977* (pp. 416–419). Innsbruck: Innsbrucker Beiträge zur Sprachwissenschaft.

Wilkins, W. (1980). "Adjacency and Variables in Syntactic Transformations." *Linguistic Inquiry, 11*, 709–758.

Winford, D. (1988). "Stativity and other aspects of the creole passive." *Lingua, 76* (4), 271–297.

Winter, W. (1965). "Transforms without kernels?" *Language, 41*, 484–489.

Wittgenstein, L. (1971 [1921]). *Tractatus logico-philosophicus*. The German text of Ludwig Wittgenstein's *Logisch-philosophische Abhandlung*, with a new edition of the translation by D. F. Pears & B. F. McGuinness. 2nd ed. London: Routledge & Kegan Paul.

Wolkonsky, C. A. & Poltoratzky, M. A. (1961). *Handbook of Russian Roots*. New York: Columbia University Press.

Zandvoort, R. W. (1962). *A Handbook of English Grammar*. London: Longmans.

Zifonun, G., Hoffmann, L., Strecker, B. et al. (1997). *Grammatik der deutschen Sprache*. Bd. 1–3. Schriften des Instituts für deutsche Sprache 7. Berlin: de Gruyter.

Бидэм, Кр. (1988). "Видовое значение конструкции «быть + страдательное причастие»." *Вопросы Языкознания, 6*, 63–68.

——. In press. "Последовательности гласный + согласный в простых непродуктивных глаголах на *-ать/-ять* и *-еть* в русском языке." *Язык и Речевая Деятельность*.

Бондарко, А. В. (1971). *Вид и время русского глагола*. Москва: Просвещение.

Виноградов, В. В. (1972 [1947]). *Русский язык (грамматическое учение о слове)*. 2ое изд. Москва: Высшая Школа.

Грамматика русского языка. Том I: Фонетика и морфология (1960). Москва: Академия Наук.

Зализняк, А. А. (1977). *Грамматический словарь русского языка*. Москва: Русский Язык.

Морковкин, В. В. (1997). *Словарь структурных слов русского языка*. Москва: Лазурь.

Обратный словарь русского языка (1974). Москва: Советская Энциклопедия.

Пупынин, Ю. А. (1980). *Функционирование видов русского глагола в пассивных конструкциях (К проблеме взаимосвязей категорий вида и залога)*. Канд. дисс., Ленинград. [Translation into English: Poupynin 1999].

Русская грамматика, т. I. (1980). Москва: Наука.

Appendix I

VCs of English strong and modal verbs (VCs of archaic forms in brackets; complete list from our data)
Ø zero consonant

æt	(em)	iːt	əʊz
æd	en	iːd	əʊl
ætʃ	ent	iːk	əʊld
æv	end	iːtʃ	əʊØ
æz	el	iːv	ʊt
æm	eld	iːz	ʊd
æn	eØ	(iːm)	ʊk
ænd	eɪk	iːn	ʊØ
æŋ	eɪv	iːl	ʌt
æŋk	eɪm	iːØ	ʌk
æl	eɪØ	ɪə(r)	ʌg
aɪt	eə(r)	ɒt	ʌst
aɪd	ɪt	ɒd	ʌm
aɪk	ɪd	ɒs	ʌn
aɪv	ɪk	ɒst	ʌŋ
aɪz	ɪg	ɒz	ʌŋk
aɪn	ɪv	ɒn	uːt
aɪnd	ɪz	(ɔɪl)	(uːv)
aɪØ	ɪm	ɔːt	uːz
aʊnd	ɪn	ɔːl	uːØ
aːst	ɪŋ	ɔː(r)	juːØ
aː(r)	ɪŋk	ɔːØ	ɜːt
ep	ɪl	əʊt	ɜːd
et	ɪlt	əʊd	ɜːst
ed	ɪld	əʊk	(ɜːn)
ef	iːp	əʊv	ɜː(r)

A total of 104 VCs from 159 verbs

Appendix II

English monosyllabic function words, ordered by part of speech, with a strong verb VC and without a strong verb VC (taken from the OALD, using its categorisation; complete list from our data).

with a strong verb VC	without a strong verb VC
Prepositions	
as	down
at	ex
bar	from
but	less
by	off
cum	plus
ere	since
for	up
gone	worth
in	9
like	
near	
nigh	
o'er	
on	
past	
per	
pro	
qua	
re	
round	
save	
than	
through	
till	
to	
26	

Conjunctions

and	how
as	if
but	lest
cos	now
ere	since
for	while
like	6
nor	
or	
save	
so	
than	
that	
though	
till	
when	
where	
yet	
18	

Verb particles

by	back
for	down
in	off
near	out
on	up
past	5
round	
through	
to	
9	

Personal pronouns

he	thou
her	us
him	2
I	
it	
me	
she	
thee	
them	
they	
we	
ye	
you	
13	

Possessive pronouns

mine	0
thine	
2	

Interrogative pronouns

who	whom
whose	1
2	

Indefinite pronouns

none	0
one	
2	

Determiners

that	own
1	such
	this
	3

Possessive determiners

her	its
his	our [aʊə(r)]
my	2
our [aː(r)]	
their	
your	
6	

Indefinite determiners

all	least
each	less
few	most
more	much
4	4

Interrogative determiners

what	which
1	1

Negative determiners

no	
1	0

Definite article

the [ði:]	0
1	

Indefinite articles

a [eɪ]	0
an	
2	

Contractions

he'd	I'll
he'll	it's
he's	they'd
I'd	they'll
I've	who'd
she'd	who'll
she'll	you'd
she's	you'll
they're	8
they've	
we'd	
we'll	
we're	
we've	
who's	
who've	
you've	
17	

Glossary of aspect terms

Aktionsart. See 'lexical aspect'.

aspect. A grammatical category which gives expression to the way in which an action or event passes through time, e.g. as an on-going or continuous activity (in English the progressive with *be* + V-*ing*), as a past action with current relevance (in English the perfect with *have* + V-*ed*), a repeated action, a single action, etc. In line with the Saussurean dictum that every language creates its own categories in its own unique system, every language has its own unique aspects, though there may be similarities between them, e.g. the English progressive, the Russian imperfective and the French *imparfait* are all similar but have important differences in their meaning and use. For this reason it is essential that our approach to aspect be formal, not semantic. In other words, it makes no sense to speak for example of an aspect called 'perfective' without specifying on what formal basis the term perfective is used in the language concerned. Aspect is realized formally in three ways: Auxiliary + Participle, e.g. the perfect in English; lexical aspect, e.g. imperfective and perfective in Russian; compositional aspect, i.e. the contribution that subject, object and adverbials make to the overall aspect of a sentence, cf. *A guest arrived* (telic) vs. *The guests arrived* (atelic). Aspect is to be distinguished from tense, the other main grammatical category which expresses time relations.

atelic. See 'telic/atelic'.

aterminative. See 'telic/atelic'.

Auxiliary + Participle aspect. One of the three formal realizations of aspect. English has three Auxiliary + Participle aspects: the progressive (*be* + V-*ing*), the perfect (*have* + V-*ed*), and the passive (*be* + V-*ed*).

bounded/unbounded. See 'telic/atelic'.

compositional aspect. One of the three formal realizations of aspect. Compositional aspect is the overall aspect of a sentence, as determined by the verb, the subject, the object, and any adverbials in it. It used to be thought that the verb alone determines the aspect of a sentence (and that a verb has an aspect which it expresses wherever it goes, i.e. in whatever sentence it appears), but it is now widely recognised that the subject, object and adverbials also determine the aspect of a sentence. Is the verb *to sing* telic or atelic (i.e. does its meaning involve an inherent end-point)? The question is meaningless, because the answer depends on what noun phrases and adverbials appear with it. A test for telic aspect is to put a verb/sentence into the progressive, imagine the action thus expressed interrupted, and to ask oneself if the action expressed has been carried out. If the action has been carried out the sentence is atelic, if not it is telic. By this criterion *John is singing* is atelic, *John is singing a song* is telic, *John is singing songs* is atelic, and *John is singing five songs* is telic again. In this example the presence or absence of an object, and the nature of the object, whether singular or plural, definite or indefinite, is dictating the overall compositional aspect of the sentence. To return to the question about the verb *to sing*, *to sing* does not have a definitive lexical aspect at all, it only has what might be called a crypto-aspect which only manifests itself in combination with other items in a sentence.

conclusive/non-conclusive. See 'telic/atelic'.

continuous perfect. A sub-meaning or use of the perfect in which the perfect expresses an action or event in the past whose effects last into the present, as in *I have lived in St. Andrews for 20 years* (and I still live there).

durational adverb. An adverbial phrase which expresses an extended period of time or duration, e.g. *for hours, all day*.

durative. 'Durative' is a term loosely used by linguists to refer to any action, event or activity which extends over a long period of time. The term 'durative' is a vague and semantically-oriented term which indicates loosely the meaning of the progressive in English, the imperfective in Russian, the *imparfait* in French, etc.

experiential perfect. A sub-meaning of the perfect in which the perfect expresses the fact that the subject has experienced the action referred to at some point in the past, as in *He has lived in Scotland*.

imperfective/perfective. Lexical aspects of Russian. Every verb of Russian has an imperfective and a perfective form. The imperfective verb views an action or event from within, as an on-going activity, whereas the perfective verb views an action or event from the outside, as a single event, from its beginning to its end. Imperfective versus perfective aspect in Russian is morphologically marked: most imperfective verbs are simplex, most perfective verbs have a prefix, e.g. *pisat'* 'to write' (imperfective), *napisat'* 'to write' (perfective). It is a mistake to use the term '(im)perfective' for a language other than Russian without specifying on what formal basis in that language one is using the term and implying that '(im)perfective' has the same meaning in that language as in Russian. Inevitably the meaning of (im)perfective in that language will differ – if only slightly – from the meaning of (im)perfective in Russian. However, in the literature on aspect one frequently encounters the terms imperfective/perfective (sometimes the terms durative/perfective) used on languages other than Russian, used to mean something approximating to an action/event extended in time versus a (single) brief or momentary action/event.

lexical aspect (or **Aktionsart**). One of the three formal realizations of aspect. Lexical aspect is most obvious in the Slav languages, because it is morphologically marked there. In Russian, for example, every verb has an imperfective form and a perfective form. The imperfective form of the verb is usually simplex, and to form a perfective one adds a prefix, e.g. *pisat'* 'to write' (imperfective) vs. *napisat'* 'to write' (perfective). Although in English lexical aspect is not morphologically marked on the verb it is syntactically there (syntax in the sense of combinatorial possibilities (not word order)) in the structure of English and can be discerned syntactically. The main syntactic tests for lexical aspect have to do with how a verb reacts to Auxiliary + Participle aspects. For example, those verbs in English which cannot combine with the progressive, e.g. *to know* (cf. **She is knowing the truth*), behave like that because of their lexical aspect. The lexical aspect in question is usually called 'stative', and it is true that the verbs in question generally express a state. But it is crucial that one adopts a formal not semantic approach to lexical aspect, and that one does not rely solely on semantic criteria to identify lexical aspect. If one did, one would say that the verb *to sit*, for example, is stative, and indeed it is semantically, but it *is* compatible with the progressive – cf. *She is sitting on a chair*. Thus what we are really saying is that 'stative' verbs are actually –[progressive] verbs, most of which are stative in meaning.

Lexical aspect in languages like English which do not have morphologically marked lexical aspect is a crypto-aspect, i.e. it only manifests itself in combination with noun phrases and adverbials in the compositional aspect of sentences. In other words, a verb like *to sing* does not have an aspect which it carries with it into every sentence in which it appears; rather, it depends on the sentence and the noun phrases and adverbials in it which aspect one ascribes to the verb, or better to the sentence. See 'compositional aspect'.

mutative. A lexical aspect. Mutative verbs express a change of location or state. The syntactic test for mutative in English is that such verbs allow attributive use of their 2nd participle, so that *to escape* and *to vanish* are mutative, cf. *an escaped prisoner, the vanished treasure,* but *to read* and *to like* are not mutative, cf. **the read book, *the liked film.*

non-conclusive. See 'telic/atelic'.

passive. An aspect of the type Auxiliary + Participle, formed in English from *be* + V-*ed,* as in *My house was burgled last night.* It expresses an action/event together with the new state which arises on the subject as a result of that action/event, i.e. its meaning is 'action + state'. A consequence of this meaning is that in passives the subject is semantically speaking patient. For a verb to form a passive it must have the lexical aspect telic, i.e. there must be an inherent end-point in the meaning of the verb (which becomes the end-state of the meaning 'action + state'). The same criterion applies to sentences, i.e. a sentence may have the compositional aspect telic, which makes a passive possible. For this reason a transitive verb which is usually non-passivizable may form a passive if the compositional aspect of the sentence is right, e.g. the verb *to resemble* in the sentence *Mary isn't resembled by any of her children.* The passive is similar in form to the perfect – cf. *be* +V-*ed* and *have* + V-*ed* - and similar in meaning to the resultative perfect – cf. 'action + state' and 'action + result'. It is for this reason that the second participle crops up in both the passive and the perfect. It is also for this reason that the same transitive verbs tend to be precluded from both the passive and the resultative perfect, e.g. *to resemble*: cf. the ungrammaticality of *?Mike is resembled by Dave* and the impossibility of a resultative interpretation of the sentence *Dave has resembled Mike.*

perfect. An aspect of the type Auxiliary + Participle formed in English from *have* + V-*ed,* which means 'past action with current relevance', as in *I have lived in St. Andrews for 20 years.* The current relevance of this sentence is that the sentence implies that the speaker still lives in St. Andrews.

perfective. See 'imperfective/perfective'.

progressive. An aspect of English of the type Auxiliary + Participle formed from *be* + V-*ing*, with two meanings, firstly 'on-going or continuous activity', as in *Fiona is reading a book*, secondly, a background time-frame against which another event occurs, as in *Fiona was reading a book when the explosion happened.*

punctual adverb. An adverbial phrase which expresses a single point in time, e.g. *at five O'clock, yesterday.*

resultative perfect. A sub-meaning or use of the perfect in which the perfect expresses an action/event together with the result which ensues from that action/event, i.e. 'action + result', as in *She has broken the doll* (the doll is now broken).

stative. A lexical aspect. As always with lexical aspect there is no point in trying to identify a class of stative verb on the basis of semantic criteria alone. Unless there are structural consequences of a verb being stative to claim that a verb might be stative is speculative and pointless. In English the syntactic criterion for recognising statives is that stative verbs are incompatible with the progressive, e.g. *to know*, cf. **She is knowing the truth*. Stative verbs are incompatible with the progressive because whilst an action can readily be described as extended in time or on-going, a state cannot.

telic/atelic (or **terminative/aterminative, bounded/unbounded, conclusive/non-conclusive**). A lexical aspect in which a verb has an inherent endpoint in its meaning, e.g. *to arrive, to break* (telic), or not, e.g. *to live, to know* (atelic). It is futile to attempt to identify telic verbs on the basis of meaning alone, it can only be sensibly and reliably done on the basis of syntactic tests. One syntactic test for telicity involves a verb's reaction to the perfect: verbs which form a resultative perfect are telic – e.g. *to break* in *She has broken her doll* – whilst verbs which form a continuous perfect are atelic, e.g. *to live* in *I have lived in St. Andrews for 20 years.*

tense. A grammatical category which gives expression to the time when an action or event happened relative to the moment of speech, e.g. as in past time relative to the moment of speech (the preterit or past tense), as co-temporaneous with the moment of speech (present tense), or in future time relative to the moment of speech (the future tense). Because tense hinges on the fulcrum of the moment of speech, i.e. tense depends on the temporal location of the speaker, it is known as a deictic (i.e. pointing) category; aspect, in contrast, is non-deictic. Most linguists today think it best to confine the notion of tense to inflected forms of the verb only, which leaves English having only two tenses, the preterit (*worked*) and the present (*he/she/it works*), with the future *(I will go)* a modal construction using the modal verb *will*.

terminative/aterminative. See 'telic/atelic'.

unbounded. See 'telic/atelic'.

Name index

Subject index

In the series *Studies In Functional And Structural Linguistics* the following volumes have been published thus far or are scheduled for publication:

59   **DREER, Igor:** Expressing the Same by the Different. The subjunctive vs the indicative in French. 2007. xxx, 272 pp.

58   **MUNAT, Judith (ed.):** Lexical Creativity, Texts and Contexts. 2007. xvi, 294 pp.

57   **DAVIS, Joseph, Radmila J. GORUP and Nancy STERN (eds.):** Advances in Functional Linguistics. Columbia School beyond its origins. 2006. x, 344 pp.

56   **JING-SCHMIDT, Zhuo:** Dramatized Discourse. The Mandarin Chinese *ba*-construction. 2005. xxii, 337 pp.

55   **BEEDHAM, Christopher:** Language and Meaning. The structural creation of reality. 2005. xiv, 225 pp.

54   **ŠTEKAUER, Pavol:** Meaning Predictability in Word Formation. Novel, context-free naming units. 2005. xxii, 289 pp.

53   **EDDINGTON, David:** Spanish Phonology and Morphology. Experimental and quantitative perspectives. 2004. xvi, 198 pp.

52   **GORLACH, Marina:** Phrasal Constructions and Resultativeness in English. A sign-oriented analysis. 2004. x, 151 pp.

51   **CONTINI-MORAVA, Ellen, Robert S. KIRSNER and Betsy RODRÍGUEZ-BACHILLER (eds.):** Cognitive and Communicative Approaches to Linguistic Analysis. 2004. viii, 389 pp.

50   **VACHEK, Josef:** Dictionary of the Prague School of Linguistics. Translated from the French, German and Czech sources. In collaboration with Josef Dubský. Translated by Aleš Klégr, Pavlína Šaldová, Markéta Malá, Jan Čermák and Libuše Dušková. Edited by Libuše Dušková. 2003. x, 216 pp.

49   **HLADKÝ, Josef (ed.):** Language and Function. To the memory of Jan Firbas. 2003. x, 339 pp.

48   **REID, Wallis, Ricardo OTHEGUY and Nancy STERN (eds.):** Signal, Meaning, and Message. Perspectives on sign-based linguistics. 2002. xxii, 413 pp.

47   **MARTÍN-VIDE, Carlos (ed.):** Issues in Mathematical Linguistics. Workshop on Mathematical Linguistics, State College, PA, April 1998. 1999. xii, 214 pp.

46   **ŠTEKAUER, Pavol:** An Onomasiological Theory of English Word-Formation. 1998. x, 192 pp.

45   **MARTÍN-VIDE, Carlos (ed.):** Mathematical and Computational Analysis of Natural Language. Selected papers from the 2nd International Conference on Mathematical Linguistics (ICML '96), Tarragona, 1996. 1998. xviii, 391 pp.

44   **JESSEN, Michael:** Phonetics and Phonology of Tense and Lax Obstruents in German. 1999. xx, 394 pp.

43   **ANDREWS, Edna and Yishai TOBIN (eds.):** Toward a Calculus of Meaning. Studies in markedness, distinctive features and deixis. 1996. xxviii, 432 pp.